THE BRITISH CROWN
AND
THE INDIAN STATES

THE BRITISH CROWN AND THE INDIAN STATES

Compiled by
Chamber of Princes

Gian Publishing House
Delhi-110 007

Gian Publishing House
29/6, Shakti Nagar, Delhi.

FIRST REPRINT : 1988

ISBN 81-212-0141-1

Published by **Gian Publishing House** and printed by **Goyal Offset Printers**, Delhi.

CONTENTS

GENERAL FOREWORD

THE GROWTH OF JOINT ACTION AMONG THE INDIAN PRINCES

By L. F. Rushbrook Williams, C.B.E.
Foreign Minister, Patiala

(With acknowledgments to *The Asiatic Review*, July, 1928)

That the Indian Mutiny brought about a revolution in the attitude of the authorities towards the Indian States is, of course, a truism. Up to the time of that outbreak, the Company's officials, remembering the days when the British themselves had been only one among many competitors for the domination of India, were wont to regard the "country powers" with a suspicious eye. The traditional policy of treating each State in isolation, coupled with the increasing material development of British India, had together produced reactions unfavourable to the States, which had tended to decline relatively and absolutely. It was apparently assumed that British India was destined for rapid advance along the lines dictated by early Victorian liberalism; while such of the Indian States as could not be absorbed beneficently under the doctrine of lapse, would inevitably dwindle into mere shadows of their former selves. But the Mutiny, while it gave a severe shock to the easy optimism characterising those who controlled British policy in India, served to demonstrate that the power of the States was still a reality. Lord Canning's famous admission that the patches of native rule served as breakwaters to the wave which would otherwise have swept us away utterly and completely, may be taken as an index of the changed attitude. Nevertheless, before many decades had elapsed the position showed some signs of approximating to that which had obtained before the Mutiny. As the nineteenth century drew to a close, the growing economic unification of the Indian subcontinent seemed to threaten the very existence of the Indian States. With the development of modern means of communication British India became welded, administratively, into something like a unit; and the disparity in resources and in importance between the territory under British rule and the isolated fragments which remained outside became more than ever accentuated. The solemn pledges given by Queen Victoria were of themselves insufficient to solve the problem presented by the survival of the Indian States. From the States' point of view the danger of the situation lay principally in the fact that the Government of India was responsible for two different sets of duties. In the first place, it governed British India; in the second place, it managed the everyday relations between the Indian States and the Crown. The inevitable tendency of the greater of these two functions to dominate the less was accentuated at the beginning of the present century by an increasing departmentalisation in the Government of India. Policies were laid down for All India by the Technical Departments of the British Indian Government; and the States were expected merely to record their acquiescence. The result, from the Princes' standpoint, was a steady, if unostentatious, encroachment upon the position guaranteed to them by Royal pledge.

They experienced considerable difficulty in devising a remedy. The policy of isolation still persisted; and although it was impossible to prevent a considerable interchange of ideas among the States, the Government of India continued to deprecate any suggestion of joint representation or joint action. But parallel with the growing realisation by the States themselves of a group of interests separate in degree if not in kind from those of British India, there may be discerned a tendency in higher quarters to look upon the States themselves as constituting jointly a factor in Indian politics. Whether Lord Curzon and Lord Minto were animated by any deliberate desire to associate the Indian Princes with the British authorities in the great task of uplifting all India is uncertain. But it is unquestionable that from the early years of the twentieth century we can trace a growing liberalisation in the policy of the Government of India towards the Indian Princes. Moreover, the new generation of Princes was possessed of ideas which, though possibly inspired by a consciousness of special interests, were quite plainly anything but hostile to the British connection. In the time of Lord Hardinge, the meeting of some of the leading Princes for certain purposes was officially encouraged, although those purposes were to begin with of very minor importance. The habit of joint consultation grew rapidly under official encouragement, with the result that even before 1914 some of the Princes, notably the present Maharajas of Bikaner and Patiala and the late Maharaja of Gwalior, had begun to envisage a scheme for the safeguarding of State interests consistently with the maintenance of the interests of British India and of the Empire.

The outbreak of the war, like the outbreak of the Mutiny, served to exhibit very prominently both the power of the Princes and their abiding loyalty to the Crown. When "boons" to British India were talked of, the Princes somewhat naturally began to consider their own position. Accordingly, when the new policy officially announced in August 1917 became the declared goal of British India, the Princes found little difficulty in securing a hearing, both by Lord Chelmsford and Mr. Montagu, for the representations they desired to put forward. For various reasons the system by which their day-to-day relations with the Crown were conducted was unsatisfactory to them. An analysis of the complaints they put forward in 1918 shows three main directions in which they believed change was necessary. They felt that they had no voice in the determination of All India policy; in other words, decisions were taken by the British Indian authorities alone which, though nominally confined to British India, in reality vitally affected the interests of the States. Secondly, they deplored the lack of any impartial tribunal to decide disputes arising between themselves and the British Indian authorities, for it seemed to them that in a number of cases the Government of India was at once party and judge. Finally, they believed that the Political Department, for all its great work in fighting the battles of the States, occasionally acted in disregard of the treaties, and in general exercised an authority which, if benevolent, was nevertheless in certain respects undeniably arbitrary. In order to remedy these defects, as they appeared to them, the Princes put forward a scheme for a deliberative assembly in which they could meet together and discuss their common interests; which assembly was to form the basis of a system for joint consultation between themselves and the British Indian authorities when matters of concern both to the States and to British India were at issue. They further proposed a system of arbitration, under which any dispute between the British Indian authorities, whether Central or Provincial, and a State, might be submitted to the decision of an impartial tribunal. Finally, they desired to associate with the Political Secretary a committee which would, as they hoped, ensure that the general policy of the Political Department should be more in harmony with the sentiments and desires of the Princes.

The plan put forward by the Princes to Mr. Montagu and Lord Chelmsford afforded a useful basis of discussion. It was not wholly endorsed by the framers of the joint Report, although some very remarkable admissions testified to the general strength of the case it was designed to meet. But the Montagu-Chelmsford Report at least recommended the externals of the machinery proposed by the Princes, even though these forms did not embody the precise content for which the Princes had hoped: It is, however, to be noticed that when the proposals of the Report came to be translated into action, the modified recommendations were so much weakened, that all that the Princes seemed to have secured as a result of nearly ten years' persistent effort was the institution of the Chamber of Princes under conditions which deprived it of initiative and rendered it merely the shadow of a name. In reality, however, the Princes secured something far more important than was at the time realised—full official recognition of their right to consult with each other; and some opportunity of acquiring that difficult art, the settlement of common interests by amicable discussion.

From that time onwards the progress has been steady, if not always easy. The policy of isolation, so long pursued, has left legacies of separation among the individual Princes which are not to be overcome without much patience and goodwill. But the Chamber of Princes, while somewhat hampered by the Rules of Business over which it had, until well into 1928, no control, has undoubtedly fostered in those who share in its deliberations a habit of co-operation. The formal sessions of the Chamber, for reasons which will be obvious, have from the Princes' point of view been less important than the informal conferences for which the annual gathering at Delhi provides the opportunity. For several years the Standing Committee of the Chamber has possessed its own headquarters in a rented building, where the Chancellor's office is located during the Session. This headquarters is the real centre of action, for it is here that the Princes assemble for the Chamber, hold their most intimate discussions, formulate common policies, and lay the foundations for joint work. Here are discussed those matters which cannot find a place upon the rather stereotyped agenda of the Chamber itself; and here are laid down the lines which will guide the Standing Committee in its discussions with Government, now held thrice a year between the sessions of the Chamber. Here also are devised schemes for putting into execution certain Chamber resolutions which would otherwise remain merely the expression of pious hopes.

The existing system of common action among the Princes is in the nature of a makeshift, for the ineffectiveness of the Chamber from the Princes' standpoint has transferred the bulk of the real business to the informal conferences. But since the informal conferences and the Chamber Sessions consist of the same Princes, the Chancellor and the Standing Committee treat mandates from either as possessing the same authority. As a result, real work is done; and several of the greater Princes who at one time stood aloof now regularly send representatives to the informal conferences, where Ministers speak by invitation—always forthcoming—even if they do not vote. The upshot is, that for every one of a long list of grievances the Princes have now a remedy to suggest, even if this remedy has not been accepted by Government. But, naturally enough, the Princes are not satisfied, nor are they content to rest upon their oars.

It was the Standing Committee, under the lead of two Princes of great experience, which first put forward a request for an impartial inquiry into the whole relationship between the Princes of India and the Paramount Power. The project was discussed at the Round Table Conference which took place in Simla in the spring of 1927 between Lord Irwin and certain members of his Government on one side and the Standing Committee on the other; and it became generally rumoured in the course of the ensuing summer that an inquiry of some sort would be undertaken. The Standing Committee next took the step of despatching to England two Ministers to obtain an authoritative opinion from eminent counsel upon certain aspects of the legal position of the Princes. This opinion had not yet been considered formally by the Standing Committee when Lord Irwin announced that the Secretary of State had appointed a

Committee of three persons—Sir Harcourt Butler, Professor Holdsworth and Mr. Peel—to inquire into the relationship between the Indian States and the Paramount Power, and to suggest means for the more satisfactory adjustment of the existing economic relations between the Indian States and British India. Once again the Standing Committee lost no time. It proceeded to formulate a plan for a central organisation to prepare a general case on behalf of the States for presentation to Sir Harcourt Butler's Committee; and, further, briefed a well-known English barrister of great experience in public life to advise it throughout on legal questions, and to present the case when ready. These steps were cordially endorsed by the next informal conference of Princes, which authorised the Standing Committee to proceed along the suggested lines, and, further, in its formal rôle as a Session of the Chamber, re-elected the Chancellor and his colleagues for a further year of office. Shortly afterwards it was arranged that as many members of the Standing Committee as could leave India should go to England in the course of the summer of 1928 to assist the Chancellor and counsel in the management of the case, and in putting forward definite suggestions, already tentatively approved, for remedying the Princes' grievances.

It was not to be expected that there would be entire unanimity among the Princes concerning these measures, particularly as certain States had not entirely thrown off their original conviction that the Chamber and all its works were alike useless. But more than three-fourths of those States who are members of the Chamber in their own right, and an equal proportion of those smaller States who are either represented by groups or who stand outside the Chamber altogether, have associated themselves with the Standing Committee. And in the meeting held at Bombay in March, 1928, it was apparent that even those States which preferred to deal directly with Sir Harcourt Butler's Committee were at one with the Standing Committee in their diagnosis of the disadvantages, from the Princes' point of view, of the present situation, although they were not yet prepared to commit themselves to the precise type of embryo Federation for All India which the Standing Committee and its advisers had by this time formulated. It is more noteworthy, from the practical standpoint, that the following resolutions were passed unanimously:

"This meeting of rulers and representatives of State Governments (*a*) appreciates the wisdom of His Majesty's Government and of the Government of India in providing for an inquiry into the relations of the Indian States with the Paramount Power and with British India; (*b*) recognises that the readjustment of these relations so as to secure the political future of one-fifth of the human race calls for the highest statesmanship on the part of His Majesty's Government and people of British India, and on the part of the Indian States; (*c*) declares its resolve to devote to the moral and material progress of the subjects of the States the advantages resulting from the equitable adjustment of fiscal and economic issues; (*d*) affirms the intention of the Indian States to join with His Majesty's Government and with the Government and people of British India in working for a solution which shall secure protection for all interests and progress for all India; (*e*) reaffirms the abiding determination of the rulers of Indian States, as recorded in the last session of the Chamber of Princes, to ensure the rule of law in their States and to promote the welfare and good government of their subjects; (*f*) emphasises the dependence of the progress and prosperity of British India and the States alike upon the creation of constitutional means for the adjustment of relations between them; (*g*) reaffirms on the one hand the loyalty of the Indian States to the Crown and their attachment to the Empire, and on the other hand their sympathy with the aspirations of British India, which they regard as legitimate."

These resolutions show that both the Princes who combined with the Standing Committee to present a joint case, and the Princes who made their individual representations directly to Sir Harcourt Butler and his colleagues, are alike envisaging the problem of the States from no narrow or selfish standpoint. They are trying to think for the Empire and for India, as well as for themselves. Without exception, they are agreed in believing that the present machinery by which their relations with the Crown are conducted needs radical alteration. They believe they have solid cause for complaint; they also believe that their grievances can be removed consistently with justice to all parties. They realise that they must first prove their case. Afterwards, they must get together and devise a remedy. Finally, they must demonstrate that this remedy is reasonable and just.

INTRODUCTION

The present generation of Ruling Princes in India differs from the last more than any generation in the past has differed from its immediate predecessors. In particular the attitude of the Princes towards the doctrine of Paramountcy has undergone a radical change.

In certain matters the Princes of the last generation yielded to the demands of the Government of India, partly from a recognition of their common interests with Britain, cemented during the Mutiny of 1857; partly, as is evident from the records of the time, from a sense —peculiarly strong in the East—of the obligations of courtesy; partly because, though tenacious of their rights as they understood them, they had few opportunities of exploring exactly what these rights were. Moreover, at that period—that is for a quarter of a century between 1860 and 1885—the British power in India was neither sufficiently centralised nor sufficiently dominated by the ardour for development, to claim that control over the internal affairs of the States which characterised the interval between the disappearance of the last generation of Princes, and the attainment by the present of the confidence, based upon age and experience, which could encourage them to put their views forward.

Towards the end of the nineteenth century many leading figures had disappeared from the Indian political stage. Jyaji Rao Scindia, Tukoji Rao Holkar, the Nizam Afzal-ud-Daula, with his great Minister Salar Jung, had all passed away, and it happened that a number of the most important States at more or less the same time fell under minority rule.

The young Princes who were to succeed to their great ancestral dominions grew up under the guidance of tutors appointed for them by the Government of India, and were strongly influenced by the example of the British officers who administered their States. Hence they could hardly fail to absorb modern ideas. As a result, when the time came for each to assume his ruling powers, he set about introducing changes into the type of government bequeathed him by his father, and—where such machinery did not already exist—a regular administrative system of modern type was set to work in most of the leading States.

The altered outlook of the Princes was not, however, in one direction only. A new recognition of their duties was accompanied by a fresh consciousness of the rights and privileges of their position; and the fact that their administrations were now provided with Government officials, who were well equipped to investigate their masters' rights, helped to insure a thorough examination of the Princes' position.

Reading the half-forgotten treaties between their States and the British Crown, the Indian Princes were roused to reflection on many questions which had not troubled their fathers. Not only did they find an unmistakable contrast between the relationship in which they themselves stood to the Government of India and the relationship of their predecessors to the Honourable East India Company, but it also grew apparent to them that the clear and definite pronouncements of the treaties on a number of particular questions were ignored in the procedure of the Political Department.

Meanwhile the steady process by which India is becoming fused into economic unity was continuing year by year, and, as the cares of the Government of India increased and the functions of each Department were extended, the tentacles of British Administration began to stretch out towards the States. Reluctant to admit the argument that efficiency and the need for centralised control made it necessary for the Indian Government to take charge of many activities within the States, the

Princes watched uneasily the gradual curtailment, now here, now there, of powers which they had imagined were for ever safeguarded by the Treaties and Engagements. In particular, they observed that during minority administrations, when the British Government virtually controlled the States, irresistible pressure was sometimes applied to achieve ends which, though sometimes but not always benevolently conceived, involved the sacrifice of some cherished privilege, immunity, or liberty on the part of the Prince concerned. They began to appeal, to protest, to memorialise.

It was an age in which India began to be disturbed by new ideas and new ambitions, and, perhaps, the same spirit which was troubling the waters of political consciousness in British India was at work in this awakening of the Princes. But if there was anything in common in the causes of the two movements, there was nothing in common in their effects, and when a wave of sedition swept over India in the time of Lord Minto (1907), the States remained staunchly loyal to the Crown. Their demands were something entirely different from the demands of the malcontents in British India.

At the time of the outbreak of the Great War (1914) the Princes had grown sensible of the dangers arising from the policy pursued by the Government when in temporary charge of States during minority administrations; and many of them had made appeals to the Viceroy in protest against the system which prevailed. As a result of such appeals the Chiefs' Conference was summoned by Lord Hardinge in 1916. The real problem before the Conference was the complaint of the Princes that the British authorities, whenever the reigning Prince was a minor, seized the opportunity to set up institutions in the States, modelled upon the institutions of British India, which were as alien from the sentiments of the people of the States as they were unwelcome to their governments. Closely connected with the problem was the question of the education of young Princes and of the working of the Chiefs' Colleges.

At the first meeting of the Princes with the Viceroy little was done by Government save to ask for the co-operation of the States in the collection of certain statistics and in spreading timely information about epidemics.

Any suspicions which may have associated the discontent of the Princes with imperfect loyalty to the Crown had been already dissipated by the response of the States on the outbreak of war. The States disappointed the expectations of Germany, not only by throwing their entire influence upon the side of the British, but by the emulation of individual rulers who vied in offering their resources to the British Power.

While the war lasted, the catchwords about the liberty of small nations, self-determination and the reward of heroes, which raised many hopes in England and Europe, and in post-war years caused many disappointments, began to have their effect in India also. The Princes in particular were given every assurance of confidence by Government, and the suspicion and mistrust with which they had formerly been regarded were admitted only to be repudiated. Conscious of the efforts which they had made, the Princes could not fail to read in these phrases an earnest of greater trust and a promise of well-deserved emancipation. At the same time it was not hard to see that the expectations aroused in British India by similar promises might easily lead to a situation in which the interests of silent loyalty would be sacrificed to the demands of vociferous politicians.

When the war ended, and the reforms of 1919 were introduced, the Princes found that their hopes had been set too high. While the creation of the Legislative Assembly and the Provincial Legislatures had given overwhelming weight to interests which were often opposed to their own, the Chamber of Princes, set up in response to the demands of the Conferences held in 1916 and after, failed to afford them any real influence in the settlement of matters vitally affecting their States. But if the Chamber has been of little weight in the affairs of India, it has served to accustom the Princes to meet and to investigate questions of common concern with a view to combined action; and to arouse in them the realisation of how many and how important those questions are.

It was not, however, only political considerations with which they were concerned. The war had left the country in financial difficulties. The Public Debt was large, and the currency system of India, without having fallen into the morasses characterising Central Europe, was sufficiently disorganised to play havoc with the Budget. New forms of taxation were introduced, and their burden fell almost as much upon the peoples of the States as upon the peoples of British India. So to the disappointment of their political hopes was added in the minds of the Princes a feeling of financial injustice and injury. While their subjects unwittingly contributed to balance the budgets of British India, the Darbars had themselves to increase taxation or to reduce productive expenditure in order to balance their own budgets, and while they were willing enough to fall in with the demand that was being made all over India for greater efficiency in administration, they were hampered by want of funds in securing the personnel required to make efficiency possible.

Even before the end of the war these considerations were in the minds of the Princes. In 1917 a scheme had been put forward very much like that which is now advanced on behalf of Their Highnesses. Later, finding the working of the Chamber of Princes little likely to secure for them greater autonomy, with corresponding opportunity to develop the resources of their States, the Princes pressed during the Viceroyalty of Lord Reading for a Round Table Conference. Their request was evaded, but it is probable that if it had been granted they would have demanded some such investigation of their affairs as that undertaken by the Indian States Committee.

The Committee, which exists "to report upon the relationship between the Paramount Power and the States, with particular reference to the rights and obligations arising from treaties, engagements and sanads, and from usage, sufferance and other causes; and to inquire into the financial and economic relations between British India and the States," must necessarily deal with the two questions which are uppermost in the minds of the Princes—the disregard of their treaty rights by Government, and the injuries which the existing fiscal system of British India inflicts upon them.

In order to demonstrate the need for a thorough investigation of these matters, it has been necessary to collect evidence from individual States. Reflections on the examination of this evidence are contained in the following pages.

The first part of this volume consists of an historical sketch of the relationship between the States and the Government of India.

Without such historical background the treaties are unintelligible, since to understand them it is necessary to understand the intentions of those who framed them. In this sketch, therefore, the statesmen of the past have been made to speak for themselves, and an examination of their utterances suggests that the views of such authorities as Lee-Warner and Tupper, like the political practices of the last sixty years, have been based upon misconception of the relationship between the States and the Paramount Power; that the construction which has been put upon such phrases as " subordinate co-operation " is unwarranted; and that the fundamental treaty position is very different from what, on the basis of a one-sided practice of recent growth, it is commonly assumed to be.

The second part of this volume deals with the economic and fiscal position of the States in relationship to British India and the central government.

The injuries of which the States are conscious were very much accentuated by war and post-war conditions, and if it were possible to believe that they would automatically disappear in the near future, there would not have been so much need to develop this part of the case.

But that possibility appears remote. It would be idle for the Princes merely to record general protests against the present fiscal policy of Government, and wait for redress; they must substantiate their complaints, secure the acknowledgment of their rights, and insist that the true remedy shall be sought in consultation with them. Thus they hope successfully to get established a system which shall work for the States as well as for British India.

Just as in the political domain a general impression prevails outside the States that the disregard of treaties by the Paramount Power has been in every instance prompted by benevolent considerations, so in the economic domain, while it is admitted that the States have been laid under contribution by the central government, excuse is sought on the ground that the States have corresponding obligations to fulfil. The chief of these obligations is considered to be their share in the defence of India, and the answer—elaborated below—that this obligation was fully discharged by each State on terms prescribed by the East India Company, at the inception of their relations, has never been adequately examined. Moreover, it has never occurred to the outside public that the operation of moncpolies controlled by Government might be unfair to the States or that the States could have any rights or even any interest in the matter.

It was apparent, at the Bikaner Conference of Princes and Ministers in 1917, that the same feeling of injustice was shared by a great number of the States. The question was discussed there, and ever since then it has been uppermost in the minds of the Princes. The desire to improve their Governments and to develop their States, combined with the post-war difficulties of the falling value of money and the increased real standard of wages and salaries, only served to give urgency to the demand for restitution which they had already felt it just to make.

The evidence contained in the great collection of State papers presented to the Indian States Committee is intended to show how the treaties of the States have been disregarded and to exhibit instances of the injustice made possible by certain inherent defects in the existing machinery for conducting the relationship between the Government and the States. The difficulties attendant upon the collection of this evidence have been considerable. Few States maintain well-organised departmental records covering anything but the last few years; and in consequence, some forty-three of the States associated with the Special Organisation of the Chamber of Princes have been obliged to admit that they have no documentary evidence to produce upon several important questions. Even when records exist, they are not always systematically arranged, and in the short time at our disposal it has been impossible for the States to seek out every instance relevant to our case from the total of available documents. Both for this reason, as also because each case has been scrutinised from the standpoint, not merely of importance, but also of demonstrability, the examples contained in the collection are typical rather than exhaustive, and if the records of the States generally had been in better order, much more would have been available. It has been our endeavour to admit no evidence which did not seem to us conclusive, and we have rejected many apparently well-founded complaints for want of formal documentary proof. The cases which we have quoted, whether of political or of economic grievances, must therefore be regarded as illustrative samples of the difficulties which exist and not as a complete account of them.

We desire, however, to emphasise one point. The following pages deal with certain general aspects of the historical and economic relations between the Crown, the States, and the Government of India. Here we desire to utter a note of warning. There is in the case of every State a separate history, a separate set of rights, a separate set of obligations, and a separate economic position. Certain of these particular aspects are brought out in the individual evidence contained in the collected evidence. But everything said in this outline sketch must be read as subject to and conditioned by the particular rights and the particular obligations of each State.

It will be clear that the following pages are not the work of a single hand. The work of compiling this historical and economic presentation of the Princes' case has been inspired by the determination to disguise no facts and strain no arguments, and by the resolution to understate rather than overstate the case which is put forward.

PART I

A CONSIDERATION OF THE EVOLUTION OF POLITICAL RELATIONSHIP BETWEEN THE CROWN AND THE STATES

I.

By the Charter issued to it by Charles II, the East India Company was permitted to wage war with non-Christian Powers, and, as a corollary, acquired the legal right to enter into treaties, alliances and engagements.

The earliest actual treaty now extant is that signed in 1723 by the Rajah of Travancore and the head of the Company's factory at Anjengo. By it the contracting parties agreed to be "in league and united in good friendship." But Anjengo was a minor factory, and the political conditions of the Malabar coast were different from those prevailing elsewhere in India. The first treaty of importance made by the Company is that made with the Maratha State of Sawantwari (1730). The ruler of this principality was suffering, as was the Company, from the raids of the Angrias, a notorious family of Malabar "pirates." The chief purpose of this treaty of "firm peace and friendship" is stated in Article 5 to be "that the joint endeavour of both (*i.e.* the Company and the Sardesay or Ruler of Sawantwari) shall be exerted to destroy the said enemy (the Angrias), the Honourable Company by their vessels of war by sea, distressing them as much as possible, and the Sardesay both by land and sea as much as in his power." This attempt at joint action, first initiated by Robert Cowen, President and Governor of the Company's factory at Bombay, does not, however, appear to have produced much result, for three years later (1733) the same Governor had to conclude with the Janjira State a "treaty of perpetual alliance and sincere friendship," again with the object of suppressing the Angrias, who had grown more powerful than ever.

For forty years yet the English settlements in India were destined to remain separately administered, each doing what seemed good in its own eyes, often not merely without reference to each other, but occasionally in direct opposition to each other's interests. The comparative importance of these factories prior to 1757 should be realised. Calcutta (Fort William) was but a minor factory of no political importance. Terrorised by the Marathas and under the threat of Ali Vardi Khan, it had no policy but of humbly carrying on its trade. The power of the Peishwa kept Bombay unimportant from a political point of view for many years to come. Only in Madras, where the quarrels of the Mohammedan Nawabs and the rivalry of the French gave them a field, the Company's factors counted politically.

It is therefore unnecessary to deal at length with the earlier treaties made by the Governors of Fort William and Bombay Castle. Only the treaties made by the Governor of Fort St. George with Hyderabad and the Carnatic are of importance for our purpose. Of these, the treaty of 1759 gave the English the seaport of Masulipatam, and certain surrounding districts in the Northern Circars which had once been assigned to the French soldier, Bussy, for the support of the French troops in the service of the Nizam. The second treaty (1766) of "Perpetual Honour, Favour, Alliance and Attachment between the Great Nawab, high in station, famous as the sun, etc., and John Calliaud, Esq., Brigadier-General, invested with full powers on behalf of the Company," stipulated that "in return for the gracious favours received from His Highness, consisting of Sunnuds (title-deeds) for the five Circars (districts) . . . the Company do promise and engage to have a body of their troops ready to settle the affairs of His Highness's Government in everything that is right and proper."

More important than either of these from the point of view of the development of the Company's relations with the country powers was the treaty made with the Nawab Vizier of Oudh after the battle of Buxar. That battle had transferred to Fort William (Calcutta) the prestige and power so long enjoyed by Madras. The treaty made with Oudh in 1765 brings out the most important point in the policy of the Company. The Company was not at that time in a position to annex the Province of Oudh, as such an annexation would have saddled it with an extensive land frontier, which was menaced on the one hand by the Afghans, under the Duranee King, and on the other by the Marathas. The result was an alliance by which Shuja-ud-Dowla was restored to the throne, and the Company undertook to defend his frontier on the condition that he defrayed the expenditure of such defence. The Company recognised that the defence of Oudh was the defence of Bengal. Thus the subsidiary system began as a method of defence without expenditure.

During the period between 1765 and 1774, the Company rose in authority and prestige owing to the grant of the *Diwani* [1] by the Moghul Emperor, and to the reorganisation of its political administration by the intervention of Parliament. *The grant of the Diwani* (1765) *raised the Company to the status of one of the Indian States.* By the financial control which it exercised over Bengal and Bihar, its political position was advanced to that of a Power which could negotiate on an equal basis with the Nizam, the Nawab of Arcot, and the Maratha rulers. By the Regulating Act of 1773, the Company was transformed from a purely trading corporation into a semi-sovereign political body, with centralised control, acting under the direction and authority of Parliament.

The first Governor-General appointed under the Regulating Act was Warren Hastings. It is in his time that the foundations of the British political system in India were laid. A brief analysis of his administration is necessary for understanding the historical circumstances under which the Subsidiary System developed.

The political position in India on Hastings' arrival in Bengal was as follows:

In Bengal, the Company was on the verge of financial ruin, the repair of which had been the main reason for

[1] The right of collecting revenue and exercising jurisdiction as vicegerents.

the appointment of Hastings by the Board of Directors. Its chief fear was a dread of Maratha raids, which might further impoverish a country already ruined by famine and misrule.

Shah Alam, the Moghul Emperor, who had been living at Allahabad on the revenues assigned to him by Clive in 1765, had solicited the help of the Marathas, and by them had been replaced on his unhappy throne at Delhi in 1771. Under cover of his name, the Marathas were each year not merely overrunning, but seizing fresh districts, and—a point that closely concerned the Company—were demanding the surrender of the districts of Kora and Allahabad which bordered not merely on Oudh, but on Bengal as well. The Company had no wish to have such turbulent neighbours at its doors.

The Punjab at this time, except for its south-eastern tracts, where the Marathas were making yearly inroads, may be said not to have come within the orbit of Indian Political History. The Sikhs were rapidly forming into a nation, and their growing strength, together with dynastic disputes in Persia and Afghanistan, prevented the Musalman rulers of these latter countries from emulating the exploits of Nadir Shah or Ahmed Shah Abdali.

Sind and the Western States of Rajputana, by their remoteness, were still secure from the Maratha scourge, but less fortunate were the Eastern Rajput States, on which Scindia and Holkar imposed a vague suzerainty.

In the centre of India the Bhosla, Scindia and Holkar had already rough-hewn their separate principalities. In the west the Gaekwar was already proving remiss in forwarding tribute to the Peishwa at Poonah, as were Scindia, Holkar and the Bhosla. Nevertheless the Company's Government at Bombay still considered the Peishwa as a power in the land by whose acquiescence they held Salsette and Bassein, which had been wrested from the "Purtugals."

Despite their mutual jealousies, the Maratha States, in combination, constituted the strongest power in the land.

Though the controlling power of the confederacy had become less effective as a result of the battle of Panipat, there was still sufficient feeling of national solidarity left in the leaders, pride of common achievement among the Maratha people, and sufficient prestige with the Peishwa, to render such a combination possible at any moment of crisis. The mutual jealousies of the leaders prevented the partition of the Nizam's territories, as the army chiefs could not agree on a division of the spoils. As it was, the Nizam's State was forced to pay *chauth*[1] with a greater regularity than any part of the Peninsula.

In the south the Nawab of the Carnatic had fallen into a position of powerless dependence on the Company owing to the rise of Hyder Ali. Hyder Ali had consolidated his power in the ancient kingdom of Mysore, whose Hindu rulers he still pretended to serve. He had attacked and devastated the whole of the Carnatic, dictating a disastrous peace to the British Company at the very gates of Madras. He nursed a strong resentment against the Company for their refusal to help him against the Marathas when he was hard pressed by the Poona Government.

Thanks partly to its geograpical position, but still more to the strength of the Marathas on the Western Ghats, Bombay at this period of its history controlled very little territory. As yet it had not by conquest or cession acquired wide dominions as Madras and Bengal had done, and for this reason was considered by the Board of Directors as the most satisfactory of its factories, since by its pacific policy it had incurred the least debt of any of the three Presidencies.

Such, in rough outline, was the position of affairs in India when Warren Hastings, by nature a man of peace, assumed control of the Company's fortunes. Students to-day can see that at this time the dominion in India lay between the Company and the Marathas. In spite of opposition and difficulties, Hastings enforced on the three Presidencies a joint policy. By their disruptive

[1] Literally one-fourth of the revenue: in effect tribute.

jealousies the Maratha Chiefs threw away their chance of succeeding to the Empire of the Moghul.

Though anxious to preserve peace, as he early informed the Court, Hastings realised that the only way to do so was to maintain an efficient army. The breakdown of the Imperial Administration of the Moghuls following the invasion of Nadir Shah had made vast provinces, where new administrations had not come into being, the happy hunting ground of desperate adventurers of every race and sect. Bands of fanatics called sanassies, "the gipsies of India," to quote Gleig, had devasted Bengal repeatedly. Hastings, by vigorous military operations, expelled them from its borders and then relieved the State of Cooch Behar from the grasp of the Booteas. These hardy mountaineers from Bhutan defended the fort of Cooch Behar desperately, but after it had been stormed, were driven out of the district. The treaty of Cooch Behar (1773) is not one of alliance, but is an admission of subjection, though the extent to which the sovereignty of that "State" may be held to have lapsed is a question not finally solved to this day. The treaty with Bhutan was one of peace. Whatever be the position of Bhutan to-day, it is not that of an ordinary Indian State.

Having restored order in Bengal, Warren Hastings turned his attention to other affairs. The British in India then held a very different position with regard to the Indian rulers from that which they were to occupy at the close of Hastings' administration. They were looked on with jealousy and suspicion by all, by none with respect. Bound by treaty to pay tribute to the Great Moghul, they had made over to him for his support the Provinces of Kora and Allahabad. But after his return to Delhi in 1771, he had become a mere tool in the hands of the Maratha, to whom he had been forced to cede those Provinces. To a sovereign who could afford the British frontier no protection, Hastings determined to pay no more tribute. The Provinces of Kora and Allahabad were given back to the Vizier of Oudh from whom Clive had taken them. As he wrote to the Board on October 4th, 1773:

"By ceding them to the Vizier we strengthen our alliance with him, we make him more dependent upon us, as he is more exposed to the hostilities of the Marathas, we render a junction between him and them, which has been sometimes apprehended, morally impossible, since their pretensions to Corah will be a constant source of animosity between them; we free ourselves from the expense and all the dangers attending either a remote property or a remote connection; we adhere literally to the United system laid down by the Honourable Court of Directors; we are no longer under the necessity of exhausting the wealth of our Provinces in the pay and disbursements of our brigadiers employed at a distance beyond them, but by fixing the sum to be paid by the Vizier for their services and their whole expense, and by removing every possible cause for their passing our own borders but at his requisition and for his defence, we provide effectively for the protection of our frontier, and reduce the expenses of our army even in employing it, and lastly we acquire a net sum of 50 lacs of rupees most reasonably obtained for the relief of the Company's necessities, and the deficient circulation of the currency of the provinces."

As the cession of Kora and Allahabad to the Vizier was intended to make for the greater security of the Company's own territories, so the war against the Rohillas, first proposed by the Vizier, was agreed to by Hastings with a similar object in view. The object of this undertaking is thus described by Hastings himself. (Letter to Col. Campion, May 28th, 1774.)

"We engaged to assist the Vizier (of Oudh) in reducing the Rohilla country under his dominion, that the boundary of his possessions might be completed by the Ganges forming a barrier to cover them from the attacks and insults to which they were exposed by his enemies either possessing or having access to the Rohilla Country. Thus our alliance with him, and the necessity for maintaining this alliance, so long as he or his successors shall deserve our protection, was rendered advantageous to the Company's interest, because the security of his possessions from invasion in that quarter is, in fact, the security of ours."

The definition of the Ring-Fence System, as well as its object, is clearly laid down by Hastings in the passages quoted above. By the Ring-Fence System, the Company's authorities meant that instead of defending their own frontier, they undertook to defend the farther frontier of their immediate neighbour—of course, at his expense. In this particular case the Company's possessions in Bengal could be attacked only by the Marathas and the Afghans. In both cases Oudh stood as a buffer State. The Ring-Fence System meant, as Hastings expressed it, the security of the Vizier's frontiers being considered as the security of those of the Company.

The objects gained by this system which Hastings established with regard to Oudh were, (*a*) the money for all defensive purposes came from the State brought into alliance, (*b*) the Company claimed and exercised the right of intervening in the internal affairs of the allied State on the ground that the defensive forces kept up in that State were not efficient enough. The Ring-Fence System was thus based on the policy of extending British authority without enlarging the line of direct defence.

Undoubtedly Hastings was more clear-sighted than the majority of his contemporaries in the matter of the relations that might be established between the Company and the States of India. In a letter to Alexander Elliot in 1777 he thus gives his views on the matter.

"You are already well acquainted with the general system which I wish to be empowered to establish in India, namely, to extend the influence of the British Nation to every part of India not too remote from their possessions, without enlarging the circle of their defence or involving them in hazardous or indefinite engagements, and to accept the allegiance of such of our neighbours as shall sue to be enlisted among the friends and allies of the King of Great Britain. The late Nawab Shuja-ud-Daula (of Oudh), who wanted neither pride nor understanding, would have thought it an honour to be called the Vizier of the King of England, and offered at one time to coin *siccas* in His Majesty's name. . . . On this footing, I would replace the *Subaship* of Oudh. On this footing I would establish an alliance with Berar (Hyderabad). These countries are of more importance to us than any other, from their contiguity to ours, and therefore it is of consequence to settle their connection with us before that of any other. But the system might be rendered more extensive by time, and the observance of a steady principle of conduct and an invariable attachment to formal agreements."

Hastings was not in a position to put this scheme of his imagination into operation. From 1774 to 1776 his time was too fully occupied with troubles in his Council to pay more attention to the affairs of Indian Powers than was forced on him by the exigency of events. But as soon as he was freed from troubles of this nature, he found himself faced with a combination of the most formidable Powers in India. For over nine years the Company had to carry on a fight against the Marathas and Hyder Ali, the latter of whom was actively supported by the French.

The Maratha War (1776–82) was largely the outcome of mismanagement during the second period when Hastings was overridden by his Council. "To this period, and to the confused and incompetent action of the Madras Council, are also to be traced the main causes of the war with Hyder Ali (1778–83) and the general disorganisation of the Company's power in Southern India. It was a fortunate thing for British India that Hastings regained his authority before the crisis came."

In this third period of the administration of Hastings were concluded the first treaty with the Rana of Gohud, now Dholpur (1779), "a treaty of perpetual friendship," and the first treaty with Gwalior (1781), a treaty of "peace and firm alliance." This latter engagement helped the termination of the Maratha war and the conclusion of the treaty of Salbai (1782).

In Lyall's[1] *British Dominion in India* (pp. 189 to 205) there is to be found an excellent summary of the wars with the Marathas and with Hyder Ali, with pertinent references to the part played by the French directly or indirectly in these struggles. The summer of 1780

[1] Lyall, Sir A., *The Rise and Expansion of the British Dominion in India.* 1910.

was the nadir of the English fortunes in India. By 1783, when the Peace of Versailles was signed, the Company was at least in as desperate straits as it had ever been. This is the only period in Indian history when a demonstration of France against the English dominion in India has failed to accelerate the expansion of that dominion. It is the only period when Britain lost, even partially, her command of the seas.

If the growth of British power in India is to be measured by the expansion of its territories, the two decades between Clive's acceptance of the Diwani (1765) and the departure of Hastings from India (1785) may be reckoned as a stationary period. And yet in an imperceptible manner the Company's authority had increased to an extent which put it in the forefront of Indian Powers. It had been able to withstand the opposition of the most formidable Indian rulers leagued together for its destruction, to carry on warfare continuously for over nine years on many different fronts, to raise, equip and maintain armies which traversed the plains of India, and in spite of all to emerge without financial bankruptcy or political discredit. The only State which had advanced in credit during the same period was that of Scindia. All others had, during this interval, become weaker and less able to undertake offensive operations. The Company's power increased by comparison, and its political and military prestige stood high. The fight for existence which Hastings undertook ended by a complete vindication of the right of the Company to be considered one of the major Powers of India. The Company was by no means supreme, nor were their military resources or political strength as yet adequate to challenge the Maratha Empire for supremacy in the Peninsula. But it was clear that their power was unshakable. Hastings had consolidated their position in such a way as to render a gradual advance not only possible but inevitable.

The Company still adhered to the policy of the Ring-Fence, which policy, if we except Wellesley's treatment of Mysore, was not abandoned until, in 1813, the Marquis of Hastings, then Lord Moira, became Governor-General. The certain failure of this policy in the future was not yet obvious to the Company owing to the indirect service done to the English by the rise of the Sikhs in the Punjab to fill the political vacuum caused there by the final disintegration of the Moghul Empire and the withdrawal of the Afghans from Northern India generally. As Lyall has said :

> " The fierce enmity of the Sikhs kept out the foreign Mohammedan and prevented the resuscitation of any fresh Islamite dynasty upon the ruins of the old empire at Delhi or Lahore."

By 1785 the Sikhs had mastered the whole country between the Jhelum and the Sutlej, were threatening the Mohammedan Provinces about Delhi, and had made pillaging excursions eastwards across the Ganges into Rohilkhand.

The position of the Sikhs astride the Sutlej was, moreover, at this time of great service to the Company in setting bounds to the encroachments of the Marathas, who were once again pressing northwards under Scindia. Having attached himself to one of the rival parties that were contending for the possession of Imperial authority at Delhi, Mahdajee Scindia had obtained his own nomination as Vice-regent of the Empire. Just before quitting India, Hastings had been much tempted to send an expedition to Delhi to set the great Moghul on his feet again and thus to make English influence paramount at his capital. " But the Company, though alarmed at this notable aggrandisement of the Marathas in a new quarter, could not yet venture to oppose Scindia's enterprise, and the project of reviving the moribund empire under European influence—which had passed across the vision of Dupleix, of Bussy and of Clive—was once more reluctantly abandoned by Hastings as impracticable."

Hastings' relations with those States which were in permanent alliance with the Company, mainly Oudh and the Carnatic, are of importance, as they show that even at that early period the question of undue intervention by Residents in the internal affairs of the allied States had arisen. Hastings was faced with this problem in an acute form in Oudh, where Mr. Bristow, instead of attempting to cultivate the Nawab's goodwill and "to show him every ostensible and external mark of respect," treated the Prince as a dependent and prescribed for him "the number of horses which he should be allowed to use and the dishes which should be cooked for his table."

Hastings tackled the matter himself and paid a personal visit to Lucknow after recalling Bristow. As he wrote to a friend, "I know that I can do much more if I am myself the immediate Agent, than I can by distant influence and delegated authority."

This incident is of importance, because it shows clearly that Hastings was not misled by the military and political impotence of the Vizier into considering him a puppet ruler. In matters of external policy Hastings was not unduly scrupulous in securing the consent of the Vizier to his own plans. *But he never forgot that the Vizier was an independent ruler in whose internal affairs the Company had no right to intervene.*

In another matter of importance also, the system of unequal treaties was showing signs of grave abuse. The force maintained by the Company professedly for the defence of the Vizier's territories was paid for by that ruler. The Company, without consulting the Nawab Vizier, reduced the number of the troops so maintained, and yet they continued to receive from the Oudh treasury the same sum as before. Hastings saw the dishonesty of "the Army subsidy being kept up at its original rate, although the number of troops employed by us in the defence of his dominions has been considerably reduced. Neither the Vizier nor any of his Ministers," he continued, "have ever mentioned to me this deficiency, but it is not the less our duty to take it into consideration. In all our adjustments of accounts with the Vizier for many years back, we have been regulated by the strictest regard to justice, and the Vizier on his part has on every occasion relied most implicitly on our justice as well as on the accuracy of our Accomptant-General. Let us then confirm that confidence which is so happily reposed in us by pointing out mistakes, even although we must be losers by correcting them."

His Council, however, vetoed Hastings' proposal to do justice to the Nawab Vizier, each of whose regiments had been reduced from one thousand to seven hundred men apiece, though he was still paying at the higher rate. Even in those days, before any bureaucrat in the Administration had thought of making "policy" a reason for forgetting justice in the solution of difficulties with the Indian States, a Governor-General might find himself thwarted in his efforts at fair play by a system which was too strong for him. In February, 1785, Warren Hastings left India, and for twenty months, until the arrival of Lord Cornwallis, the affairs of the Company were administered by Sir John Macpherson, Senior Member of the Bengal Council.

II.

In England, Indian affairs had been arousing increased attention in Parliament. The provisions of the Act of 1773 had proved inadequate, and in 1783, Fox had introduced an India Bill which had been thrown out in the House of Lords only by the personal influence of King George III. The India Bill introduced by Pitt in the following year was a compromise. Unlike Fox's Bill, it left political and commercial powers in the hands of the Company, but the Directors of the Court were now subjected to the strict supervision of a new department of State, the Board of Control. The President of this Board was the officer ultimately responsible for the Government of British India, and continued to be so until, in 1858, the Crown took over the Company's Indian possessions and appointed a Secretary of State for India in place of the President. The old powers of the Directors of the Company were transferred to the Secret Committee of their body, which was not to exceed three in number.

Hastings considered the policy laid down in the Act to be a censure on his administration and decided to leave India as soon as possible. The preamble was a repudiation of the policy followed by Clive and Hastings; it ran as follows :—

"And whereas to pursue schemes of conquest and extension of dominion in India, are measures repugnant to the wish, the honour, and policy of this nation; be it therefore further enacted, that it shall not be lawful for the Governor-General and Council, without the express command of the Court of Directors or of the Secret Committee, in any case (except where hostilities have actually been commenced or preparations actually made for the commencement of hostilities against the British Nation in India, or against some of the Princes or States whose territories the Company shall be engaged by any subsisting treaty to defend or guarantee) either to declare war or commence hostilities, or entering into any treaty for making war, against any of the country Princes or States in India, or any treaty for guaranteeing the possessions of any country, princes or states . . . and in all cases where hostilities shall be commenced or treaty made, the Governor-General and Council shall, by the most expeditious means they can devise, communicate the same unto the Court of Directors, together with a full statement of the information upon which they shall have commenced such hostilities, or made such treaties, and their motives and reasons for the same at large."

Lord Cornwallis, who was specially selected and sent to India to carry out this policy, was a statesman who, by virtue of his exalted rank and his previous experience as an officer of the Crown, was well fitted to pursue a steady line of action without being unduly worried by the criticism of the Court of Directors or by the jealousy of the Company's servants in India. Moreover, he firmly believed that the policy laid down in the Act was the correct one. The object of that Act, which Pitt had declared to be "to prevent the Government of Bengal from being too ambitious," seemed to Cornwallis a most laudable one. Yet in vain did he try to avoid all war and all entangling relations with the Indian States. The alliances and treaties which he had inherited forced his hands and compelled him to wage war against Tipu Sultan, who had invaded the State of Travancore, which the Company had undertaken to protect.

In a letter written early in 1790 to Mr. Malet, who was the Company's representative at the Court of the Peishwa, Cornwallis is forced to admit—

> " Some considerable advantages have no doubt been experienced by the system of neutrality which the Legislature required of the Government of this country, but it has at the same time been attended with the unavoidable inconvenience of our being constantly exposed to the necessity of commencing a war without having previously secured the assistance of efficient Allies.
>
> " The late outrageous infraction of the treaty of peace by Tipu furnishes a case in point. We could not suffer the dominions of the Raja of Travancore, who was included by name as our ally in that treaty, to be ravaged or insulted without being justly charged with pusillanimity or a flagrant breach of faith, and without dishonouring ourselves by that means in the view of all the Powers in India, and as we have been almost daily obliged for several years past to declare to the Marathas and to the Nizam that we were precluded from contracting any new engagements with them for affording them aid against the injustice or ambition of Tipu, I must acknowledge that we cannot claim as a right the performance of those promises which the Marathas have repeatedly made to co-operate with us whenever we should be forced into a war with that Prince. . . . I thought it right, in order to obtain the aid of the Marathas, to offer them a defensive alliance against Tipu, to which they would in reason and equity have a good title if they were to take an active part with us without having made such a previous engagement."

To secure the Nizam's aid against Tipu, an alliance similar to that with the Marathas had to be made, and so the Triple Alliance of the three Powers which was formally concluded in 1792 became a definite factor in Indian politics.

Cornwallis himself, as Commander-in-Chief, conducted, but with only moderate success, the operations against Tipu. To support him in his campaign he also entered into a treaty of friendship and alliance against Tipu with

Coorg (1790) and a Treaty of Vassalage and Alliance with Cochin (1791).

But it was not only the orders against entangling alliances which Cornwallis was forced to violate. He was compelled, too, to add to the territories of the Company. After the defeat of Tipu, so as to secure the Carnatic against such incursions as those made by Tipu and his father, Hyder Ali, Cornwallis annexed in 1792 part of the Mysore dominions. The Company, the Marathas and the Nizam all took equal shares in the territories annexed, whereby, thanks to a control of the passes into Mysore, the power of Tipu to attack his neighbours was much curtailed. In his letter explaining the necessity of the new acquisitions of territory, Cornwallis appears almost apologetic, though he gives most valid reasons for his action.

The policy of non-interference by the British in the affairs of Indian Principalities which was followed by Cornwallis had two distinct results. It had the most beneficial effects on the internal administration of the Company's dominions. Trade recovered, and the financial prosperity of the Government was restored. Externally, it had the effect of indirectly helping Scindia to establish himself as the leading ruler in North India and to consolidate his authority in Delhi. Mahadaji Scindia died in 1794, and "a menace which must have been serious to the establishment of the political power of the Company in Hindustan vanished with him." Sir John Shore (Lord Teignmouth), who, after the departure of Lord Cornwallis, acted as *ad interim* Governor-General until the arrival of Lord Mornington (Marquess Wellesley), had to deal only with Doulat Rao Scindia. During Sir John Shore's tenure of office the only treaty made was a treaty "of friendship" with Travancore (1795).

The most important event during Shore's administration was, perhaps, his refusal to help the Nizam when, in 1795, the latter was attacked by the Marathas. At the battle of Kurdla, where for the last time all the Maratha chieftains ranged themselves under the orders of the

Peishwa, the Nizam's forces suffered a disastrous defeat. For a time this completely altered the balance of power, as the Subadar of the Deccan was entirely at the mercy of the Marathas, whose power became more formidable than ever.

From the point of view of the British power in India, the policy of non-intervention in this case proved a sorry failure. The Nizam, Tipu and the Indian States generally lost all respect for and confidence in that power. Shore's refusal to allow the subsidiary force to help the Nizam alike estranged the principal ally of the Company and encouraged its principal rivals. Incensed at the Company's action, the Nizam increased his regular troops and placed them under the supervision and control of French officers. This revival of French influence in the Deccan and the hostility of the Nizam alarmed Sir John Shore, who intervened to protest against the augmentation of the Nizam's troops, without realising that his own refusal to render help to that ruler at the time of his need was what had inclined him to rely upon French support.

III.

Many years later, in a letter to Lord Ellenborough, Lord Wellesley professed to have discovered, even before his arrival in India, " how vain and idle was poor old Cornwallis' reliance on the good faith of Tipu, and on the strength to be derived from treaties with the Marathas or the Nizam." Whether or no the new Governor-General was really gifted with such prevision, Marquess Wellesley (or Lord Mornington, as he was then styled) had certainly started to take an interest in the Indian States before he reached Calcutta.

On the voyage out to India his ship stopped for some time at the Cape of Good Hope, where he met Major Kirkpatrick, who had been Resident at the Nizam's Court. In a long letter written to Mr. Dundas, President of the Board of Control, and dated Cape of Good Hope, 23rd February, 1798, Wellesley gives an interesting account (supplied by Kirkpatrick) of the different troops under the command of French officers at Hyderabad, and makes various suggestions dealing with a situation which, owing to the state of affairs in Europe, was undoubtedly fraught with danger to the British in India. Even if Wellesley was occasionally too prone to suspect French intrigue where none existed, there is no doubt that " the formidable Corps d'Armée of fourteen thousand sepoys under French officers that was maintained by the Nizam " formed a good nucleus round which might gather the French adventurers in Scindia's and other Maratha armies, as well as those with Tipu.

Since 1793 England had been engaged in a life-and-death struggle with the French Republic, and the idea behind almost every action of Wellesley was to checkmate the real or possible machinations of France.

In the month of April, 1798, on the very day on which the Marquess Wellesley landed at Madras on his way to Calcutta, at Mangalore, on the west coast of India, there disembarked some ambassadors whom Tipu had sent to the Isle of France (Mauritius). They brought with them a rather shabby collection of volunteers and a promise from the French Governor that his Republic would soon entertain with pleasure Tipu's offer of " alliance and amity." By this assurance " Citoyen Tipu " was much elated. It helped to counteract the depression he had felt at the retirement of Zeman Shah of Afghanistan. That ruler, in the previous year, had invaded the Punjab and occupied Lahore, but owing to a Persian attack on his own western provinces, had been forced to withdraw, much to the relief of the Bengal Government. Tipu now redoubled his efforts to unite the Marathas and the Nizam against the English, but met with comparatively little success. The Maratha confederation still suspected the ruler of Mysore, and the Nizam, though furious at the refusal of the British assistance at Kurdla, had grown to fear the French corps at his capital almost as much as the Marathas who had temporarily reduced him to a state of vassalage.

Wellesley gladly enough would have declared war upon the Sultan of Mysore immediately on learning of the arrival of the French volunteers. But the condition of the Company's finances and credit, as well as the unprepared state of the Madras army, forbade that step. Further, the policy of non-interference pursued by Cornwallis and Shore had led the Marathas to despise the British alliance, while Daulat Rao Scindia, the most considerable prince among them, whose influence at Poona at this time overawed the Peishwa, urged the impolicy of assisting the English to overcome Tipu. Lastly, the Nizam, thanks to the subjection to the Marathas and his dependence on his French corps, was more likely to be a source of danger to his allies than of strength. His potential resources, however, were of value, as Wellesley saw. So, against his inclinations, Wellesley was forced to temporise with Tipu in order to consolidate his own position and to make adequate preparations to undertake an offensive war. The first step necessary in this direction was to remove the French control over the Nizam's forces, which might, in case of a war with Tipu, develop at any time into a serious menace. Wellesley therefore entered into an alliance with Hyderabad—the first Subsidiary Alliance, as we now know it—by which the Nizam was forced to disband the French battalions and to agree to receive a force commanded by English officers to be stationed permanently in his territory. This treaty was unlike the former agreements negotiated by the East India Company, and an analysis of its principles is necessary for an understanding of the subsidiary system.

So far the Company had only offered alliance to Indian States as an inexpensive method of defending their own frontier (the Company's). There was no attempt to restrict the authority or independence of the rulers concerned. Even the Nawab of the Carnatic and the Vizier of Oudh were not prohibited from entering into relations with other States or from carrying out any policy not inconsistent with the main purpose of the safety of the Company's frontier. The treaty with the Nizam and most of the treaties made by Wellesley are, however, based on a wholly different policy. The object of the treaty was to restrict the Nizam's freedom of action, and, as Wellesley himself put it, "to place the States in such a degree of dependence as to deprive them of the means of prosecuting any measure hazardous to the security of the British Empire."

On the same principle, it was also laid down that the ruler should have no external relations.

An alliance of a similar nature was offered to the Peishwa, but the Poona Court refused to walk into Wellesley's parlour.

But though the Peishwa had refused a subsidiary force, he, like the Nizam, agreed to join the English against Tipu. Accordingly, in 1799, with the Madras army now fully organised, Mysore was attacked. Tipu in vain looked for help from the French. Soon driven into the fortress of Seringapatam, he met his death when that stronghold was stormed. The short-lived Musalman dynasty of Mysore came to an abrupt end. The kingdom which lay at the mercy of the allies was broken up, each receiving a share, while the remainder was made into the modern principality of Mysore and given to a scion of the old Hindu family which had been expelled by Haidar Ali.

Very stringent conditions were imposed on the Maharajah by the new treaty, Writing to the Court of Directors on the 3rd August, 1799, Wellesley explained :—

> "In framing the engagement (with Mysore) it was my determination to establish the most unqualified community of interest between the Government of Mysore and the Company. . . . Recollecting the inconveniences and embarrassments which have arisen to all parties concerned with the double Governments and conflicting authorities unfortunately established in Oudh, the Carnatic and Tanjore, I resolved to reserve to the Company the

most extensive and indisputable rights of interposition in the internal affairs of Mysore, as well as an unlimited right of assuming direct management of the country."

The Mysore treaty is, of course, an exception, but just for that reason it is of supreme importance, as it demonstrates that the clauses relating to the complete internal independence of the States which find a place in other treaties are not merely the language of courtesy nor hypocritical phrases employed to dupe the unwary; they are genuine clauses which were deliberately inserted, from considerations of honour and in order to limit the Company's responsibilities; and they express solemn guarantees which were thoroughly understood and meant to be discharged.

The fall of Seringapatam brought to light the correspondence which Tipu had conducted with various Indian and other Powers. Among the many letters found were some from Muhammad Ali, the late Nawab of the Carnatic, and the son who had succeeded him. On the pretext that this correspondence with Tipu constituted disloyalty to an ally, Wellesley annexed the Carnatic without hesitation. The real reason was that as Mysore had ceased to be a hostile independent State there was no need to stick to the Ring-Fence policy in Southern India.

In his dealings with Oudh, as in his dealings with the Carnatic, Lord Wellesley did not set great store by treaties and obligations. By pressure, the treaty of 1801 was forced upon the ruler of Oudh. In 1799 the Nawab Vizier had proposed to abdicate, and Wellesley was not unmindful of the opportunity such a step offered to force Oudh to accept new conditions. Writing to the Secret Committee of the Court of Directors (28th November, 1799), the Governor-General observed with commendable frankness:

"Whatever may be the motives or whatever shall be the ultimate decision of His Excellency on this occasion, it is my intention to profit by the event to the utmost practical extent, and I entertain the confident hope of being able either to establish, with the consent of the Vizier, the sole and exclusive authority of the Company within the Province of Oudh and its dependencies, or at least to place our interests in that quarter on an improved and durable foundation."

Wellesley claimed that the Company had the right to augment their forces within the Nawab Vizier's dominions, even without his consent, "to whatever extent the British Government in India may judge requisite to the permanent security of our common interests," and that the Nawab Vizier was bound "to defray the expenses of any force which the British Government shall deem necessary" for the effectual protection of Oudh. This extraordinary claim, meant to establish, as the Governor-General himself said, "the sole and exclusive authority of the Company within the Province of Oudh and its dependencies," the Vizier was not in a position to resist. He, however, refused to abdicate, though the price of continuing to reign in Oudh was his acceptance of a new treaty which reduced that State to a position of absolute vassalage. As Lord Wellesley explained in his despatch to the Secret Committee, dated 14th November, 1801, the sixth article of the treaty "reserved the positive right of interference in the internal management of that part of the country retained by the Nawab Vizier." The military power of Oudh was completely extinguished. At the same time the treaty exonerated "the British Government from the obligation of maintaining any definite or specified number of troops in the province of Oudh, the Company being charged with the general defence of the Vizier's dominions, and being relieved from all special engagement with regard to the description or amount of the force to be employed for that purpose." For the maintenance of the subsidiary force—the specific upkeep of which was, by the way, dispensed with by treaty—Wellesley forced the Vizier to surrender a considerable portion of his territory. The principle on which the subsidy was to be commuted was on the basis of the Hyderabad precedent, where "in commutation of 40 lakhs a country rated at the annual value of 62 lakhs of rupees was taken away in full sovereignty." (Wellesley's Despatches, p. 205.)

The Vizier of Oudh gave the Governor-General some trouble, but the Nizam proved less difficult to deal with. The treaty of 1798 had converted that ruler into a really serviceable ally in the war against Mysore, and by Wellesley's own account rendered him far more worthy than the Marathas to profit by the division of territories made among the victorious allies. But the Nizam's share of those territories was surrendered to the British so as to provide for the expense of the augmented subsidiary force. Probably the Nizam's easy consent to this arrangement was due to the promise to undertake his defence against all enemies, and, since his humiliation at Kurdla, the Nizam had been desperately afraid of the Marathas. He now was promised by Wellesley relief from the exaction of *chauth* by them. It could, however, hardly be expected that the Peishwa and other Maratha chiefs would be willing to forego their claim to *chauth* in the territories of Hyderabad, and the Company's demand that they should do so, "almost unavoidably involved a war with the Marathas, whenever that people should have the courage to undertake one." That, in fact, was Wellesley's idea. Since Hyderabad had been reduced to helplessness and the power of Tipu extinguished, only the Maratha States remained to be dealt with. Wellesley offered the Peishwa a subsidiary alliance, and he made no secret of his view that as the Peishwa was the acknowledged head of the Maratha Confederacy, the acceptance by him of a subsidiary alliance would be held binding on the other Maratha Chiefs. The Peishwa had originally, on the advice of Scindia, Holkar and other princes, refused the alliance offered. But when Scindia withdrew to the north, the Peishwa signed the treaty of Bassein and accepted a subsidiary force, for the maintenance of which he ceded territories. Wellesley had now rounded off his system. Of the five important Indian Powers outside the Punjab, the Marathas, the Nizam, the Sultan of Mysore, the

Nawab of the Carnatic and the Vizier of Oudh, he had conquered Mysore, annexed the Carnatic, extinguished the military power of Oudh, reduced the Nizam from an independent Power to a dependent ally, and finally, by the treaty of Bassein, attempted to convert the Marathas into a subordinate confederacy. The treaty of Bassein was naturally enough repudiated by the Maratha leaders, and the war that followed, though it broke up the power of the Peishwa, did not establish British authority over Scindia, Holkar or the Bhosla rulers of Nagpur.

Though the final effort to bring the whole Maratha empire under British suzerainty by a single stroke did not meet with success, Wellesley could still claim with justification that the political system of subsidiary alliance was mainly of his creation.

Wellesley did not conceal his purpose of acquiring for the Company "imperial paramountcy" in India. In a speech to the European inhabitants of Calcutta on the eve of his departure he stated: "My public duty is discharged to the satisfaction of my conscience by the prosperous establishment of a system of policy which promises to improve the general condition of the people of India and unite the principal Native States in the bond of peace under the British power." If he was not wholly successful in this, in spite of the victories of Arthur Wellesley, it was because the Maratha rulers were still strong enough to resist direct encroachments on their sovereignty.

The process of expelling Scindia's soldiers from the Eastern Punjab, however, brought the Company into touch with the Cis-Sutlej Sikh States, and prepared the way for the admission of these Powers, six years later, into the general system.

Guided, as Wellesley was, by the idea of controlling the States brought under the subsidiary alliances to suit the policy of the Company, he did not hesitate to advise his Residents at the Courts of his allies to intervene officially in the internal affairs of Government. In Mysore he had expressly reserved for the Company full powers of interposition in all matters. In Oudh also he had tried to establish, with the consent of the Vizier, "the solid and exclusive authority of the Company." In Hyderabad he took advantage of the succession of Secunder Jah to insist that the Nizam shall "engage to pay at all times the utmost attention to such advice as the Company's Government shall occasionally judge it necessary to offer to him with a view to or objects connected with the advancement of his interests, the happiness of his people and the mutual welfare of both States."

For the purpose of forcing the Nizam to accept these conditions, which materially reduced his powers of internal government, Wellesley proposed to use the very subsidiary force which was maintained at the Nizam's own expense for the defence of his dominions. "It is manifest," the Governor-General wrote to the Resident at Hyderabad, "that our power of settling the succession in the manner described and of obtaining the advantages which I have enumerated will depend in an eminent degree, if not absolutely, on the local position of the subsidiary force at the time of His Highness' death. It is therefore of the last importance that the force should not only be kept together, but stationed as near as possible to the residence of the Nizam."

Wellesley was recalled in August, 1805, and Lord Cornwallis was appointed in his place. He was sent out to liquidate the grandiose scheme which Wellesley had undertaken, "which annually calls for reinforcements of men and for remittances of money, and which yields little other profits except brilliant Gazettes." (Cornwallis to Lord Lake. Letter 30th July, 1805.) Before he could undertake the work of pacification and settlement Cornwallis died.

Sir George Barlow, who succeeded him, carried out the policy of the Court of Directors and withdrew from the doubtful liabilities which Wellesley, in his policy of expansion, had undertaken. The subsidiary alliance which was offered to Scindia was not pressed, and that ruler was left completely independent.

The Company also deliberately dissociated themselves from concern in the internal affairs of those States not directly bound by treaties. The Rajput States and the Central Indian rulers were left to be dealt with by Holkar and Scindia as they chose. But in the affairs of Hyderabad, Oudh and other States closely bound to the British Government by definitive treaties and military obligations, Sir George Barlow intervened to support the Company's interests. This policy of leaving the independent States alone (known at this period as non-intervention), which had the support of the Court of Directors, did not meet with the approval of the Company's political officers in India. Metcalfe characterised it as unworthy, weak, and described some of the arguments advanced in support of it as monstrous.

Lord Minto, the next Governor-General, came out to India in 1807 with instructions to follow the same policy as that inaugurated by Lord Cornwallis.

Lord Minto was quite determined to avoid entangling alliances, such as those of Lord Wellesley's time. The recognition by Sanad of certain minor States in Bundelkhand to the claims of the Peishwa in those areas was no more than a confirmation of the existing rights of those chiefs in relation to their suzerain, and could by no chain of reasoning be held likely to create fresh political relations.[1] The same claim may be made for the Kathiawar settlement when the chiefs in that peninsula signed a security bond against misbehaviour on the entry into Kathiawar, in 1807, of the joint forces of the Company and the Gaikwar.

But, though Lord Minto would have been quite content to devote all his energies to the work of organising the new provinces acquired for the Company by Lord Wellesley, he could not entirely avoid war. He had to intervene in Travancore, to support the ruler of that State against his rebellious subjects. He was also compelled by circumstances to take under the military protection of the Company the powerful Sikh *misls* [2] on

[1] *See* Aitchison (9th ed.), 30, V. pp. 108–111, for an instance.

[2] Clans.

the eastern side of the Sutlej, thus putting an effective barrier to the expansion of the newly-founded Lahore State under Ranjit Singh.

As can be seen from his instructions to Malcolm, Metcalfe and Elphinstone, his envoys to Persia, the Punjab and Afghanistan respectively, as well as by his despatches to the Board of Control, Minto was at least as anxious to counteract the danger of a French invasion as Wellesley had ever been. But Napoleon's projects were upset by the revolt of Spain and the ensuing Peninsular War; thus all fears of his designs on India faded away. So that though Malcolm's mission to Persia was a failure, Elphinstone's to Afghanistan productive of no result, good or bad, and only Metcalfe's to Ranjit Singh fruitful, the later years of Minto's regime were a peaceful time.

IV.

At the end of Wellesley's administration, in the year 1805, the Company was in actual alliance by treaty with the following States:

Oudh,	Coorg,
Hyderabad,	Mysore,
Travancore,	Poona,
Cochin,	Baroda.

The basis of alliance was everywhere—except in Mysore—the same. The Company undertook (*a*) to protect the rulers of these States from internal and external aggression, and (*b*) to maintain a force for that purpose, which was to be subsidised by the State concerned. The State entering into this alliance agreed to give up its right of foreign relations, but was guaranteed full and absolute internal sovereignty. During this period most of the States entering into alliance with the Company were considered equal in status with the Company and possessed of full sovereignty. It was on this basis that alliances had been offered to Scindia and to Holkar.

Since the treaties made by Wellesley form the basis of

the political system of India as it developed during the course of the next half-century, a few general considerations of importance arising from Wellesley's policy may be discussed here.

(1) In the treaties between the Company and the States there is a spirit of equality of status, and the States are recognised as being in the enjoyment of *sovereign independence*. The treaties with the Nizam and the Marathas, who were, in theory and fact, in the enjoyment of absolute external and internal sovereignty, both show a spirit of reciprocity. In the treaty with the Nizam, which was entered into for the purpose of taking "means for the mutual defence of their respective possessions," it is stated, "whatever transactions, whether of great or small import, may in future take place between the aforesaid Rao Pandit Pradham or his dependents, a *reciprocal* communication of the same shall be made to the other contracting party without delay and without reserve." (Separate article in the Treaty of Alliance, 1st of September, 1798, page 170, *Wellington Despatches.*) Again, the preamble of the Treaty of Defensive Alliance with the Nizam, dated 12th October, 1800, mentions as the object of the treaty, "the complete and *reciprocal protection* of their respective territories, together with those of their several allies and dependents." It will also be of interest to note that even up to 1829, the Governor-General, in his correspondence with the Nizam, used such terms as "Niyaz Mund," a recognition of his superiority of rank, while the Nizam, speaking of himself, used the royal "we." It is not only in agreements with powerful rulers like the Nizam and the Peishwa that equality of status was recognised. In the treaty with the Rao Raja of Alwar, concluded in 1803 during the campaign against the Marathas chiefs, the Raja is authorised to demand aid from the British Government "if from the obstinacy of the opposite party no amicable terms can be reached," an admission of Alwar's rights of separate and direct negotiations with other States.

(2) The Company at that time had no intention of

claiming for themselves or the Crown the rights of an overlord, or of encroaching otherwise on the sovereignty of their allies. In fact, after the victory over Scindia in 1804, Lord Wellesley wrote to the Secret Committee of the Court of Directors that the object of the Company should be security; and Scindia was given the option of coming into the defensive alliance or keeping out. The policy later on pursued of evolving a State system in which the British Company would stand as a paramount power over subordinate allies did not come into being until a later date. It can be seen from the contemporaneous documents that neither in the case of the Nizam, nor of the Peishwa, nor of any of the Powers which came into alliance, even though subsidiary, was there any limitation of the armies to be maintained by them.

(3) A third consideration is that by a most unequivocal declaration the independent Powers brought into the defensive system were guaranteed by the Company full and absolute sovereignty in their internal affairs. Every treaty with a State previously independent, or taken into alliance for help in campaigns, lays this down in express terms. That the clause was no empty profession, but a legal obligation intentionally assumed to respect the sovereign rights of the allies, is clear from the fact that Wellesley frankly recognised its baneful effects and implications, and tried to remedy it wherever he could by the provisions of subsequent treaties. Even Dalhousie at a much later period recognised the implications of this clause when on the 27th May, 1851, in a minute he thus commented on the Treaty of 1800:

> "The several obligations which those treaties imposed have been faithfully observed by the contracting parties on either side. *Among them all no article was more distinctly or emphatically worded* than that wherein the Honourable Company's Government distinctly declared that they have no manner of concern with any of His Highness' children, relations, subjects or servants, in relation to whom His Highness is absolute. . . . We have bound ourselves by treaty to shield him from every enemy and we have guaranteed to him the exercise over his own subjects of his sole and exclusive authority."

But the establishment of a subsidised force within the territory of the Ruler was an important feature of these treaties. This force was ostensibly for the purpose of defending the ruler from external and internal enemies, and a subsidy was undertaken by the protected ruler for its expenses. The Government of India themselves writing to England explained the true object of this force: "When for our private views that Prince (the Nizam) was constrained to support a body of our troops stationed near his capital, the then Government disguised the interested oppressiveness by the steady declaration that His Highness had spontaneously sought the aid of a subsidiary force to secure his person and territories." (Bengal Political Letter, 20th December, 1822.) And we saw in the case of the Nizam, that far from protecting the ruler, this force which was paid for by him was used by Wellesley to coerce him into accepting clauses affecting his own sovereignty. We saw in the case of the Nawab Vizier of Oudh how on the basis of this clause it was claimed (without justification) that the Company had the right to intervene in any matter of its choice, and to increase the force to any extent, charging the whole amount to the Vizier.

The subsidy which the State agreed to pay for the maintenance of the security troops reached generally to about a third of its revenues. The Company's Government knew well enough that such a demand on the State's revenue could not be met with any regularity in a country like India, where revenues shrink and expand according to the monsoon. Practically the position was like a mortgage. The States would naturally fall into arrears, and opportunities were thus bound to arise for the Company to enforce its security and annex valuable portions of the territories of its defaulting ally. On two occasions large areas of the Nizam's dominions were thus acquired. On successive occasions Oudh was deprived of valuable districts to defray the expenses of the subsidiary force. On a later occasion (1844) Scindia was made to yield provinces on the same ground.

The pay and allowances of the British officers of these contingents maintained at the expense of Indian States were many times more than what prevailed in the Company's forces or in the British army. The Commandant of the Nizam's contingent was paid £5,000 a year—a salary larger than the Commander-in-Chief of the Company's forces received—and other officers were paid in proportion.[1]

The restriction of sovereignty with regard to the right of external relations was not a part of the original treaties of alliance made with Arcot, Oudh or Travancore. This clause was only introduced in the treaty with the Nawab of Arcot in 1787. No other ruler before the time of Wellesley had been restricted in his right of negotiating with other Indian rulers. But Wellesley made this clause an essential condition in the treaty with the Nizam, and in all other treaties which he negotiated or offered to negotiate, introduced it as a consideration for the Company's undertaking to defend the territories and possessions of the ruler against external aggression and internal rebellion.

Although, with Wellesley, the policy of the subsidiary alliance came into existence in all its essential features, and although from that time—the early years of the nineteenth century—the practice of active intervention in internal affairs, restriction of sovereign powers, forced appointment of ministers and control of succession began to take shape, and although the problems incidental to paramountcy began to agitate Anglo-Indian statesmen, it must not be thought that a political system embracing the whole of India had been brought into being at that time. The treaties with Scindia left him a sovereign Power whose independence was acknowledged up to 1833. The treaty with Holkar in 1806 was also not of a kind which reduced him to the position of a subordinate ally.

During the period between the recall of Wellesley and the appointment of Lord Moira (later the Marquess of

[1] Kaye's *Life of Metcalfe*. 1854. Vol. II. p. 15.

Hastings) the following States were brought within the system of subsidiary alliances:

Chatarpur (1806) . .	Recognition by Sanad.
Maihar (1806) . .	do. do.
Baoni (1806) . . .	do. by letter.
Panna (1807) . . .	Confirmation by Sanad.
Ajaigarh (1807) . .	do. do.
Kathiawar Settlement (1807) (Col. Walker) .	A security bond for regular payment of tribute to the Gaekwar, and good behaviour signed by the principal Chiefs, in return for a guarantee of the integrity of their States as then possessed.
Nagod (1809) . .	Submission.
Patiala and other Cis-Sutlej States (1809) .	Proclamation of guarantee against encroachment from Lahore.
Bijawar (1811) . .	Sanad on Submission.
Mahi Kantha Agency, Idar and other States (1812)	Settlement by security bonds on the same lines as Kathiawar.
Nawanagar (1812) . .	Submission.
Rewa (1812) . . .	Protection.
Orcha (1812) . . .	Subordinate alliance.
Radhanpur (1813) . .	Relations with Baroda mediated by treaty.

How the Company in India, as well as the British authorities in England, looked upon the States at this epoch is well brought out in the "Fifth Report from the Select Committee of the House of Commons on the affairs of the East India Company" (1812). That celebrated document was issued just before the renewal of the Company's charter for another twenty years (from 1813 to

1833). From the point of view of the relationship of British India with Indian States it is an illuminating document. It is difficult from a perusal of the Report to imagine that any relationship at all existed. The very few cases in which the name of any State or ruler is mentioned occur only in reference to the territories ceded by or taken from Indian Princes. The inference is clear. In 1812 the Company considered these States as foreign territories, territories, it was true, in which they had some interest, and which they had undertaken to protect, but still foreign territories in the real sense of the word. Whenever they had intervened, as in Hyderabad at the time of Sikandar Jah's succession, it was to secure a ruler who would be friendly to them, and not with a view to encroach on his sovereign rights. The intervention was a manœuvre of international diplomacy, adroit, perhaps even not too straightforward, but not a measure of executive control in exercise of any claim of right based on precedent or agreement or paramountcy. This was true even with regard to some of the minor States brought into alliance in the time of Lord Minto, when the policy of non-intervention was officially in vogue; and in the case of important States, like those of the Cis-Sutlej rulers, no claim of suzerainty or right of control was ever put forward. The Company took them under protection as a safeguard against the growing power of Ranjit Singh.

V.

Lord Moira (later the Marquess of Hastings), who succeeded Lord Minto in 1813, was a different type of statesman. With Wellesley and Dalhousie he shares the claim of having followed a consistent, if often aggressive, policy towards the Indian States.

All fear of France was now past, and it seemed that the work of any Governor-General lay merely in improving the condition of the British Provinces. So far as this sketch is concerned the main events of his period of rule may be summarised as follows:

(1) The War with Nepal (1814–16).
(2) The Defeat of Holkar's Army at Mehidpur (1818).
(3) The Operations against the Pindaris (1814–17).
(4) The Outbreaks at Poona and Nagpur (1817).
(5) The surrender and deposition of the Peishwa in 1818 and the creation of the State of Satara.

With the details of these wars and settlements it is not proposed to deal here. Suffice it to say that, as the successful outcome of the war with Nepal, various dispossessed Hill Chiefs in the tract from the Gogra to the Sutlej were reinstated in their ancestral dominions and given deeds of title (Sanads) (1815), while Sikkim, which abuts on the eastern border of Nepal, in 1817 entered into a treaty of subordinate alliance with the Company. Further, as the firstfruits of the Pindari war, Amir Khan, a prominent free-booting chieftain, came to terms with the British and was assigned various lands in Rajputana and Central India which are now known as the State of Tonk.

After the last Maratha war the Peishwa was deposed and the Poona State annexed. Thus the central circle and unity of a Maratha Confederacy finally disappeared. The Rajah of Nagpur was mulcted of a large portion of his territory, and a treaty was forced upon Scindia (1817) with a view to rendering him incapable of offensive action.

The suppression of the Pindaris and its aftermath, the final Maratha war, not only led to the destruction of the Maratha Confederacy, they resulted in the establishment of a protectorate over the States of Rajputana and certain principalities in Central India from which the Marathas had claimed the right to levy tribute.

These Rajput States had for years been soliciting the Company to enter into treaty relationships with them, but owing to the treaty with Scindia the British Government was forced, often reluctantly, to refuse such agreements. It was only after the treaty with Scindia in 1817 that the Company secured a free hand with regard to the Rajputana States. The treaties concluded by Lord Hastings after this make an impressive list, viz.: Karauli in Eastern Rajputana (1817), protectorate; Samthar in Central India, N.E. of Jhansi (1817), subordination; Bhopal (1817) (pending negotiation of the treaty of 1818, the correspondence (No. XCVI) of 1817 was declared to have "the force and validity of a treaty"); Kotah (1817), protectorate; Jaora (1818), protected by treaty with Holkar; Jodhpur (1818), Udaipur Mewar (1818), Bundi (1818), Bikaner (1818), Kishengarh (1818), Jaijur (1818), Patabgarh (1818), all protectorates; Alirajpur (1818), mediatised, Dungarpur (1818), Dewas (1818), Jaisalmer (1818), Banswara (1818), all protectorates, the engagements for their protection mediated by Sir John Malcolm; Dhar (1819), protectorate; Jhabua (1821), guaranteed by engagement. In addition to these Rajputana and Central India States, Lord Hastings made treaties with Cutch (1816), protection and subordinate alliance; Palanpur (1817), mediated treaty of subordination; Tributary Mahals of Chhota Nagpur (1817 to 1825), engagements of subjection taken from the chiefs in these territories ceded to the Company in 1817; Satara (1819), created by Lord Hastings; Tehri Garhwal, E.S.E. of Simla (1820), Sanad of restoration after Nepal war; Rajpipla (1821), agreement to submit to British settlement; Chhota Udaipur (Central Provinces) (1822), engagement of subordination. It will be observed that this list shows a network of treaties thrown over a large area in the middle of India.

Lord Hastings' policy with regard to the Indian States deserves special attention, because it was during his time that the Simla States—the numerous sovereignties on the lower ranges of the Himalayas—were taken under the Company's protection, Central India was pacified, and the Rajputana Agency came into existence. He "established the State of Satara with sovereignty sufficient for the maintenance of the family in comfort and dignity," a charitable, if strange, principle of sovereignty which is met with in no other case in India. Most of the treaties he entered into contained a clause establishing "subordinate co-operation," a phrase new in Indian political language, between the British Government and the allied State. For the exact significance of this phrase a reference is invited to No. 19 (p. 105 below), from which it would be apparent that the subordinate co-operation was intended merely for war and other external relations, and did not mean subordination of the State in matters relating to its internal government, as is plain from the fact that the same treaty laid down unequivocally that the ruler so allied was absolute within his State.

Another aspect of the Marquess of Hastings' settlement was the "guarantee" given to subordinate chieftains, a provision which gave rise to constant friction and trouble.

Though Lord Hastings was in favour of the extension of subordinate alliance and the maintenance of even the small tributary chieftains in Central India, especially those whose overlords he deposed or deprived of their rights of tribute, he was firm against the principle of intervention in the internal affairs of these rulers. He laid down the policy in unequivocal terms, with a clarity that left nothing to be desired.

To Mr. C. T. Metcalfe, who had suggested intervention on behalf of the British Power in the affairs of the Nizam, in the interests of good government, the Governor-General in Council replied as follows:

"In the second paragraph of your first letter you say that 'you suppose our interference in the Nizam's affairs to be not merely right, but also a duty, arising out of our supremacy in India, which imposes on us the obligation of maintaining the tranquillity of all countries connected with us, and consequently of protecting the people from oppressions, as no less necessary than the guaranteeing of their rulers against revolution.' The assumption of our possessing an universal supremacy in India, involving such rights as you have described, is a mistake. Over States which have, by particular engagements, rendered themselves professedly feudatory, the British Government does exercise supremacy; but it never has been claimed, and certainly never has been acknowledged in the case of Native Powers standing within the denomination of allies.

Although a virtual supremacy may undoubtedly be said to exist in the British Government, from the inability of other States to contend with its strength, the making such a superiority a principle singly sufficient for any exertion of our will would be to misapply and to pervert it to tyrannical purposes.

. . . .

"Paragraphs 4 and 5 plead necessity for our interposition because the Nizam does not rule his subjects with equity and prudence. The fact of maladministration is unquestionable, and must be deplored. Does that, however, decide the mode in which alteration is to be effected? *Where is our right to determine that the amount of the evil is such as to demand our taking the remedy into our hands? His Lordship in Council observes that the necessity stated is altogether constructive. Were such a pretence allowable, a powerful State should never want colour for subjugating a weak neighbour.* The consequence is so obvious that no principle in the law of nations leaves room for acting in such a presumption. It is admitted that if convulsions rage so violently in one State as clearly to threaten the excitation of ferment in a bordering one, the latter may be justified in reducing to order the nation by which its tranquillity was menaced. This, however, is an extreme case, at the same time that it is of a description strictly defined. No analogy exists between indisputable exigency and an asserted convenience, where vague arbitrary charges, if tolerated on the ground of procedure, would furnish ready pretext for the foulest usurpations."

Lord Hastings' policy of non-intervention differed materially from the previous policy of so-called non-intervention followed by Cornwallis, Shore and others. What the earlier statesmen understood by non-intervention was a close-border policy, of keeping the Company free from entanglements. They held that it did not really matter to the interests of the Company what the relations were between the Marathas and the Nizam or between Scindia and the Rajput States. Lord Hastings, on the other hand, held that the external policy of the States was a matter of vital importance to the Company, but that the rulers in subordinate alliance retained absolute independence in internal matters, and should not be interfered with. The distinction which the Marquess of Hastings clearly brought out in his letter to Metcalfe quoted above is vital. That letter expresses in historical fact the true nature of Paramountcy; and it was upon the basis of a relationship so understood that the treaties of his time were accepted by the States who signed them. And it is of the utmost importance to the true analysis of the relationship of Paramountcy to realise that whatever their past history had been, the contracting States contracted from the standpoint and in the capacity of independent States.

VI.

The period of Lord Hastings' administration had roughly coincided with that of the foundation, rise and collapse of the firm of Palmer & Co. in Hyderabad. The unsavoury scandals in this connection, from which it is impossible entirely to exonerate Lord Hastings, had been the main cause of friction between him and the Court of Directors, and eventually led to their refusal to grant the old nobleman the honorarium proposed by his friend Mr. Douglas Kinnaird.

The monopoly of the Company's trade had been taken away by Parliament in 1813, and in 1823 the Company was actually forbidden to engage in trade. This gave a great impetus to private merchants, among whom were many who were only too glad of an opportunity to make the dishonest gains that Palmer & Co. had made in Hyderabad, and who doubtless considered themselves shrewd enough to avoid the fate of bankruptcy which had been that of Palmer. Such men were bitterly opposed to the Act of 1797, which had prohibited all financial transactions with the Indian Princes without the express consent of the Governor-General, and were the keenest critics of those officers of the Company who opposed interference in the concerns of the States. Such persons were only too ready to bleed "poor old Nizzy" or any other Prince if opportunity offered.

Until the arrival of Lord Amherst in Calcutta the

Government rested with Mr. John Adam, the Senior Member of Council.

The only incident of Lord Amherst's period of government (1823–28) which may be mentioned is his relations with the Bharatpur State. The story of the capture of Bharatpur, the fortress which in 1805 had baffled Lord Lake, and of the seizure of the State treasures and jewels in the citadel and their immediate distribution among the attacking force, is well known and need not be repeated, though it is but fair to quote Sir Charles Metcalfe, who wrote: "Our plundering here has been very disgraceful and has tarnished our well-earned honours. Until I can get rid of the prize agents, I cannot establish the sovereignty of the young Raja whom we came professedly to protect, but have been plundering to the last lotah (water pot) since he fell into our hands."

More pertinent is it to remember that interference in the affairs of Bharatpur, though it was in support of a minor against a usurper, was strenuously opposed by Lord Amherst, despite the fact that the investiture of the child ruler had, "in obedience to the express orders of the Governor-General in Council, been performed by one of the political officers of the Residency." He only yielded to the solicitations of Metcalfe, whom he had called from Hyderabad to replace Sir David Ochterlony, after disgracing the latter for assembling a field force to expel the usurper. Portions of Metcalfe's Minute on the subject may be quoted, for there is little doubt that he represented the opinion of all the ablest political officers of the Company at the time. He writes:

"We have become the paramount State in India. In 1817 it became the established principle of our policy to maintain tranquillity among the States of India . . . and we cannot be indifferent spectators of anarchy therein without ultimately giving up India again to the pillage and confusion from which we rescued her. . . . We are not bound by any positive engagement to the Bharatpore State, nor by any claim on her part, but by our duty as supreme guardians of general tranquillity, law and right to maintain the legal succession of Bulwant Singh. . . . Our supremacy has been violated or slighted under the impression that we were prevented by entanglements elsewhere from sufficiently resenting the indignity."

Lord Amherst accepted this view, stating that he had altered his opinion as the result of Metcalfe's Minute. Bharatpur was stormed and the usurper, Doorjan Sal, confined at Allahabad and Benares for the rest of his life.

"The boy Rajah," to quote Marshman, "was conducted to the throne by Sir Charles Metcalfe and Lord Combermere, but the laurels of Bharatpur were dishonoured by rapacity. The siege was undertaken to expel a usurper and to restore the throne to the rightful Prince, yet all the State treasures and jewels found in the citadel, to the extent of forty-eight lacs of rupees, were unscrupulously pronounced by the military authorities to be lawful prize and at once distributed among the officers. Six lacs fell to the share of the Commander-in-Chief. This procedure was defended by the sophism that 'as Doorjan Sal had been in quiet possession of the throne, and acknowledged by all parties as the Maharajah, no individual either openly or secretly supporting the claims of Bulwant Singh, naturally gave the former the full right to all the property in the fort, and deprived the latter of any claim which he might be supposed to have to it.'"

As has been mentioned above, Sir Charles Metcalfe protested against this dishonourable conduct. The Governor-General, however, took no notice of it.

Lord Amherst's only other action which is of importance in connection with Indian States was in relation to the public debt. Having dissipated the funds left by Lord Hastings he increased the public debt by ten crores. Of this sum, about "one-fourth was obtained from the hoards of the King of Oudh, the perennial reservoir of the Calcutta treasury. Large sums were likewise subscribed by native chiefs and bankers after the capture of Bharatpur, and Bajee Rao (the ex-Peishwa) was induced to invest in the Company's paper some portion of the accumulations of his annuity."

Early in 1828 Lord Amherst retired, and was succeeded by Lord William Bentinck. In 1833 Lord

William became, on the renewal of the Company's charter, the Governor-General of India in place of Governor-General of Fort William in Bengal. With the Indian States he had few dealings, and his policy would seem to have been to leave the States to look after their own affairs without intervention from outside. Only in Mysore, where the original treaty gave the right of taking over the administration in case of misrule, did the Governor-General intervene forcibly. Mysore was put under British administrators, and for half a century it was held in fact, though not in name, as a British province.

In Hyderabad a new Nizam came to the Musnud in 1829, and the Governor-General took advantage of the occasion to revise the style in which the correspondence with the Court of Hyderabad had hitherto been carried on. In speaking of himself, the Nizam used the Imperial phrase of *Ma ba Dawlat*, or royal self, while the Governor-General made use of terms such as *Niaz Mund*, etc., which admitted an inferiority of rank. These were discontinued and the correspondence of the parties thenceforward was conducted on a footing of equality.

Whatever his reasons, Lord William Bentinck favoured non-intervention in the internal affairs of the States. On the new Nizam requesting a discontinuance of the civil interference, introduced by Sir Charles Metcalfe chiefly with a view to counteract the undue influence of Palmer & Co., the Governor-General readily acceded to the demand. An extract from the letter giving this consent may be quoted :

"As Your Highness entertains the desire, worthy of a great Prince, to take the Government of your country into your own hands, I have most readily ordered the Resident to withdraw all interference on his part. Only it will be necessary that the Kowls (promises) which have been issued with the cognizance of British officers and the confirmation of your Minister be maintained inviolate. This is required by good faith.

"In every other respect your authority will be absolute whether in the selection or removal of Ministers or other servants of the

State, or in the administration of justice, or in revenue affairs, or in any other branch of the Government of your country, there shall be no interference."

Metcalfe's successors at the Hyderabad Residency, a Mr. Martin and Colonel Josiah Stewart, a protégé of Malcolm, were ready enough to follow out this policy, and this led to the common saying at the time, that "there was a Resident at Hyderabad but the Residency had gone to sleep." The Mandamus Papers express in strong terms Lord William Bentinck's opinion of Mr. Martin's conduct. He had retired under a cloud, "distrusted by every man on his staff, who lived on barely civil terms with him." Colonel Stewart, though accused by some Indian newspapers of jobbery perpetrated in certain appointments in the Contingent, was a man of strict probity, but he was quite content to follow out the orders of his Government.

By Lord William Bentinck, fully occupied with his reforms in British India, the doctrine of absolute non-intervention towards the Indian States was strictly enforced. Thus at Gwalior in 1833, according to Aitchison, the British Government declared it was "a matter of indifference whether the Maharajah or the Bai (Baiza Bai) was at the head of the Gwalior State, and that the only object of Government was to preserve the general tranquillity and its own reputation, recognising such ruler as might be placed by the popular voice at the head of the administration."

Beyond question up to this period Gwalior was in fact a State independent of the East India Company and was so treated by it. To quote from Lord William Bentinck's own Kharita, dated December 18th, 1832:

> "I do not possess any authority either to confer or take away the ruling powers because the Maharajah Scindia is the absolute ruler of his country. The British Government have neither seated anyone on the Gadi nor can they depose. There is no reason why the principles of Government should be altered to suit the times."

Again, to quote the evidence of Major Close, Resident

at Gwalior from 1816 to 1823, given before the Select Committee on the Affairs of the East India Company (1833):

> "The treaties with him (Scindia) are not such as to abrogate his independence or to place him in acknowledged submission to the British Government."

In the same report, Gwalior is mentioned along with Nepal, Lahore and Sindh as not under British protection, its relations with the Company being merely those of amity and friendship.

The same policy was followed in Indore, whose ruler had also been declared in the treaty to be absolute over his subjects. In 1835, when the discontented subjects of Holkar rose in rebellion and the Resident was anxious to intervene, the Governor-General refused to be moved from his attitude of neutrality, because interference would have required a prolonged treatment of the internal affairs of the State, which was inconsistent with the position of the ruler and the policy of Government.

This neutrality was the result, not of any unfriendliness to the States, but of a firm conviction that the States in treaty alliance were independent and foreign, and that, therefore, any interference in their affairs would not be legitimate. That Lord William Bentinck and others of his school considered the States as foreign territories is illustrated by the fact that they were willing enough to profit by the internal quarrels of such States to secure their territories for the Company. The best illustration of this is provided by the case of Gwalior. Lord William Bentinck had ostentatiously refused to intervene in the affairs of Gwalior on the ground that the Company had no power to do so. But when the Maharajah Jankoji Rao was faced with serious trouble, the Governor-General's Foreign Department wrote to the Resident asking him to suggest that the Maharajah should abdicate and allow the Company to annex the State. When the Hon. Mr. Cavendish refused to be a party to this suggestion, he was accused of having allowed "a favourable chance to escape of connecting Agra to the Bombay Presidency."

Again, when the Governor-General thought of intervening in Coorg, then still an independent State, he did so, not on the basis of Paramountcy or of any claim vested in him by treaty, but on the basis of international law. The Raja of Coorg was solemnly told that his conduct in putting the emissary of a friendly State in prison was "a gross outrage upon the established rule of all civilised nations." War was declared on the State of Coorg.

Considering the States as independent and foreign, Lord William Bentinck saw no moral or legal objection to a policy of frank annexation, if a State repudiated its treaty obligations or other legitimate occasion arose. In fact, with many persons holding high office in India at the time, Lord William Bentinck believed that all the territories under the rule of the Indian Princes were destined to eventual absorption by British India. Like Dalhousie in later days, he could brook no opposition to his views by the Residents in the various States, and his visits to several of the Indian Princes would seem to have been occasioned by a desire to see how great was the disorganisation existing in their territories. For practical purposes the subsidiary and contingent forces stationed in the various States were at liberty to do as they liked, provided they paid attention to the orders of the Resident. These forces were only nominally under the orders of the Commander-in-Chief. Their discipline was usually far below that of the Company's regular forces, but at the same time greatly superior to that of the armies maintained by the Princes themselves. Posted usually in the neighbourhood of the capitals of the States, they overawed the lawful authority in the State and were the real masters of the situation. Outwardly the Indian Princes were treated with great personal respect. No one questioned their sovereignty; some of them besides the King of Oudh were addressed as "Majesties"; "Royal" salutes were fired in honour of their accessions to their thrones. But in practice they were *rois fainéants* possessed of little power, and any attempts by them at organising their States into compact political entities were looked upon with the utmost suspicion. With a policy which was designed to enfeeble their administrations and indirectly to teach their subjects to look to the Company as their master and not to themselves, it is no wonder that the progress of the States was slow.

VII.

In tracing the relationships of the Indian States with British India the administrations of Sir Charles Metcalfe (1835–36) and of Lord Auckland (1836–42) call for little comment. The former was definitely opposed to interference in the affairs of the States. He was opposed also to Bentinck's forward policy to counteract real or imaginary Russian designs on India.

The blighting effects of the subsidiary system which Lord Cornwallis had noticed when he wrote in 1805 to Lord Lake that: "From Reports I have received from the Residents, I am sorry to find that the States which are most intimately connected with us are reduced to the most forlorn condition; that these States possess no funds or troops on which they can depend; that anarchy and disaffection prevail universally throughout their dominions," became more and more evident. The meddlesomeness of Residents and the resultant diminution of the sovereign's authority naturally led to an almost complete breakdown of State administration. Conditions had become so bad in Mysore that it had to be taken over for direct administration by the British Government under a convenient clause which Wellesley had introduced into the treaty of 1799.

The condition of the States saddled with a subsidiary force or made to pay large sums for its upkeep was even worse. Conditions in Hyderabad were so disorganised as to prove a standing testimony to the blighting effects of this system. Affairs fell into such disorder, and the Administration was so much in debt, that the provinces were for a time put under British Commissioners. In Oudh, where anarchy had become the normal state of affairs for over half a century, a worsening of conditions was considered a matter of indifference. The King, Nasir ud den Shah, was, however, made to sign a treaty in 1834, wherein he declared his willingness "to sign any new treaty which the Governor-General may dictate." Though the Court of Directors repudiated this clause, and refused to ratify the treaty, the King of Oudh was not informed of the fact!

In Gwalior an army of 40,000 troops made civil administration impossible. That state had lost its military power, though the civil administration continued to be based on military rule. The case of Holkar was even more lamentable. The administration of Hari Har Rao became so unbearable that in 1835 his subjects besieged him in his own palace. In Baroda, Anand Rao Gaikwar's administration was so disastrous that on his death the successor was not able to pay his (Anand Rao's) debts to private creditors. A proposal was actually made for the annexation of Cochin on the ground of extreme maladministration. The Rajputana States, which had been relieved of the vexatious supremacy of the Marathas, had not yet emerged from a feudal system of polity in which rebellious and unruly Thakurs (nobles) defied the ruler and set at naught his authority. In fact, in every State which had come under the subsidiary alliance, the old edifice of administration reared up to suit the peculiar conditions of the State had broken down. The subsidiary force, the presence of the Resident and the guarantee of the ruler's position from external aggression, had combined to undermine initiative and responsibility of rulers and sap the foundations of social well-being in the States. That they recovered from this almost complete breakdown was due to the energy, ability and farsightedness of a new school of statesmen represented by Salar Jung of Hyderabad, Dinkar Rao of Gwalior, Sankurni Menon of Travancore, and Madhav Rao of Indore, who laid, truly and well, the foundations of modern administration in Indian States.

The disasters in Afghanistan brought about the retirement of Lord Auckland and the appointment of Lord Ellenborough (1842–44), who had been President of the Board of Control. The new Governor-General succeeded to some extent in re-establishing British prestige in Afghanistan, and then proceeded to annex Sindh. The annexation of Sindh was an act of gross injustice, as Sir Charles Napier himself recognised when he communicated his achievement in his classical pun, "peccavi." It was recognised as such by Parliament, which was already offended by the rhetorical tone of Ellenborough's proclamations and "the absurd solemnity with which the (spurious) Somnath gates were brought back from Ghazni." Lord Ellenborough had for some time been actually contemplating what action to take against Gwalior, and on what pretext to annex it. That the measures of coercion later employed towards Gwalior, nominally as a punishment for the resistance offered by its troops to the British Army, had been contemplated before there was any idea that there would be any fighting, is shown by Lord Ellenborough's own letters to the Queen at a time when he anticipated nothing beyond an armed demonstration to restore order in the interests of the minor ruler. For example:

"The late Maharajah of Gwalior had allotted certain revenues for the maintenance of a corps of about 1,400 men, to be commanded by British officers, and constantly stationed in Gwalior territory. This corps has done excellent service, and it is proposed to obtain from the Gwalior State the assignment of further revenues for the purpose of raising very considerably the amount of this useful force."

Or again:

"This measure of increasing the force under British officers which is paid by the Gwalior State, taken in conjunction with that of reducing the number of their own ill-regulated army, will, it is expected, give full future security and permanently place the Gwalior State in the relation towards the British Government in which it was Lord Wellesley's object to place it, and in which he thought he had placed it by the treaties of Sirjee Arjengaum and of Boorhanpore, which were concluded by the Duke of Wellington on the 20th of December, 1803, and the 17th of February, 1804."

Again, in a letter to the Duke of Wellington before there was any likelihood of any fighting with the Gwalior troops, he writes:

"I am acting upon your treaty of Boorhanpore, carrying into effect the spirit of that treaty by rescuing the person and the Government of the Maharajah from the real subjection in which both are to the army. . . . I shall carry into effect, too, Lord Wellesley's views as to the future relations of Scindia with our Government, which would have been entirely defeated had we permitted this really unfriendly Government, with an overgrown and mutinous army, to exist at Gwalior."

The real motive of his intervention became evident as soon as the Governor-General was in a position to show his hand. The Governor-General had intervened, nominally in order to support the rights of the minor Maharaja. But as soon as the Gwalior army was dispersed, the Governor-General proceeded to institute a Council of Regency, whose members were to act in accordance with the advice of the Resident, and were not to be changed except with the sanction of the Government of India. That Gwalior was not annexed, as one school of officials had always wanted to do, was due to the recognition by the Governor-General that his aggression on Sindh had already made him unpopular with the Cabinet in London.

Lord Ellenborough's chagrin at his recall by the Directors of the Company was mitigated somewhat by the fact that Sir Henry Hardinge, his successor, was his own brother-in-law, and so likely to be fairly tender to his reputation. The new Governor-General was a soldier of ability and one who did not hesitate to serve under his own Commander-in-Chief and lead a brigade in certain battles during the first Sikh war. As a result of that hard-fought struggle, several Indian States came into treaty relationship with the Company. At the end of the war Rajah Gulab Singh of Jammu was recognised as the ruler of Kashmir (treaty of 1846). The treaty with the Sikhs (1846) recognised Mandi and other Trans-Sutlej States. Jind by its engagement (1847) received a grant of new territory, while in the following year the chiefship of Shahpura in Rajputana (adjoining Ajmer-Merwara) was taken under British protection.

VIII.

The policy of annexation which began with Auckland, and was continued by Ellenborough, found its most avowed champion in Lord Dalhousie. A remarkable and masterful personality, Dalhousie stands in relation to Indian States and to British India on the same eminence as Warren Hastings, Wellesley and the Marquess of Hastings. His Governor-Generalship in India is marked by the annexation of the Punjab, Oudh and Nagpur, as well as of those States to which his famous " policy of lapse " was applied. The theory and practice of " lapse " need not be discussed here, as the problems raised by them have been set at rest once for all by the assurances conveyed to the Princes in 1858 of their right to adopt successors.

Dalhousie's policy of annexation, based on what he claimed to be his desire to bring under " one just, efficient, and systematic rule," as one apologist (Ramsay Muir) puts it, needs examination. Many of the States that were annexed were no worse governed than the rest. Oudh, where the administration was scandalously corrupt, was annexed by a diplomatic sharp practice which even the best of motives could not condone.

Though an annexationist—and his annexations need not be discussed here, since the conditions which led to them are not relevant to our puprose—Dalhousie was, like the Marquess of Hastings and all other Governors-

General who understood the true relations between Indian States and the Government of India, a believer in the principle that the treaties gave the Government of India no right to meddle in the internal affairs of Indian States. When General Fraser, Resident in Hyderabad, suggested that the Government of India should intervene to set affairs right in the Nizam's dominion, Lord Dalhousie wrote:

"I desire to record my entire dissent from, and disapproval of, the policy which the Resident has suggested for the adoption of the Government of India. For more than half a century relations of amity and intimate connection have existed between the British Government and the Nizam, and they have been strengthened on both sides by the stipulations of formal treaties.

"The several obligations which those treaties imposed have been faithfully observed by the contracting parties on either side. Among them all, no article was more distinctly or emphatically worded than that wherein the Honourable Company's Government distinctly declared that they have no manner of concern with any of His Highness's children, relations, subjects or servants, with respect to whom His Highness is absolute. . . .

"Lastly, the course of events during the several administrations that have succeeded the rule of Chandu Lal have shown how fruitless have been our endeavours to exercise a beneficial influence in the management of His Highness's affairs through the medium of a minister recommended by our approbation; and have demonstrated that a minister not selected by the Sovereign's favour, though he may be supported by all our authority, is rendered powerless for good by the passive obstruction which it is and ever will be in His Highness's power to place in the way of his servant's exertions. . . .

"Again, it is often maintained that such is the misgovernment of His Highness the Nizam, that so great are the violence and lawless confusion which pervade every part of his dominions, that it has become the moral duty of the British Government, as the Paramount Power in India, to assume to itself the Government of His Highness's dominions, in order to correct the evils of his rule, and to rescue his subjects from the sufferings which are alleged to proceed therefrom.

"I desire to repudiate all adhesion to a doctrine which leads, in my humble judgment, to a system of unwarranted and officious meddling.

"In too many instances, I fear it proceeds not from sentiments of enlarged benevolence but from the promptings of ambitious greed. Even where the motive from which it springs is pure and sincere, the doctrine is, in my view, not the less unsound. The acknowledged supremacy of the British power in India gives to it the right, and imposes upon it the duty, of maintaining by its influence, and (if need be) compelling by its strength, the continuance of general peace. It entitles it to interfere in the administration of Native Princes if their administration tends unquestionably to the injury of the subjects or of the allies of the British Government.

"But I recognise no mission confided to the British Government which imposes on it the obligation, or can confer upon it the right of deciding authoritatively on the existence of native independent sovereignties, and of arbitrarily setting them aside, whenever their administration may not accord with its own views, and although their acts in no way affect the interests or security of itself or its allies.

"Still less can I recognise any such property in the acknowledged supremacy of the British Government in India as can justify its rulers in disregarding the positive obligations of international contracts, in order to obtrude on Native Princes and their people a system of subversive interference which is unwelcome alike to people and prince.

"In the case of the Nizam, the British Government is bound by the solemn obligations of a treaty to abstain from all interference in His Highness's internal affairs. The sovereign has been and still is strongly and consistently averse to any the slightest evasion on our part of these obligations. His people have shown no desire for our good offices, nor have ever furnished us with the slightest pretext for interposition. And, whatever may be the tenor of His Highness's administration, it cannot be said as yet to have materially affected the security of any portion of British territory, or to have damaged the interest of British subjects. . . .

"I refuse to entertain them because we acknowledge the Nizam as an independent Prince. We have bound ourselves by treaty to shield him from every enemy, and we have guaranteed to him the exercise over his own subjects of his sole and absolute authority. The British Government therefore cannot honestly entertain, and has never entertained, any intention of open aggression on the independence of this Prince. It nourishes no secret and insidious design of standing aloof while his sovereignty is fast crumbling under the weight of his own incapacity and folly. The Resident at His Highness's Court continues, and will continue, to persevere in the endeavours he has made in past times to support His Highness's power and to promote the good of his people. He will be instructed to give on every fit occasion the services of the contingent troops, or, if need be, those of the subsidiary force also, for the maintenance of the sovereign's just authority. In so doing he will exercise the power with which he is vested, of judging in each case of the fitness of the purpose for which the troops are required, and of demanding subsequently the adoption of such measures as are the proper consequence of his interposition.

" He will address the Nizam, as heretofore, on every occurrence which may seem to call for an expression of its sentiments by the Government which he represents, and which is entitled by its position of supremacy and by long-standing alliance to address His Highness in the language of remonstrance and reproof.

" He will warn him on every fitting occasion of the evils which his administration may involve; he will point out the remedy for the abuses he may have denounced, and he will tender freely to His Highness all the aid which the Government of India can supply, whether by his counsel or by force of arms, for meeting the opposition which may be roused to the application of the remedies he may have suggested.

" But so long as the alleged evils of His Highness's Government are confined within its own limits, and affect only his own subjects, the Government of India must observe religiously the obligations of its own good faith. It has no just right to enter upon a system of direct interference in the internal affairs of His Highness's kingdom, which is explicitly forbidden by the positive stipulations of treaty, which would be utterly repugnant to the wishes of the sovereign, our ally, and is unsought by the people over whom he rules.

" If, indeed, the effect of His Highness's misgovernment should be felt beyond his own bounds, if the safety of our territory should be placed in doubt, or the interests of our subjects in jeopardy, I shall be prompt to demand and to enforce reparation for the aggrieved, as well as the infliction of signal punishment on the aggressors. . . ."

The corollary in Dalhousie's mind to the impossibility of interference so long as a State continued to exist was to abolish the State; hence his radical remedy of ruthless annexation, which he applied to old-established kingdoms like Oudh and Berar, and whenever his policy of escheat and lapse found an opening. In the result he left India a cauldron of discontent which boiled over in the Mutiny. The importance of Indian States even, in their existing condition of disorganisation, was never better illustrated than at that time of crisis. What saved the British Empire in India was the ready help rendered by the Princes of Northern India, and the wise policy pursued by Salar Jung in Hyderabad. It is unnecessary in this connection to do more than refer to the officially published "Honours and Rewards for Mutiny Services," in which a full recognition of the part played by the Indian States in those critical days is recorded by grateful contemporaries.

IX.

In theory the position of the Indian States underwent no change as a result of the Mutiny. The transfer of the Government of India from the Company to the Crown did not, and could not, affect the treaty position of the States. This was made amply clear in the Act of 1858 and in the Proclamation of Queen Victoria.

One important result of the Mutiny was the repudiation of the doctrine of lapse—though not in entirety the doctrine of pseudo-feudalism. The aggrandisement of the Company's dominions by a convenient interpretation of the theory of lapse had been one of the contributory causes of the Mutiny.

Lord Canning, who had arrived in Calcutta fully convinced of the wisdom, if not of the justice of Dalhousie's policy of "escheatment," was one of the first to recant this view. Queen Victoria, who had from her accession regarded the Company's Government as an anomaly, who had disliked the Company's gift of medals for military services in India, and who had allowed the Governor-Generals to correspond direct with her as if they had been the rulers of a royal province, had from her accession taken a keen interest in the Indian States. This interest continued unflagging throughout Her Majesty's life, and, though press of official work made it impossible for the Queen to go through all the Indian despatches, as on the assumption by the Crown of the Government of

India she had at first arranged, she always insisted on seeing any important papers dealing with the affairs of the States, if such papers came to London.

When the horror of the Mutiny dawned upon the minds of men in England, all were agreed that the Company must go, except the Directors in Leadenhall Street and certain hirelings whom they employed to present an unconvincing case for the retention of the Company's ruling powers.

This is no place to go into the details of the political settlement arrived at when the Crown took over the charge of India. Suffice it to say that the executive power of the Government of India remained practically what it had been in the last days of the Company.

In England it was recognised that the harmful impression created by Dalhousie's annexations must be removed, and in the Proclamation which, after several redraftings at the Queen's wish, was issued in the name of Her Majesty, the Crown announced its intention of making no fresh extensions of territory in India.

Her Majesty is believed to have wished to go further, and to have had a desire that in future matters at issue between the Government of India and the States should be settled by some form of judicial tribunal to be set up, but the idea unfortunately came to nothing. It is, however, certain that in 1859 the Queen asked the Secretary of State whether some procedure could not be devised for dealing in a more judicial manner with cases in which a State was threatened with sequestration, in order to " secure the Queen from acts being done in her name which might not be entirely justifiable, morally as well as legally." Sir Charles Wood proposed measures to ensure this, but on Lord Canning's objections the Queen suggested that the Viceroy himself should indicate a more suitable plan. What answer was returned is not known, but, perhaps, the procedure followed in the Gaikwar's case in 1874–5 resulted from this correspondence.

The Proclamation of the Crown was not considered enough, and so in 1861 Lord Canning issued Sanads

(Letters of Recognition) to about one hundred and forty of the more important States, giving the Princes the right of adoption in the case of failure of direct heirs. These Sanads, which were of two kinds, for Hindu and Musalman rulers respectively, cannot be regarded as more than an acceptance on the part of the British Government of the right of Indian rulers to perpetuate their succession, a right which Dalhousie had strenuously denied.

But it should be remembered that the right of adoption already belonged to the Princes, according to the law of their States, as an attribute of their sovereignty, so that the Sanads were a mere recognition of all inherent rights.

The issue of the Sanads by Lord Canning to some extent relieved the feeling of insecurity remaining, a feeling which had been heightened by his declarations in 1860, that the Government of India was not debarred from intervening in the affairs of a State under certain conditions. " Neither," he had then said, " will the assurance diminish our right to visit a State with the highest penalties, even confiscation, in the event of disloyalty or flagrant breach of engagement."

From the point of view of the States the Crown's assumption of rule in India was a great thing. The Sanads were accepted as a statement of the British Sovereign's goodwill, but as the Princes thought succession was their legal right, they did not regard them as grants conferring a privilege. That the acceptance of a Sanad would eventually be perverted to an unwarranted political use, viz. as a means of curtailing existing rights, never occurred to any Indian ruler at the time, nor, it may be safely asserted, to the advisers of the Queen who proposed the issue of such Sanads. Those Princes whose loyalty during the Mutiny had been conspicuous received various rewards for their services; they little anticipated that the course of political practice and economic development in India was shortly to entail many infringements of their sovereignty.

For the first few years after the Mutiny the Government of India was too busy restoring order after the chaos caused by the rebellion and in setting right the disrupted finances of the Provinces to have much time to pay attention to the States. When in a Darbar Lord Canning announced that " for the first time the Crown stands face to face with its feudatories," there was no one on either the Government's or the States' side likely to point out how loose and dangerous was the use of the term " feudatories." The psuedo-mediævalism of Dalhousie had been repudiated only to the extent of guaranteeing States from annexation and escheat. Its potentialities in the evolution of a political practice which could be made a cover for a course of encroachment upon the States' treaty-rights could not at that time have been in anybody's mind.

The general attitude of the Princes after the Mutiny was one of relief except in those exceptional cases where they felt they had been unjustly treated.

Holkar no doubt felt aggrieved that, owing to the personal animosity of Sir Henry Durand, his right to a recognition of his services during the Mutiny had not been conceded despite its admission by Sir Robert Hamilton in open Darbar: the Nizam was sore that only the Raichur Doab and not Berar had been given back to him: but, as a whole, the Princes felt that the era of insecurity had gone. If Upper India was devastated by famine, the cotton districts were flourishing, thanks to the outbreak of the Civil War in America. Alike with British India, the States should have been able to look forward to an age of great development.

In 1862 Lord Canning retired and was succeeded by Lord Elgin. He spent his first year in Calcutta attending to official matters and the improvement of official routine: next year he died at Dharmasula. His influence on the policy of the British Government in regard to Indian States was therefore negligible. His published letters, however, show how strongly he was impressed with the necessity of avoiding undue interference in the States.

During the Viceroyalties of Lords Canning and Elgin

no definite policy seems to have been evolved, though tendencies were becoming more and more evident which showed that a new attitude was being officially adopted at Simla and Calcutta towards problems affecting Indian States. The Government of India was too much preoccupied in balancing its budget after the debt incurred by the Mutiny and in restoring economic prosperity and the order on which such prosperity depends to have much time to consider its relations with the States. The Sanads had been distributed and the States were for the moment forgotten.

It is possible that the abandonment of the annexationist principles of Dalhousie was regretted by a section of the Government of India, which had only decided to tolerate the States because they could not abolish them. For example, in 1868, speaking in the House of Commons, Mr. Samuel Laing, who had recently retired from the Finance Membership of the Viceroy's Council, said:

> "The existence of the Native States in India, except as far as it was based on treaty and sanctioned by the allowing of hereditary possessions, was a doubtful policy either for British interests or for the welfare of the inhabitants of British India. If we looked at the past conditions of the Punjab, Oude, and other districts which had been recently annexed, and compared it with their present condition, we should see how much the people themselves had benefited by the change of Government."

This attitude of Mr. Laing's has been described as one of toleration of the States, reluctantly, without hope, and without any fixed intentions for the future. Laing's declaration, though not official, represented the common official position of the day.

X.

Sir John Lawrence was appointed to succeed Lord Elgin in response to public opinion in England. The appointment of an Anglo-Indian official was a departure from precedent, but Sir John Lawrence's great services were considered a sufficient justification for such a change.

After his notable work in the settlement of the Punjab, and his later services during the Mutiny, Lawrence's term of office as Viceroy must seem an anti-climax. Though honestly anxious to conciliate the States he caused considerable trepidation in some of them. Keene, a contemporary and admirer of Lord Lawrence, writes:

> "This was the more tragic in that originally an annexationist (and able to point with just pride to the bright side of annexation in his model Province, the loyal and prosperous Punjab), his zeal was now tempered by the shock of the great revolt, which had fallen on no one with more astonishment than on him. He had come to see the great value of the Native States, and he got a glimpse—it may be doubted if he ever attained to a full perception—of the danger of hurrying Western ideas into the moulds of antique Eastern civilisation. We should be struck with the absurdity of blaming Solomon for not establishing a penny post from Dan to Beersheba; yet some of our Anglo-Indian reformers would think nothing of disarming a Pathan chief and then asking him to subscribe to a dispensary. At all his Darbars Lawrence used to harangue the chiefs, assembled out of all corners of mediæval barbarism, on the evils of infanticide and the blessings of female education."

Lawrence, as has been said before, seriously alarmed certain of the States. In the case of Tonk, the ruler of which was said to have abetted murder, the Nawab was deposed, but the infant heir was installed in his place. It is, however, significant of the persistence of the old tradition of annexation that the opportunity was taken to mulct the State of certain territories. It is difficult to see on what logical grounds or with what justice.

In 1868 the Maharaja of Mysore died after thirty-seven years of retirement.

> "Contrary to the Viceroy's wishes, the adopted son of the deceased was proclaimed Rajah of Mysore; but he was only six years old, and the State was put under a Regency for the next few years, Major Malleson being appointed Chief Commissioner. It was on this occasion that Lawrence was led to issue his famous circular asking the provincial officials if they did not think the natives were

happier under the British sway than under that of their own rulers. By this indication of his own views the Viceroy seemed to anticipate the conclusion; at any rate it was generally favourable to him. The universal testimony of those consulted was that the people were, indeed, possessed of much more security, and provided with far more sources of prosperity under the just and punctual system of which His Excellency was the head."

Lord Lawrence viewed with suspicion the forces maintained by certain States, despite the fact that the number maintained did not violate treaty stipulations. In a letter, the politeness of which did not conceal its peremptory nature, he ordered that "Scindia's little army should at once be broken up, the several corps dispersed about the country, and that no such large assemblage of troops should again take place." This action had been the result of inviting the Political Agent at Gwalior to witness a review of all the "drilled soldiers" permitted by the treaty of 1860, which troops he had massed at his capital. The Report of the Central India Agency for 1866–67 states that the measures of the reduction and dispersal of these troops were taken in February, and "a full and detailed report of the circumstances was furnished in a despatch dated 15th March, 1867." In para. 62, p. 13, the Agent to the Governor-General says "it would be hardly possible to overstate the soreness caused by the check that has thus been given to the indulgence of his (Scindia's) passion for military organisation and parades, and of his desire to keep his whole force with this object at the capital under his personal control and command."

It is hardly strange after this, in paras. 65 to 68, to find that the Agent to the Governor-General, while "cordially admitting" the Maharaja's "friendly personal bearing," declaring His Highness to be "accessible and courteous and prepared to discuss most subjects in a pleasant way, and to listen with attention to the arguments addressed to him," and giving his testimony to the "Maharajah's respect for the authority of the British Government," should still find the Prince occasionally "suspicious and distrustful," and that he sometimes

" considers the intervention of the British Government, or its officers, unwarrantable.

It was during the period of Lawrence's Viceroyalty and largely under his encouragement that Mr. (later Sir Charles) Aitchison compiled the first edition of that extensive work which is supposed to contain all the treaties of any importance made between the British Government and the Indian States, prefixed in the case of each State by a narrative giving a résumé of its history.

Like the other departments of the Government of India, the Political Department, of which the Viceroy held the charge, was becoming more strictly organised than in past days. Matters were moving towards the stage when decisions affecting one State would become regulations to be applied to all, because the pressure of economic interests seemed to demand it.

In a curiously prophetic letter written by Canning in 1860, when discussing the selection of his successor, he asks :

> " Who is to be my successor ? If John Lawrence, he will go far towards upsetting in a year or two all that I hope to have accomplished in my last three years both in Oudh and in the Punjab. He will not do so by direct means—I can make that very difficult for any man—but by giving a cold shoulder to all measures for increasing the consequences of and placing trust in the native chiefs and gentry generally."

Sir John Lawrence, as Viceroy, may, indeed, be said to have given the cold shoulder to the States. At his Darbars he would lecture the Princes on the need for more modern administration, but of practical sympathy, even towards his old friends the Phulkian States, he showed little trace. It was said of him during his Viceroyalty that he looked upon the Provinces as sons, and on the States as stepsons, but that he was a sympathetic parent to neither.

XI.

Lord Lawrence was succeeded by the Earl of Mayo, who was chosen for the post by Disraeli, though that statesman resigned office before the appointment actually came into effect. Mr. Gladstone, the new Premier, did not interfere with the appointment, and so, early in 1869, the new Viceroy took over the responsibilities of his office, trusted by both the political parties in Parliament.

Lord Mayo was deeply interested in the relationship of Indian States with the Crown. He toured constantly and held great Darbars and addressed the Princes on their duties and rights. In his speeches on these occasions and in his correspondence may be seen the enunciation of the new policy of Paramountcy, in which the claim for intervention in other interests besides the maintenance of the treaty obligations is put forward on behalf of the Government of India. In his great Darbar in Rajputana he said to the assembled Princes:

"Be just and mercful to your people. We do not ask whether you come to us with full hands, but whether you come with clean hands. No presents that you can bring will buy the British favour. No display which you may make will raise your dignity in our eyes; no cringing or flattery will gain my friendship; we estimate you not by the splendour of your offerings to us, nor by the pomp of your retinue here, but by your conduct to your own people at home.

". . . Be assured that we ask you to do all this for no other but your own benefit; if we wished you to remain weak, we should say to you, be poor and ignorant and disorderly. It is because we wish you to be strong that we wish to see you rich, instructed and well-governed. It is for such objects that the servants of the Queen rule in India, and Providence will ever sustain those rulers who govern for the people's good. . . .

"If we respect your rights and privileges, you should also respect the rights and regard the privileges of those who are placed beneath your care. If we support you in your power, we expect in return good government. We demand that everywhere throughout the length and breadth of Rajputana, justice and order shall prevail; that every man's property shall be secure; that the traveller shall come and go in safety; that the cultivator shall enjoy the fruits of his labour and the trader the produce of his commerce; that you shall make roads and undertake the construction of those works of irrigation which will improve the condition of the people and swell the revenue of your States; that you shall encourage education and provide for the relief of the sick."

As an exhortation by the representative of the Queen Empress in India, and addressed personally to the individual Chiefs before him on the general aims of good government which he advised them to pursue, and as an expression of the sympathetic interest which he felt in their success, the speech was unexceptionable. And yet in some of its phrasing it was perilously near language which its hearers might interpret as a warning, and as an intimation that their internal administration was the concern of the Government of India and would be closely watched, and as a threat that failure in any of the respects to which His Excellency adverted in his homily would entail that very interference of Government which their treaties expressly forbade. For it was the Princes of Rajputana who were his audience: and there is in most of the treaties made with the States of Rajputana a clear and unequivocal declaration that the British Government shall have no manner of concern whatever with the internal administration of the States, and that within their territories the rulers "shall be absolute."

This theory of interference on the basis of Paramountcy manifested itself in a number of ways. The claim was put forward that the appointment of a Diwan (Prime Minister) by a Prince should be subject to the approval of the Government of India. According to Aitchison's narrative, in the case of Baroda during Lord Lawrence's Viceroyalty in 1867, "the Government of India waived their right to have formally submitted for sanction any appointment which the Gaekwar might wish to make to the post of Diwan of his State. They retained, however, the right to veto any nomination of which they might disapprove." It is not known how the Government of India acquired such a right of sanction or how they could retain a right of veto without some cession of authority from the ruler.

The point, however, to be emphasised here is that during Lord Mayo's time the officers of the Political Department were very zealous in seeing that the Chief Ministers in any State were persons of whom they approved.

In Hyderabad Salar Jung, who had proved so good a friend to the British in Mutiny days, still remained at the head of the administration, as he was destined to do until his death in 1883. Though in 1869 the Nizam was succeeded by a child of three years old, Salar Jung, from a loyal jealousy for the rights of Hyderabad, succeeded in preventing the sovereignty of his master from being unduly infringed.

By the force of their personalities the Maharajahs of Gwalior and Indore managed to prevent serious infractions of their privileges at the time. The former had an able but unscrupulous Diwan who contrived to keep on the right side of both his master and the British Government; the latter had engaged as his Chief Minister Sir T. Madhava Rao, a statesman of great ability. In neither State was there any opportunity for direct encroachment on the rights of the ruler.

To Lord Mayo's time may definitely be assigned the origin of a fixed policy during minorities in the States. Annexation had been abandoned, but the direct or indirect control of a State while its ruler was a minor was now to become a dominant rule of policy, always tending and too often intentionally used by Government to promote the financial or general interest of the Paramount Power in India at the expense of the individual State.

As each year the railway system of the country grew in extent, its lines traversing British Province and Indian State indifferently, so was India more and more being knit into an economic whole. In the process the interests of the States as the weaker partners were being insensibly subordinated to those of the Provinces. An Imperial policy was in process of development by the Home Government, and it is probable that neither the Viceroy nor the Secretary of State ever contemplated that what was certainly for the economic good of the British Empire and, perhaps, for the benefit of the Indian Provinces, was likely to react unfavourably on the Indian States, their rulers and subjects.

Certainly during the Viceroyalty of Lord Mayo interference in the internal affairs of the Indian States became more frequent, due in part to Lord Mayo's idiosyncrasy for systematising things.

During his tenure of office the policies of the various departments tended to crystallise into a bureaucratic mould. This was particularly noticeable in the Political Department, which was under the Viceroy's special direction. Lord Mayo was not content with the idea that Princes in possession of their powers should govern their dominions well: he wished to ensure that the younger generation which would grow up to rule should be educated for its responsibilities, and to him is due the foundation of the Rajkumar College at Rajkot for the education of the Chiefs of Kathiawar and other States then under the supervision of the Bombay Government.

But it was not merely the education of boy Princes which occupied Lord Mayo's attention: he was anxious about the administration of the States themselves when their rulers were still too young to exercise administrative powers. The subject of minority administrations exercised his mind considerably. He wished to see the States prosperous, but such prosperity must come in co-operation with the ideas and policy of the Government of India. Holding the portfolio himself of not merely the political but also the Public Works Department of his Government, he had had much to do with the construction of railways through the territories of the States. To his Viceroyalty is to be dated the construction of the metre-gauge line which was "to connect the great salt lake of Rajputana with the chief marts of Hindustan." This was the result of the acquisition by lease in 1870 of the Sambhar Lake.

In most cases the construction of railways in or through the States involved the surrender of railway jurisdiction by each particular State over the land given free for the construction of the line. While at this period it was common talk that the extension of railways would completely alter economic conditions of India, the general idea was that such alteration would come by making the relief of famine easier, by benefiting both import and export trade, and generally by making communications quicker and easier. The military authorities again made a great point of the increased facility for putting down any disturbances as the result of the improved mobility by rail of their troops. But no one on the side of either the Government or the States seems to have foreseen that the extension of railways in the States might, and indeed must, lead to the extension of the political predominance of the Government of India over the States' own internal authority. Given the cession of jurisdiction, such predominance is an inevitable sequence of the construction of railways, but it becomes harmful to the economic and political life of the State if it be not confined to railway jurisdiction pure and simple, but be extended to other purposes.

At this period everybody wanted railways, in the States as in British India. A decade had still to elapse before certain States were to discover that the construction of railways, often built with their own funds, tended unduly to bring about infringement upon their sovereignty. Under Lord Lawrence the expensive guarantee system of railway construction was given up. The Government of India decided to build their own railways or to leave their building to private enterprise. But they had no temptation to build railways in the States, except where from the strategic point of view it seemed important to link together two systems in British India, or two portions of a through route. To private enterprise the comparatively poorer States offered less attraction than British India for the investment of capital. It remained, therefore, for the States to construct their own railways with their own money: and this from Lord Mayo's time they began to do.

XII.

In 1872 the new Viceroy, Lord Northbrook, had had a certain amount of experience of Indian problems, since he had early in life joined the India Board under Sir Charles Wood (Lord Halifax), and later had been the first Liberal Under-Secretary for India during the Palmerston Ministry. In neither case, however, had he shown so keen an interest in Indian problems as to refuse political advancement in favour of the Board of Control or the India Office. He had followed Sir Charles Wood to the Admiralty and later had left the India Office for the War Office. As a whole the idea of a Liberal peer as Viceroy did not commend itself to official circles in India. They need not, however, have been unduly perturbed. Lord Northbrook never made any attempt to alter the existing system. While taking the keenest interest in the Foreign side of the Department, which was his special charge, and worthily maintaining what he considered the true interests of India in avoiding the forward policy in the relations of India with Afghanistan, Russia and Central Asia, he did not interfere to modify the system of encroachment on the rights of the States which was growing up on the political side.

Despite Lord Mayo's geniality of manner, the States already felt that they were distrusted. In a confidential despatch, Lord Napier of Magdala, the Commander-in-Chief, wrote to the Home Government:

> "Our whole experience in India should warn us that we cannot always depend upon tranquillity; that disturbances arise when they are least expected; and, when they commence at one point, unless immediately checked, they are sure to be followed by others.
>
> "There are considerable forces under Native Chiefs, who may be individually friendly, but whose troops can never be relied on not to join against us.
>
> "Our military force at Gwalior is much inferior in strength to that which Scindia could bring against it, and nothing but the possession of the fort could justify our position at Morar, even with the garrison originally appointed for it.

"We are aware that the Deccan, Central India and the Border States of Rajputana, such as Kerowlee and Kotah, could furnish larger bodies of men than those which gave such ample occupation to General Stewart's and afterwards Sir Hugh Rose's and Sir John Mitchell's forces.

"We know that Holkar has a foundry and makes good guns for his own amusement. We do not know how many may be made in other places, but we may be certain that guns will not be wanting whenever there are people to use them."

Such is a typical statement of the view expressed in high places by the military authorities of Lord Mayo's time, a view adopted generally by the Political Department.

Some may doubt whether the States were aware that such a view was held. Certainly they were. The extract given above was printed publicly in a pamphlet issued in Calcutta in 1872, and, though few of the Princes of the time knew English, most of them were careful to have the gist of the Anglo-Indian Press and other publications referring to the States translated into vernacular for their benefit.

About this time the *Spectator* had dealt with the question of the armies maintained by the States, but had treated it from another angle, though still echoing a similar want of confidence. It commented thus:

"If we could persuade the Native Princes to disarm on condition of a guarantee of quiet possession from any exterior force, we should be relieved from one of the causes of danger which make our military expenditure so heavy. These Princes amuse themselves by keeping on foot and equipping with arms of the newest pattern armies of very considerable size for no apparent purpose whatever. These forces are ten times what they need for internal police of their territories, and there is no external enemy that could touch them. The real object of these armies is that their masters, if bad times came for the English, might rule the situation and ask their own terms. We are at present on excellent terms with these Princes, but we are obliged to watch their armies and keep armies of our own to hold them in check. The consequence is that the vast majority of the natives in India bear the burden of taxes which they hate, and which grind them terribly, in order that the Princes of a small minority may enhance their dignity by keeping up armies to frighten us with."

The exaggeration of such a statement must have been apparent to the political authorities of the time. For example, the assertion that the Princes were equipping their armies with the latest pattern of weapons was obviously untrue.

Allowances must be made for the fact that a large part of official India had talked themselves into the belief that they were still living on a powder magazine. It is unnecessary here to analyse this feeling or to consider whether it was not in reality the heritage of a natural reaction after the period of undue confidence which had led up to the Mutiny; but at the time Lord Northbrook reached India, few members of the Government would have accepted the truth of Lord Canning's words:

> 'Should the day come when India shall be threatened by an external enemy, or when the interest of England elsewhere may require that her Eastern Empire shall incur more than ordinary risk, one of our best mainstays will be found in these Native States. But to make them so we must treat their Chiefs with consideration and generosity, teaching them that in spite of all suspicions to the contrary their independence is safe, that we are not waiting for plausible opportunities to convert their country into British territory."

In his farewell speech at Southampton, Lord Northbrook had voiced the following sentiments:

> "I hope I have learnt one great lesson which I shall carry with me to India—that is, the difference between the Eastern and Western civilisation and the danger of being carried away by the ideas that what may be right and politic and wise in this country must be the same for a people with different sentiments, different religions and a different education, different tone of thought from ourselves. That lesson at any rate I hope to carry with me to India."

He lived up to his professions. He was fully prepared "to trust the man on the spot," and despite his native ability was very chary of interposing his own opinions. He maintained the friendly personal relations with the Indian Princes which Lord Mayo had done, but he also continued in full force the system which had begun to crystallise in the latter's time.

From the point of view of the States, the incident for which Lord Northbrook is most remembered is "the trial" and deposition of Malhar Rao, the Maharajah Gaikwar of Baroda in 1875. The Gaikwar was accused of having tried to poison the Resident, and for this he was ordered to be tried by a tribunal consisting of two Indian Princes, two Ministers and three high officers appointed by the Government of India. The legal authority of this tribunal and of its proceedings must not be assumed. The step was not justified by any treaty agreement nor had it the sanction even of previous practice. Baroda was a State in treaty alliance with the British Government. As Tupper himself says, the action was taken apart from treaty obligations. The objections to the validity of the procedure adopted were plain from the beginning, and their realisation probably accounts for the fact that under the orders of the Conservative Government which had just succeeded Mr. Gladstone's Ministry, the Gaikwar was deposed not for any action of which he had been accused, but on general grounds of maladministration.

The proceedings in connection with the Gaikwar's case aroused distrust in many of the States, and the feeling was only partially allayed by the gracious demeanour of the Prince of Wales, who shortly afterwards visited India. A shrewd observer of men and affairs, His Royal Highness, in a letter to the Queen in November 1875, commented on the attitude adopted by Political Officers towards the rulers of the States to which they were accredited. His Royal Highness wrote:

> "What struck me most forcibly was the rude and rough manner with which the English Political Officers (as they are called who are in attendance or native Chiefs) treat them. It is indeed much to be deplored and the system is, I am sure, quite wrong."

Disagreeing with the Home Government on a matter of the foreign policy to be followed by his administration, Lord Northbrook in 1876 resigned the Viceroyalty.

XIII.

Lord Lytton was sent out primarily to put into execution the policy of the new Tory Administration towards Afghanistan, where Russian influence was held to have gained the upper hand. Lord Northbrook and his Council had been anxious not to interfere with the *status quo* in the relations of the Indian Government with the Amir's dominions, but to pursue "the policy adopted by Canning, Lawrence and Mayo," towards this buffer State. Such a policy, according to Lord Lytton, was "not a question of letting well alone but of letting bad alone." There was considerable anxiety and nervousness felt about the approach of Russia to the Indian frontier. The fear of France which had blinded statesmen in the beginning of the century was now replaced by a fear of Russia. There was general anxiety lest the influence which Russia was said to have gained in Afghanistan should penetrate India.

At the date of the arrival of Lord Lytton in Calcutta the centralising policy of the Government of India had already produced a great effect on the relationships between that Government and the States. As we have indicated in the preceding chapters, during the two decades which followed the outbreak of the Mutiny, the whole attitude towards the States had changed. The Government of India had put forward and exercised the claim either to depose or try the rulers of States (*e.g.* the Gaikwar and the Nawab of Tonk [1]); to interfere high-handedly in internal affairs (.*g.* Datia,[2] Jodhpur [3] and other States), and to deprive a ruler of salute (*e.g.* Datia). In 1876 the theory of feudalistic relations was being consciously developed.

[1] Sequestration of Lawa (see evidence presented to Indian States Committee).

[2] Appointment of British Superintendent (1861) after the State had been pacified.

[3] See evidence presented to Indian States Committee.

The new subjection of the States was as serious to them economically as politically, and pursued with equal persistency. The Government of India was taking every opportunity afforded by the minority administrations or temporary embarrassments of the rulers to force them into the economic system of British India. That the States cannot exist without being knit up with the economic life of British India is plain to every student of the question, but that the States are entitled to a fair give and take was not acknowledged by the Government of India, sorely harassed as it was by famine, by unduly expensive railway construction, by equally extensive but less productive foreign wars, and finally by an exchange which had started to fall with the demonetisation of silver in Europe.

Because the States did not share the enthusiasm for public works and social services which characterised official policy in British India they were being already regarded as backward areas. The Government of India would not at that time even admit that some of the backwardness may have been due to the economic fetters which they themselves were riveting on the States.

In 1876, Disraeli revived an idea, often previously mooted, that the Queen should assume the title of Empress of India. His wish coincided with that of Her Majesty. It had, indeed, been the desire of the Prince Consort for his wife and sovereign in 1858. Accordingly, in the spring of that year, a Royal Titles Bill was introduced in the House of Commons. During the debate, on March 14th, Disraeli emphatically asserted that the addition of the title "Empress of India" did not in the least affect the rights, dignity and honour of the Indian Princes as guaranteed in the Proclamation of 1858.

Lord Lytton held a Darbar at Delhi to announce publicly the new title assumed by the Queen. Lord Hartington described it in the House of Commons as "the assumption of the fallen estate of the Moghuls." The Princes and rulers were invited to attend and do homage to the representatives of the Queen Empress.

Orders of chivalry were conferred on them, and their precedence *inter se* was settled.

In any case, from the Viceroy's point of view, indeed, from that of the Government of India, the Delhi Assemblage of 1877 was a great success, and so in April Lord Lytton is found writing to Disraeli:

"Nothing has struck me more in my intercourse thus far with Indian Rajahs and Maharajahs than the importance they attach to their family pedigrees and ancestral records. Here is a great feudal aristocracy which we cannot get rid of, which we are avowedly anxious to conciliate and command, but which we have as yet done next to nothing to rally round the British Crown as its *feudal* head. Every Rajah I have yet conversed with has been curiously and amusingly anxious to convince me of the antiquity of his family, and the extent to which its importance has been recognised by the Suzerain Power at various times. Many of them have presented me with printed and illustrated genealogies and family records, lovingly edited by themselves and published at their own expense. Several of these genealogies are composed and printed in English. But what is worthy of notice is that in all of them I find evidence that small favours and marks of honour bestowed from time to time by the British Government on the head of the family (such as an additional gun to his salute, the right to a return visit from the Viceroy, or a more honourable place in the Durbar, etc.) are quite as highly prized and appreciated as the more substantial benefits (of augmented territory or revenue) conferred in earlier times upon their family by an Aurengzebe or an Akbar."

In a letter to Lord Salisbury about ten days later, Lord Lytton writes:

"I am convinced that the fundamental political mistake of able and experienced Indian officials is the belief that we can hold India securely by what they call good government, that is to say, by improving the condition of the ryot, strictly administering justice, spending immense sums on irrigation works, etc. Politically speaking, the Indian peasantry is an inert mass. If it ever moves at all, it will move in obedience, not to its British benefactors, but to its native Chiefs and Princes, however tyrannical they may be. The only representatives of native opinion are the Baboos, whom we have educated to write semi-seditious articles in the native Press, and who really represent nothing but the social anomaly of their own position. Look at the mistakes which Austria made in the government of her Italian provinces. They were the best governed portions of Italy; she studied and protected the interest of the native peasantry; but, fearing the native *noblesse*, she snubbed and repressed it; when that *noblesse*, having nothing to gain or to hope from the continuation of her rule, conspired against it, the peasantry either remained passive or else followed the lead of its national superiors in attacking its alien benefactors. But the Indian Chiefs and Princes are not a mere *noblesse*. They are a powerful aristocracy. To securely, completely and efficiently utilise the Indian aristocracy is, I am convinced, the most important problem before us. I admit that it is not easy of immediate solution. For whilst, on the one hand, we require their cordial and willing allegiance, which is dependent on their sympathies and interests being in some way associated with the interests of the British power, on the other hand, we certainly cannot afford to give them any increased political power independent of our own. Fortunately for us, however, they are easily affected by sentiment and susceptive to the influence of symbols to which facts very imperfectly correspond."

Had Lord Lytton been given his way he would have established orders of Indian nobility and an Indian Privy Council. The first proposal came to nothing; the second was whittled down into the empty title of "Councillor to the Empress."

This was a period in which India was particularly "fertile of administrators, barren of statesmen." The Indian budget was becoming more and more difficult to balance, thanks to a severe famine and a grossly expensive war with Afghanistan. The Government of India was eager to drive hard bargains with the States in many economic matters, and especially in the matter of salt, of which they had made up their minds to acquire a remunerative monopoly.

In Lord Lytton's time were concluded the most important of the various salt agreements with the States. Undue, if polite, pressure was put on many States to conclude such agreements; and some examples will be found in the evidence. Usually the States were induced to accept a policy which fixed for good and all on an unfair basis the amount of compensation to be paid for a source of revenue which had every prospect of expansion. But, if persuasion failed, the Government of India was ready to apply other pressure, or even, as in the case of the Mandi State, to put in its own supervising agency without the consent of the State.

XIV.

The Marquess of Ripon who succeeded Lord Lytton as Viceroy came out with direct orders to reverse the foreign policy of his immediate predecessor as well as certain internal regulations like the Vernacular Publications Act. Perhaps no Viceroy has ever lived up to the political theories of his party in the way in which Lord Ripon did. But even he found the India Office was inclined to interfere too much with the administration of India. Years before he had written :—" The Government in India ought, as it seems to me, to be made as much as possible the real executive of that country."

The Viceroyalty of Lord Ripon is memorable in the history of the relationship of the States with the Government of India for the return of the great State of Mysore with its 30,000 square miles and population of 5,860,000 to the direct administration and control of its ruler, a measure carried through by the joint agreement of Lord Ripon and Lord Hartington, the Secretary of State for India at the time.

In 1868 the death took place of the Maharaja whose maladministration had in 1831 resulted in Mysore being placed under British management. He left no son, but only a boy whom he had adopted despite the firm refusal of the Government to sanction any such adoption. Had he died in Dalhousie's time, there can be little doubt that Mysore would have "lapsed." In 1868, however, Lord Lawrence and Sir Stafford Northcote, then Secretary of State for India, decided on the preservation of the Principality. The unauthorised adoption was accordingly recognised, though no Sanad of adoption had been given in 1861, and the Government of India agreed to restore the State to the boy if, on reaching manhood, he were found competent for his duties as a ruler. In 1881 the promise of the Government was carried out and Mysore was given back to the control of its Prince.

The Government of India was doubtless aware of the uneasiness that had been created by the trial of the Gaikwar. It was true that Baroda had not been annexed, but only its ruler punished; yet Holkar's dictum to Sir H. Daly, "The person for the time being is little; the State with its rights is the point for consideration," did not express the whole of what the Indian Princes thought about the Baroda case.

The restoration of ruling powers to the Maharaja of Mysore was an important event. The fact of rendition appealed strongly to all the Princes. "Now that annexation is at an end," commented Scindia, "we breathe freely, even when our failings are proved and our shortcomings discussed." But it was also an opportunity for the Government of India not merely to retain effective control over Mysore, but to make a precedent of the kind of relationship which they would like to see established between the Paramount Power and all the Indian States. The rendition of the State gave them the opportunity, because on the one hand the young ruler, just eighteen, was in no position to look his gift-horse in the mouth; he had to take his kingdom on whatever terms the Government chose to offer it or not get it at all; and consequently he took what was offered with gratitude. On the other hand, it was a great State, occupying nearly 30,000 square miles and containing nearly 5,000,000 subjects with a great revenue, and an efficient administration created by the British. The Maharaja had just been given a salute of twenty-one guns, and the State was therefore on the same level of importance with the greatest States in India. What a chance to create a permanent example on the grand scale of the kind of relationship between Government and State which they wanted to see become universal throughout India! And so naturally enough the Instrument of Transfer contains an elaborate constitution with many clauses defining the duties of the Maharaja and the powers over him of the Government, the net result of which is to subordinate his authority to Government supervision in every department and to leave the real internal Sovereignty of the State in the hands of the Government of India.

It opens with an explanatory introduction showing that it was made with the idea of continuing the improved system of administration introduced into Mysore after 1831. So far as future successions are concerned, it states that the lineal descendants by blood or adoption of the Maharaja should succeed except in case of disqualification through manifest unfitness to rule. But no succession was to be valid until recognised by the Governor-General in Council, who, in the failure of lineal heirs, was left the discretion of selecting " as a successor any member of any collateral branch of the family whom he thinks fit."

The Maharaja and his successors are bound at all times to " remain faithful in allegiance and subordination to Her Majesty the Queen of Great Britain and Ireland and Empress of India, her Heirs and Successors, and perform all the duties which in virtue of such allegiance and subordination may be demanded of them."

The State in return for defence and protection against all external enemies (internal security is not mentioned) undertakes to pay an annual tribute of thirty-five lakhs of rupees.

Without the sanction of the Government of India the ruler of Mysore is not to " build any new fortresses or strongholds or repair the defences of any existing fortresses or strongholds."

Except with the permission of the Government, the importation of arms, ammunition or military stores is prohibited, and their local manufacture is to be discontinued whenever Government may require it.

No objection must be raised by Mysore to the maintenance or establishment of British cantonments whenever and wherever the Governor-General in Council may consider them necessary. Land for them is to be given free and all jurisdiction over such land renounced. Every facility is to be given for the provision of supplies to troops in cantonments, and no duties or taxes are to be levied on goods imported or purchased for the troops without the consent of the Government of India.

The strength of the State troops, their terms of enlistment, organisation, equipment and drill are to be in accordance with the orders of the Government of India.

Mysore is allowed no dealings with any other State or Power except with the previous sanction and through the medium of the Governor-General in Council.

Any person not a native of India may not be employed by the Mysore State without the previous sanction of the Government of India, which is empowered to demand the dismissal from State service of any person so employed.

The currency of British India is to be legal tender in Mysore and British Indian currency laws adopted by the State. The old right of State minting is not to be revived.

All land required for the construction and working of telegraph lines in the State is to be given free of charge. Similarly lands for railway construction are to be given without charge.

On demand by the British Resident the State is made responsible for arresting and surrendering any persons accused of offences in British India.

Plenary criminal jurisdiction over European British subjects in Mysore is to remain with the Government of India.

The State must comply with the wishes of the Government of India in the prohibition or limitation of the manufacture of salt and opium.

The laws and rules in force at the time of the transfer of Mysore are to remain unchanged and not repealed nor modified without the previous consent of the Government of India.

The system of administration is not to be materially changed without a similar consent.

All title-deeds granted and land revenue settlements made by the British Government and in force at the date of the transfer are to be maintained unless rescinded or modified by a competent Court of Law or the consent of the Governor-General in Council. Section 22 of the Instrument reads:

"The Maharajah of Mysore shall at all times conform to such advice as the Governor-General in Council may offer him with a view to the management of his finances, the settlement and collection of his revenues, the imposition of taxes, the administration of justice, the extension of commerce, the encouragement of trade, agriculture and industry, and any other objects connected with the advancement of His Highness's interests, the happiness of his subjects, and his relations with the British Government."

The Instrument of Transfer concludes thus:—

"This document shall supersede all other documents by which the position of the British Government with reference to the said territories has been formally recorded. And if any question arises as to whether any of the above conditions have been faithfully performed, or as to whether any person is entitled to succeed, or is fit to succeed to the administration of the said territories, the *decision thereon of the Governor-General in Council shall be final.*"

In considering this instrument it is important to realise that rightly or wrongly the Government considered the Sovereignty of Mysore to be then vested in the Crown or at least to be at the Crown's free disposal. In 1799 Mysore had been won by force of arms from Tipu [1] and annexed, but on grounds of policy Wellesley had proceeded to partition the larger part of its territories between Hyderabad, the Peishwa and the Company, whilst conferring what is substantially (subject to an exchange in 1803) the present Mysore on the then representative of the Hindu ruling family of forty years before, a boy of three years old. The Peishwa did not accept his share, but the plan of conferring the present Mysore on the young Maharajah was carried out. The

[1] It is interesting to note the part played by the Patwardhans of Sangli in the defeat of Tipu.

Treaty of 1799 between the Company and the young boy (Aitchison IX, p. 220) contained two articles important to our investigation, Nos. 4 and 14. By the former the Company reserved the right "to assume and bring under the direct management of the Company" any part of the territory which they thought necessary in order to enforce payment of the annual payment covenanted by Article 2 for the maintenance of a military force in the State by the Company. And by Article 14 the Maharaja had to accept the advice of the Company in every department of his internal administration. When in 1833 the Maharaja was hopelessly in debt, his payment in arrears, and the State grossly mismanaged (Aitchison IX, p. 184), the British Government under the reserved powers took complete charge, and retained it until the rendition in 1881.

This history shows that no complaint can be made against the Government for the bargain they then drove with the young Maharaja. Firstly, they had in 1799 annexed the State and were then free to grant such limited powers of sovereignty as they chose. The child Maharaja of 1799, as donee, had no ground of complaint at Articles 4 and 14 of his Treaty. The resumption by the Company in 1833 was therefore in accordance with the contract. And when the rendition took place in 1881, even granting that the Government had not actually annexed in the long interregnum and still remained under an obligation to restore the State to self-government, nevertheless, in so far as the limitations of the "Instrument of Transfer" were within the terms of the original Treaty of 1799, there could be no ground of complaint at their imposition. And many if not most of the limitations were so covered.

But there is a further point. The Government in 1881 undoubtedly *thought* themselves free to impose any limitations they chose as if it were a pure case of creating a State *de novo* out of British territory. Whether that view was legally sound or not is immaterial. It is sufficient to preclude the Government from treating the rights of control which they reserved for themselves by the Mysore instrument as any guide to the rights which they possess over other States which have not originated in grant, but were already in existence when the British first came into treaty relations with them. States like Baroda, Gwalior, Udaipur, Alwar, Nawanagar or Tripura existed already as full-powered States when they first accepted British Paramountcy. Their sovereignty was their own, not granted to them by the British. Indeed they were the donors and the Crown the donee. For Paramountcy was created by their cession of certain sovereign rights to the Crown. And this conclusion is equally true whether the State came into relationship with the Crown by treaty or by some other form of contractual adjustment like Tripura or Nawanagar or Seraikella without any treaty. Every State having its own independent existence retained whatever powers of sovereignty it did not give away to the Crown. The whole of the "residuary jurisdiction" remained *ex necessitate* vested in it.

And this contrast between Mysore and the generality of States leads to a general proposition. Every State in existence when the British first came into relation with it still possesses all sovereign rights and powers which it then had, except in so far as it had then or subsequently ceded any of them to the Crown. Theoretically no doubt the case is possible of a State which, at the time of first contact with the British, only possessed particular powers, the whole State having originated (like Mysore) at some earlier date in a grant from some greater State which had conferred only limited powers and reserved to itself the residue of sovereignty. But the burden of proof would be upon the Crown to establish such facts, and to show further that it had itself acquired the succession to the rights of the earlier grantor State. Such a succession could not be established by claiming as successor to either the Mughal Empire or the Maratha Power, because the former had evaporated long before the era of British Paramountcy, and the latter merely exacted tribute without exercising sovereignty, whether over the great Maratha States like Baroda or Indore, or Gwalior or Nagpur, or over States ruled by non-Maratha Princes like the States of Kathiawar and other States in the Bombay Presidency. A further difficulty of an insuperable character in the way of making any effective case out of the theory of succession to the "reserved" powers of some suzerain State is that its "reserved sovereignty" over its Feudatory would have to be still a reality at the time when the Crown acquired its Paramountcy over the Feudatory. This the Crown cannot establish. No such suzerainty was acknowledged by any State which agreed to accept the paramountcy of the Crown; no treaty contains any such admission; and no treaty, either by preamble or article, treats the Crown or the Company as contracting in the shoes of any suzerain power to which it has succeeded. Historically the contention that the Crown acquired any actual rights over any State (other than tribute) in virtue of its succession to the defunct Mughal Empire or its defeat of the Peishwa and its succession to the Peishwa's powers in 1817 is a myth.

But these considerations were not present to the mind of the Government of India in 1881. It was a period when the Government were obsessed by the need for centralisation, for uniformity of procedure, and for simplicity of system. They were engaged in driving hard bargains with the States generally in economic matters, and especially in matters connected with railways and opium. The Government of India were utterly at a loss to counterbalance the financial difficulties caused by the fall in exchange after the drop in the world price of silver.

A confirmed believer in the virtues of Free Trade, Lord Ripon would have liked to see all the customs duties imposed by the States abolished, but he was too busy in introducing Liberal principles into the administration of British India or in watching the machinations of Russia in Central Asia to have much time to devote to the problems of the Indian States. Indeed, it may be said that, having dealt with the case of Mysore in a manner which exemplified the views of the Department which was his special charge, he forgot more or less that that Department had a Political as well as a Foreign side. But, directly or indirectly, the Instrument of 1881 has had a considerable influence upon the relations of the Government of India with other States which historically and legally are in no such dependence as Mysore. The officers of the Political Department have not generally analysed the position and have not understood that whilst the Government may have been strictly and properly entitled to insist on every one of their powers under the Instrument of Transfer to Mysore, their rights *vis-à-vis* other States are on a wholly different footing. A consequence of the confusion has undoubtedly been to create an impression that what is good enough for the great State of Mysore is good enough for other States, and to make the powers over Mysore a sort of standard to be attained over other States also.

XV.

Lord Dufferin had served his apprenticeship at the India Office as an Under-Secretary in the days of Sir Charles Wood (Lord Halifax). For years he had devoted his talents to diplomacy, and incidentally had gained an insight into Eastern problems. Mr. Gladstone considered him a suitable person to hold the Viceroyalty at a moment when negotiations with Russia were in progress. Despite his years (he was nearing sixty when he reached India in 1884) he proved a very able Governor-General.

Soon after he assumed charge of his great office, the Penjdeh incident of 1885, on the far northern frontier in the Pamirs, nearly brought England and Russia to war. Throughout his Viceroyalty, Russian affairs occupied a very large part of Lord Dufferin's attention; indeed, even in the important dealings which he had with the Indian States, he could never forget Russia.

The effect of this preoccupation of his mind was mainly

felt in Kashmir. That State had been hitherto outside the Indian political system. A treaty had been made in 1870 for the control of the great trade route to Central Asia through Kashmir, under which by agreement with the Maharaja a "British officer on duty" had been appointed, and a joint jurisdiction had been conferred upon him and an officer of the Durbar, limited to road affairs, to be exercised in accordance with certain regulations issued in 1872 with the full consent of the Durbar. But there was no Resident appointed to Kashmir and no claim had been put forward to any control over its internal administration. After the death of Maharaja Ranbir Singh in 1885 the British Government appointed a Resident to the Kashmir Court, and in 1887 an attempt was made to bring the frontier area of Kashmir touching the Russian Pamirs under the control of the Political Department. In 1888 the Maharaja was accused—though the accusation was later on dropped as founded on spurious information—of having been in correspondence with the Russians, and his powers of administration were taken away and handed over to a State Council presided over by the Resident and placed in reality under his orders. And immediately after the deprivation of the Maharaja's powers, the Gilgit Agency was established, and the political control of a large area of the State was in fact committed to the British Political Agent.

The Russian scare, however, had a happier issue in another way. To it was due the institution of the Imperial Service troops, by which the States voluntarily offered troops for the defence of the Empire.

Lord Dufferin was the first Viceroy to pay regular official visits to the States. Before his time the usual practice had been for Viceroys during their tours to hold Darbars sometimes in some important city in British India, sometimes in their camps when pitched in a convenient position in some province. But the visit of the Prince of Wales a few years earlier made a precedent for such ceremonial visits as now became customary for Lord Dufferin and all succeeding Viceroys. There can be no doubt that the innovation was a good one, as it has led to a personal intercourse between the Representative of the Crown and the Indian Princes, and to better political understandings generally.

The practice followed by the Political Department towards the States, however, was not as yet modified in any way, and in official reports of this period denunciations of these "backward" territories are constantly to be found. And the most backward States were alleged to be those which offered most resistance to the centralising policy of the Government of India, so far as can be judged from official reports.

Personally Lord Dufferin showed himself very sympathetic towards the Indian Princes, and displayed a genuine interest in their affairs, but his primary concern was with the Russian negotiations which occupied his attention during the greater part of his Viceroyalty. He is, however, gratefully remembered for various graceful acts, such as, for example, the rendition of the Gwalior fortress to Scindia.

In the summary of the work performed during his tenure of office,—he says,

> "I had never any ambition to distinguish my reign by a sensational policy, believing as I did that in the present condition of affairs it is best for the country that the administration should be driven at a low and steady pressure."

In the policy of the Political Department he introduced no innovations. Aided by the occurrence of several Minority Administrations in Rajputana, Central India and the Punjab, the control of that Department over certain States steadily grew. There is little doubt that the idea of Political Officers generally was that it would be for the advantage of all the States as well as for British India if the principles laid down in the Mysore Instrument of Transfer were applied without discrimination to each Indian State.

The Marquess of Lansdowne, who succeeded Lord Dufferin at the end of 1888, also proved himself a very able administrator. To him must be given the credit of placing on a sound basis the system of Imperial Service troops inaugurated in the time of his predecessor. Lord Dufferin had asked " those Chiefs who have specially good fighting material in their armies to raise a portion of those armies to such a pitch of general efficiency as will make them fit to go into action side by side with Imperial troops." The States recognised that the old suspicion entertained concerning the military forces in their States was passing away. Individual Political Officers might still be unduly nervous at any efficiency in the armies of the States, but the ideas of the higher military command at least had changed for the better. Like the Viceroys, the Commanders-in-Chief became frequent visitors in the States, and no longer wrote minutes pointing out the danger of the troops maintained by the Indian Princes.

Responses to the invitation to establish Imperial Service troops had poured in from all sides, but when Lord Lansdowne took up the practical working of the scheme he found it necessary to discriminate. Many of the offers made in the enthusiasm of the moment, when war with Russia seemed imminent, were clearly beyond the resources of the Princes who had made them, " or held forth no likelihood of advantage in the military sense."

For the elimination of useless or unacceptable offers, Lord Lansdowne laid down the following rules:

" The Government of India will on no account accept assistance of this kind from the Feudatory States except in instances where there is the clearest possible evidence to show, first, that the ruler of the State in question is honestly and sincerely desirous of placing his troops at our disposal, and esteems it an honour to have those troops brought into line with those of the Imperial Government; secondly, that such service will not impose too heavy a burden on the State, and that there is to be found among its people a genuine loyal desire to accept such service; and thirdly, that there exists in the troops themselves that military spirit so conspicuous in some of the races of India which has given to our native armies some of the finest fighting material in the world. The essence of the whole scheme is that there should be no compulsion in the matter, that only those States should be singled out which are not only willing but anxious to bear their part with us in defending the Empire in the hour of need."

This honest declaration of a sound policy has unfortunately not always been acted up to, and pressure has been applied to certain States which did not provide Imperial Service troops—pressure coupled with the hint that their failure to do so would be considered disloyal. That by their treaties the States had fully paid for external protection and internal security was not the view accepted by the Political Department under the control of which the Imperial Service troops were placed.

It is unnecessary to go into the question whether sometimes, as has been thought, in the name of efficiency the Imperial Service troops were made an excuse for undue interference by the Political Department in the internal affairs of the States. Thanks to the lessons of the Great War and the sympathy of various Commanders-in-Chief, the Imperial Service troops have to-day developed into the State Forces, a system which, while securing increased military efficiency, has relieved considerable political friction such as was common in the past.

Another act of Lord Lansdowne's administration which affected the States was the closing of the Mints to the free coinage of silver, and the fixing of the sterling value of the rupee at 1*s.* 4*d.* To aid in this policy it was expedient for the Government of India that as many States as possible should close any Mints they might own. Indeed, prior to 1893, and especially during minorities in the States, pressure had been applied to force the States to abandon their rights of minting, but, at the same time, no arrangements were in existence by which the Imperial Government should allow the States a share of the profits from coinage.

In cultivating close relations with the Indian Princes, Lord Lansdowne followed the policy of Lord Dufferin. During a visit to Hyderabad, in the course of a speech he thus expressed himself:

"I have always recognised the advantages of the arrangement under which a considerable portion of the Indian Empire continues to be governed by its hereditary rulers, and to be subject to forms of administration differing to a considerable extent from our own, but inspired by our proximity and stimulated by our example. No one would be more averse than I should be to any change in our relations with the Native States inconsistent with the measure of local autonomy which they now enjoy."

Despite repeated requests, however, he did not give back Berar to the control of the Nizam.

Early in his Viceroyalty occurred the rebellion in Manipur. The case as stated by a recent writer was as follows:

"The brother of the ruling Rajah rose in rebellion and installed the Jubraj on the *gadi*. The British Government recognised the Jubraj, but demanded that the brother who had raised the standard of revolt should be expelled. This the Jubraj refused to do, and a British force entered the Territory, deposed the Jubraj, and tried him. He was sentenced to be hanged. The subjects of the Manipur State were enjoined by proclamation to take warning by the punishment inflicted. This was an attempt to claim direct allegiance from the subjects of Indian States. The question whether, in an act of resistance by a ruler, the subjects of the State should loyally obey a Maharajah cannot be answered completely by a proclamation from the Government of India. Subjects of a State like that of the Nizam owe their immediate duty and allegiance to their sovereign. The claim put forward that the Imperial authorities can dissolve this allegiance by proclamation is tenable rather on the basis of superior strength or political expediency than of law or of treaty obligations. The idea that new obligations can be created or established rights taken away in the case of States in alliance, by the Government of India issuing either a circular letter or a proclamation, is not sound. But such action, though it could establish no legal claim, is a clear enough indication of the tendency towards Imperial authority. The Government of India has exerted itself to push forward new claims, and to extend old ones. For this purpose, constitutional, legal and feudal theories have been brought into use. Each in its turn has served to deprive the rulers of some part of their authority, or to give to the Central Government some new basis for intervention."

We are not vouching for either the completeness or accuracy of the above account of the facts. But it does not differ materially from that given by Lee-Warner (Chapter 6). What we are concerned to notice is the claim put forward by Government:

"In the exercise of their high prerogatives, the Government of India have, in Manipur, as in other protected States, the *unquestioned right to remove by administrative order any person whose presence in the State may seem objectionable.* The rule was, therefore, laid down that 'any armed or violent resistance to the arrest of such person was an act of rebellion, and can more be justified by a plea of self-defence than could resistance to a police officer armed with a magistrate's warrant in British India.'"

The words in italics (ours) have in our view no justification whatever either in law or history. It is an invasion upon the internal sovereignty of the ruler of the State, and if he orders resistance to it by his subjects they are bound to obey him. For the Government of India to intervene and arrest or indict for rebellion a subject of the State so acting is wholly illegal. The conclusion by Lee-Warner that such persons are within British jurisdiction and therefore amenable to British criminal justice is in our view a conclusion from premises which are false.

In 1893 Lord Lansdowne announced his intention of not staying in India beyond four years, and Mr. Gladstone after much deliberation announced the appointment of Sir Henry Norman, who, however, withdrew from the high appointment to which he was designated. The choice then fell on Lord Elgin.

XVI.

Lord Elgin's administration may be described as the calm that preceded the storm of Lord Curzon's Viceroyalty. Considerate, just and well-intentioned, not even his admirers ever said of Lord Elgin that he had either a policy of his own or the strength of character to make his mark on the complicated polity of India.

Lord Curzon, who took over the Viceroyalty from Lord Elgin at the end of 1898, was genuinely interested in the

States and their welfare. The first speech in which he outlined his policy was delivered in Gwalior in November 1899. He expressed a firm conviction when on that occasion he uttered the words: "The native Chief has become, by our policy, an integral factor in the Imperial organisation of India. He is concerned not less than the Viceroy or the Lieutenant-Governor in the administration of the country. I claim him as my colleague and partner." The terms of partnership were, however, to be those which the Viceroy himself from time to time considered best for the ruler and his State.

Lord Curzon's regime witnessed the high-water mark attained by the policy of considering Indian rulers as administrative Agents of the Government of India, deriving their rights, powers and dignities from the Crown. The theory had been one of slow development. But on that basis the political system of India was being, in fact, evolved by the Political Department, although so far it had not found public expression in any high official utterance. Lord Curzon was the first openly to state it. "The *sovereignty* of the Crown is everywhere unchallenged. It has itself laid down the limitations of its own prerogative," were his words at the installation of the Nawab of Bhawalpur: a claim not to Paramountcy but to complete sovereignty; and an assertion that the prerogative of the Crown reached out to any length it chose, entitling it as of right to impose on every State what control it thought fit, although in its forbearance it had graciously elected to submit to certain self-imposed limitations. Again, at the installation of the Maharaja of Alwar, Lord Curzon declared unequivocally that the Government must satisfy themselves "that the young Chief has received the education and training that will qualify him to rule over men," before entrusting him with the task of administration.

This attitude of considering the rulers of Indian States as servants of the Government of India, bound to take orders from Simla and Calcutta and having no rights of their own, was best illustrated in the circular issued by

Lord Curzon's Government, stating that before an Inc ian ruler left India the permission of the Viceroy should be obtained.

There was, however, one matter on which Lord Curzon took a strong attitude. During the preceding fifty years which marked the change in the status of the representatives of the Government of India from that of diplomatists at a friendly court to a Political Officer in control, the Residents had come to be in the enjoyment of many valuable privileges at the expense of the States, such as rent-free houses, free furniture, free travelling and other perquisites, for which there was no justification of any kind; the practice was so widespread that these advantages acquired, in ordinary discussion, a name of their own, "easements." Lord Curzon found, during his visits to various States, that the Residencies were often furnished and maintained by the State. In some cases even the household bills of the Resident and his staff, his "touring" expenses, etc., were charged to the State. Lord Curzon strongly objected to this, and caused a circular to be issued prohibiting this custom. Though its success has only been partial, the growth of a very objectionable evil was stopped by this act of the Viceroy. It is obvious that it is not a State's duty to defray the expenses of a diplomatic agent accredited to it. The practice, if encouraged, might easily degenerate into pressure upon the States to continue or increase a very substantial aid to the Government's exchequer; and even if merely tolerated might be abused by rulers to influence Political Officers in their favour. The system *must* be corrupt in tendency and ought to be stopped absolutely and everywhere.

Lord Curzon's general attitude at the Imperial Darbar, where the rulers thought they were treated with indignity, even in petty details (*i.e.* as when the Government of India required the Gaikwar to change the livery of his servants), also created uneasiness in their minds.

Lord Minto's Viceroyalty (1905–11) was an interval of reduced pressure, after the tempestuous excitement of Lord Curzon's regime. Though his appointment was made under a Conservative Government, his viceregal term in India synchronised with the Liberal administration of 1906 and the tenure of the India Office by Lord Morley. So far as his dealings with the States were concerned, he worked on the sound principle of first getting to know intimately as many of the rulers as possible, recognising doubtless that for practical purposes each Prince was his State. He inaugurated the habit of consulting the Indian Princes on matters affecting the welfare of India as a whole, of the Provinces as well as the States, and so indirectly helped to create a sense of unity of interest among the Princes which had previously been non-existent.

Lord Minto frequently visited the States, and he utilised his visits not merely for sport, but also for the frankest discussions with the rulers on matters of general concern and of particular interest to individual principalities. He was careful not to abuse the hospitality of the rulers, as an occasion for extracting some concession from a State which its ruler might have been unwilling to make. He not merely listened sympathetically to the grievances which his kindly attitude made it easy for the Princes to express frankly, he encouraged a clear facing of the difficulties which last practice had brought about in the relationship of the States with the Government of India. Lord Minto took a keen interest in the history of their relationships, and the previous official connection of his family with many of the States gave him additional interest in the welfare of the rulers.

Indeed Lord Minto's administration was important from the point of view of the States in many ways. First, it saw the enunciation of a new policy of trust and co-operation. After the hectoring, patronising and often unfriendly attitude of Lord Curzon's time, this policy of cordial co-operation was a welcome change. It was based on a policy of non-intervention, and on a sympathetic understanding that the conditions in different States were not identical and were often far from similar to those existing in British India. His speech at Udaipur in 1909 made this amply clear. He said:

"I have made it a rule to avoid the issue of general instructions as far as possible, and have endeavoured to deal with questions as they arose with reference to existing treaties, the merits of each case, local conditions, antecedent circumstances and the particular stage of development, feudal and constitutional, of individual principalities."

This was indeed fundamentally different from the policy that Lord Curzon enunciated when he said that the relations of States with the Crown had "conformed to a single type."

Secondly, he inaugurated, as above mentioned, the policy of discussing with the Princes general questions of Indian interest. The growth of the nationalist movement in British India caused him alarm, and he saw in the Princes a strong bulwark against subversive movements. He took counsel with them, and may thereby be said to have sown the seeds of the association of the Indian States in the general policy of the Empire. He said:

"The foundation stone of the whole system is the recognition of identity of interests between the Imperial Government and the Durbars, and the minimum of interference with the latter in their own affairs. . . . I can assure Political Officers I am speaking in no spirit of criticism. . . . My aim and object will be, as it has always been, to assist them, but I would impress upon them that they are not only the mouthpiece of Government and the custodian of Imperial policy, but that I look to them also to interpret the sentiments and aspirations of the Durbars."

A third act of Lord Minto which helped the Princes to realise the changed attitude of the Government of India was the re-establishment of the State of Benares.

Lord Minto, like his ancestor who succeeded Lord Cornwallis, realised that the policy of indiscriminate intervention was not likely to be productive of good results, and that the right policy to pursue towards the States was that of strengthening their hands and leaving them to evolve political systems suited to their own conditions. Lord Minto left the Princes of India in a happier frame of mind than ever before.

XVII.

At the time of the retirement of Lord Curzon, the Political Department was acting on the principle that, as against the Provinces and the Government of India, the States possessed no rights except on sufferance.

From that extreme position the last twenty years have witnessed a recession. During the decade 1908–18 the isolation of one State from another was as a rule of policy to some extent modified by the action of different Viceroys who consulted the Princes on various particular matters (and especially so during the war)—consulting them as a class if not as a political body.

When the Government of India thus set the example, it would have been illogical for them to continue to forbid the States exchanging views on political matters which very definitely affected them, and so consulting together. The conferences of Princes, summoned by Lords Hardinge and Chelmsford, eventually paved the way for the Chamber of Princes, which the Reforms brought into being.[1]

In their informal meetings the Princes, while discussing the infringement of their political rights, grew to recognise that equally important for the future prosperity of their dominions was the question of their economic relationship with British India. The more progressive of the rulers of the Indian States did not fail to see that, while it was irritating to their *amour propre* or derogatory to their dignity that the former precedence accorded them by the Government of India or the India Office was being set aside, it was a matter of life and death to their States that the relationship with the Paramount Power should be placed on its true legal basis of rights and obligations and that the unjust economic treatment under which they suffered at the hands of British India should speedily terminate.

It was freely recognised in the Montagu-Chelmsford

[1] For the origin and working of this body *see* General Foreword *above* p. xi *et seq.*

Report that the position of the States as it had evolved during the preceding few decades required reconsideration. The authors of the joint report recognised the injustice which had been done by the attempt of the Political Department to attain uniformity of practice. "The practice appropriate to the minor Chiefs has been used in the case of the major ones," confessed the Report. It was also recognised that the present system by which the Government of India sits as accuser and judge in cases against States and rulers was fundamentally wrong, and that the Princes had a right to claim a voice in matters affecting them jointly with British India.

The anomaly of the position is recognised now by the Government of India, but it is doubtful whether they yet realise how vicious the present system is and how radical an alteration is required in their attitude towards Indian States if common justice is to be meted out to them.

The statement made at a meeting of Princes and Government officers held on September 22nd, 1919, by Colonel (now Sir Robert) Holland throws an interesting light upon the position.

> "Lt.-Col. Holland proceeded to observe that there had been in the past a constant development of constitutional doctrine under the strain of new conditions as the British Power had welded the country into a composite whole. That doctrine, as, for instance, in the case of extraterritorial jurisdiction, railway and telegraph construction, administration of cantonments and various other matters, had been superimposed upon the original relations of many States with the Crown, but had evolved in harmony with the needs of the Indian body politic and had not been inspired by any desire to limit the sovereign powers of the Indian rulers. The rulers' consent to such new doctrine had not always been sought in the past, partly because it was often evolved piecemeal from precedents affecting individual States, and partly because it would have been impracticable to secure combined assent within a reasonable period. It was admitted, however, that, while the justice and necessity of the new measures were clearly seen, their effect upon the treaty position was not appreciated at the time, with the result that a body of usage influencing the relations with the States had come into force through a process which, though benevolent in intention, was nevertheless to some extent arbitrary."

It may, with some justice, be said that with the inauguration of the Chamber of Princes a new era has dawned in the relations between the Government of India and the States; that with the frank recognition of the Government that mistaken policies have been pursued in the past and that treaties though declared inviolable and inviolate have often been treated as non-existent or obsolete, the rights of the Princes stand better chance of recognition. It is true that the Government of India do not now claim, as they did in Lord Curzon's time, that their sanction is required before succession, or that the interests of the States should give way before the interests of Indian Provinces. It is unlikely that the Political Department would now give orders to any Indian State as the Lieut.-Governor of the Punjab did to Patiala in 1900. On that occasion, in dealing with the construction of a railway and the cession of full jurisdiction over the lands given for railway purposes, it was said:

> "Upon a full review of the case the Government of India have come to the conclusion that for Imperial reasons which apply throughout India, and which are of the utmost importance for the administration of the whole system of Indian railways, it is necessary that the Patiala Darbar should comply with the wishes of the Government in the matter as the majority of Native States have already done in India. His Honour must therefore ask the Patiala Darbar now to carry out the request, etc., etc."

The Government of India of to-day have no doubt modified in favour of the States' contentions certain of the autocratic views it once held. But Lord Reading, writing to H.E.H. the Nizam of Hyderabad as recently as March 27th, 1926, claimed that the supremacy of the British Government in India "is not based only upon Treaties and Engagements, but exists independently of them"; and that "it is the right and privilege of the Paramount Power to decide all disputes that may arise between States or between one of the States and itself, and, even though a Court of Arbitration may be appointed in certain cases, its function is merely to offer independent advice to the Government of India, with whom the decision rests." Lord Reading further based upon the supremacy of the British Crown a general claim to a right to intervene in the internal affairs of the States, limited at the sole discretion of the Crown to certain cases. Thus any change which may have taken place in the Government of India's policy appears to have arisen rather from an altered view of what is politically expedient than from a frank admission of the fundamental rights of the States. But the Princes as an Order feel that radical changes in the Government attitude are still needed, and in particular that the whole problem of the welding of India into a whole depends for its solution on four fundamental factors:—Firstly, the States have rights—absolute rights—rights based on contract with the Crown—rights which are ascertainable by the application of well-known legal principles. Secondly, there must be judicial machinery for the fair adjustment of disputes—so that the Government of India shall no longer be judge in their own cause, and that the aggrieved State may know what case it has to meet and not be left by official secrecy in ignorance which breeds distrust. Thirdly, there must be constitutional machinery for the adjustment of differences of opinion and conflicting interests between the States and British India and Great Britain. The fourth and last, and perhaps the most important factor of all, is that the States and their rulers are loyal to the King, the Empire and India, and are ready and willing to co-operate in building up a successful and united India within the Empire—if only they are given the opportunity, by the institution—in consultation with them—of appropriate Federal machinery, to play their rightful part.

This end must be attained ultimately by agreement. On the side of British India, and perhaps for all India, the Statutory Commission will contribute much. The Indian States Committee is working under terms of reference formulated in response to a demand pressed by the Princes for several years that their position should be investigated. But those terms contain no reference to the work of the

Statutory Commission nor to the problem of building up a united India. The task of co-ordinating Indian India and British India will necessitate not only the linking up of the recommendations of the Indian States Committee with those of the Statutory Committee, but the consideration of all those aspects of the States and their activities and rights and duties which are not covered by the terms of reference of the Indian States Committee, but none the less must form the subject of definite decisions before Parliament can legislate for British India after the report of the Statutory Committee has been considered. And those decisions are beyond the legislative jurisdiction of Parliament and beyond the executive authority of the Paramount Power; they rest solely within the sovereign power of the States themselves. They will necessitate much joint consideration and united action by the States in order that between the States, British India and the Crown an agreement may be reached, to be put into force by the joint action of the three parties interested. The States recognise that Parliament is the final authority for British India. But just as the Statutory Committee represents the conviction of Parliament that the opinions, the wishes and the aspirations of all classes in British India must be ascertained before Parliament legislates, in order that the result may be just, politic and acceptable in the eyes of British India as well as of Great Britain; so before legislation for British India can be proposed in Parliament it is essential that the opinions, wishes and aspirations of the States should be ascertained in regard to the effect upon them, both of proposals for British India and as to the constitutional machinery which will best ensure wise, harmonious and easy co-operation between the Governments of British India and the Governments of the States in the future. The Indian States Committee can make a valuable contribution to this great work by supplying information and stating opinions on both parts of their reference, and by making recommendations on the second. But after their report will come for the States the further stages indicated

The theory evidently has its basis in a *personal* relationship between the King-Emperor and the Indian rulers. It seems to have been argued that by the abolition of the Company new rights were created in the Crown: that the authority, legal and constitutional, supposed to have been vested in the phantom Mughal Emperor became transferred to the British Crown. This idea that the Queen became the inheritor of the Mughal pretensions is really at the basis of the feudal and imperial idea, although it was expressly repudiated both at the time of the transference from the Company in 1858 and at the assumption of imperial dignity in 1876. If the Company did not possess these feudal rights—and admittedly they did not—it seems almost inexplicable that the Government of India should, not many years after the Mutiny, have put forward such a claim. The explanation may be found in the curious reasoning about the supposed feudal position which is discussed in XX, p. 113.

THE THEORY OF PARAMOUNTCY.

The theory of a kind of feudal Paramountcy which thus came to be elaborated in the time of Lord Mayo was a radical departure from the relations that existed between the British Government and the States up to that time. We have noticed in an earlier section that both the Marquess of Hastings and the Marquess of Dalhousie expressly repudiated any claim to a Paramountcy which justified interference in internal affairs. The Governor-General in Council stated in 1821:

> "In the second paragraph of your first letter you say, that 'you suppose our interference in the Nizam's affairs to be not merely right, but also a duty, arising out of our supremacy in India, which imposes on us the obligation of maintaining the tranquillity of all countries connected with us; and consequently of protecting the people from oppressions, as no less necessary than the guaranteeing of their rulers against revolution.' *The assumption of our possessing an universal supremacy in India, involving such rights as you have described, is a mistake.* Over States which have, by particular engagements, rendered themselves professedly feudatory the British

Government does exercise supremacy; *but it never has been claimed, and certainly never has been acknowledged in the case of Native Powers standing within the denomination of allies.* Although a virtual supremacy may, undoubtedly, be said to exist in the British Government, from the inability of other States to contend with its strength, the making such a superiority a principle singly sufficient for any exertion of our will would be to misapply that strength and to pervert it to tyrannic purposes."

Lord Dalhousie was equally emphatic:

"I acknowledge no mission confided to the British Government which imposes on it the obligation, *or can confer on it the right*, of deciding authoritatively on the existence of independent Native Sovereignties and of arbitrarily setting them aside whenever their administration may not accord with its own views, and although their acts in no way affect the interests or security of itself or its allies.

"Still less can I recognise any such property in the acknowledged supremacy of the British Government in India as can justify its rulers in disregarding the positive obligations of international contracts in order *to obtrude on Native Princes and their people a system of* subversive interferences which is unwelcome alike to people and Prince."

The Government of India did not at any time before the Mutiny claim any general Paramountcy over Indian States investing it with the right to order the rulers to conform to the wishes of the Government (apart from external relations) or to intervene in any matters outside the express provisions of the treaty. Whenever such a policy was put forward by an over-zealous subordinate, the Government of India brushed it aside on the ground that it had no legal or constitutional authority justifying such a course.

After the Mutiny the position slowly changed. Lord Canning stated that the assurance against annexation did not "diminish our right to visit a State with the highest penalties, even *confiscation*, in the event of *disloyalty* or flagrant breach of engagements." The implications of the words "confiscation" and "disloyalty" will be discussed later. Here it is sufficient to note that this statement contains a claim which the Government of

India had expressly repudiated before the Mutiny, and no Indian ruler had by agreement or by sufferance accepted.

This policy became clearer during the course of the next ten years. Lord Lawrence deposed the ruler of Tonk. This was essentially on the claim of Paramountcy. Again, Lord Canning had declared in 1860 that

> "the territories under the sovereignty of the Crown became at once as important and as integral a part of India as territories under its direct domination. Together they form one direct care, and a political system which the Moghuls had not completed and the Marathas never contemplated is now an established fact of history."

Lord Mayo's words in his speech to the Rajput rulers, with which we have dealt more particularly on p. 63 above, were:

> "If we support you in your power we expect in return good government. We demand . . . that you shall make roads, undertake more works of irrigation which will improve the condition of the people and swell the revenues of your States; that you shall encourage and provide for the relief of the sick."

In form no doubt this was Viceregal advice to the rulers personally. But it was easily understood by them and by officers of the Political Department as a guide for political conduct conveying an official view that the internal administration of the States would be conducted under the supervision of the Government of India because the Government of India was "the Paramount Power."

We have seen that the East India Company, though politically and in a military sense paramount in India, never claimed to be the Paramount Power with a right to intervene in the internal affairs of the States. If, in 1857, the Government of India did not possess those rights, on what basis and through what process did the Government of India become invested with these powers subsequently?

The claim that the assumption of the Government of India by the Crown invested the Government of India with suzerainty over the States, hardly needs examination, as the only rights transferred to the Crown were those possessed by the Company. The Act of 1858 made it perfectly clear that no additional rights by that transfer accrued to the Crown. Its last clause provided that "all treaties made by the Company shall be binding on Her Majesty"; and the historic proclamation of the Queen made the position perfectly clear:

> "We hereby announce to the Native Princes of India that all treaties or engagements made with them by or under the authority of the Honourable the East India Company are by us accepted and will be scrupulously maintained, and we look for the like observance on their part."

Thus the fact that the Mughal Empire disappeared, or that the Queen assumed the direct governance of India, or later took the style of Empress, did not, and could not, alter the legal position of the Princes or convert them from allies to feudatories and the Government of India—or the Crown—from a predominant partner bound by treaties into a suzerain whose mandates were law. The policy which Canning began and Mayo developed (to be continued and elaborated in its legal and constitutional ramifications by successive Viceroys up to Lord Reading's time) was thus in violation of treaty rights and subsequent pledges of the Crown.

XIX.

"SUBORDINATE CO-OPERATION."

Subordinate co-operation is a phrase which is met with for the first time in official documents in the time of the Marquess of Hastings. In the treaty concluded by that Governor-General with the Maharana of Udaipur in 1818 it is laid down: "The Maharana of Udaipur will always act in subordinate co-operation with the British Government and acknowledge its supremacy, and will not have any connection with other Chiefs or States." The same phraseology is repeated in most of the treaties made by Lord Hastings.

Persistent attempts have been made to interpret the phrase "subordinate co-operation" to mean the subordination of Indian States to the policy of the Government of India. The Government of India has in many cases (*e.g.* Bhopal in 1863) founded upon this clause a pretension to force upon the States policies or measures which encroached upon their rights.

It will be found that the clause in the treaties laying down subordinate co-operation, particularly if taken in conjunction with other articles of the treaty and construed in the light of the surrounding circumstances, *i.e.* of the political facts existing at the time, cannot bear any such interpretation.

Firstly, it can be seen from the text of the treaties that the clause deals exclusively with the conditions of external relations or military co-operation. The purpose was to see that the ruler taken in alliance did not disturb the general peace. The Udaipur treaty, for example, mentions actually in the same article that the Maharana will not have any connection with other Chiefs and States.

Secondly, these treaties lay down emphatically that the rulers will remain absolute in their own territory and that their internal sovereignty will not be encroached upon.

Thus the Jaipur treaty, which also lays down the condition of subordinate co-operation, has the following clause:

> "The Maharajah and his heirs and successors shall remain absolute rulers of their territory and their dependents according to long-established usage; and the British Civil and Criminal Jurisdiction shall not in any manner be introduced into that principality."

Similar clauses exist in most other States allied by treaties of subordinate co-operation.

Lord Hastings expressed himself unequivocally as to what he meant by the "absolute rulership" which the treaty guarantees. In the letter written to Metcalfe, who was then Resident of Hyderabad, the Governor-General negatived all suggestion that a right of interposition existed in the case of States "standing within the denomination of allies." "Our treaties characterising the Nizam as an independent sovereign authorise no such latitude." This being Lord Hastings' view with regard to States whose rulers are declared to be absolute, it is impossible to argue that he thought any degree of subordination, except in military matters, was intended by the phrase in question. It could not be that Lord Hastings declared a ruler to be internally absolute and internally subordinate at the same time, especially when we know that he had laid down as a principle of his policy that where a ruler was declared to be (independent) absolute master in his own territory, the British Government had no right to intervene.

Though meant originally to limit the external relations and military activity of the States, the phrase was expanded and came to be constructively interpreted in official circles to mean almost the complete subordination of the States to the opinions and views expressed by the Residency. The transformation of the Residency from the representatives of an allied Government to the controllers of Indian States, and the consequent growth of their political importance at the expense of the authority of the ruler, have been the result of this wide and comprehensive misinterpretation of this term.

Originally the Agents and Residents had the diplomatic function of controlling the external relations of the States, and of watching over the Company's interests, and the earlier agreements contained arrangements for mutual appointment of Agents. Later, by applying the policy of "subordinate co-operation" in its mistaken sense, the Company gained an advantage, in that it retained the right to station its Agent in the Indian States, whilst withdrawing the States' reciprocal corresponding privilege of having its Vakil at the seat of the British Government. The true duties of Agent, however, were precise and comprised only the transaction of the external affairs of the States. Or rather their duties were to watch that the States concerned had no external relations except with the Company. The treaties bargained for this and nothing more.

At a later stage the presence of the Political Agent enabled the Government to charge him with additional duties and thus indirectly to enlarge his powers and correspondingly curtail the ruler's rights. For this there was no authority except the interpretation that the Government gave to the term "subordinate co-operation." The Bhopal case illustrates the silent advance.

In 1863, when the Government of Bhopal appealed against the exercise of jurisdiction by the Resident which was against the clear provision of the treaty of 1818, declaring that "British jurisdiction in any matter will not be introduced into that principality," it was stated in reply that "as Bhopal by its treaty has undertaken to act in subordinate co-operation with the British Government, it may be reasonably expected to accept arrangements of that nature." Again, in Patiala, when the Darbar refused its sanction to arrangements proposed in connection with railway extension, which policy the Patiala authorities considered to be an encroachment on their rights, the Chief Secretary to the Punjab Government wrote as follows:

> "Upon a full review of the case the Government of India have come to the conclusion that *for Imperial reasons which apply throughout India* and which are of the utmost importance for the administration of the whole system of Indian railways, it is necessary that the Patiala Darbar should *comply with the wishes* of the Government in the matter as the majority of Native States have already done in India. *His Honour must therefore ask the Patiala Darbar now to carry out the request* and return duly signed two copies of the agreement forwarded with this office letter No. 567, dated 24th July, 1899, in respect of each of the Railways mentioned in that letter."

A right thus assumed could be enlarged in various ways, and was enlarged to the detriment of the rulers' powers. With the entire authority of the Indian Government and its military resources behind them, the Political Officers ceased to be any longer mere intermediaries between two parties in alliance. They became dictators in the States. As one writer has put it, "The whisper of the Residency became the thunder of the State."

The doctrine, dear to the heart of the Government of India, of maintaining the prestige of the man on the spot, made it possible for every officer to dominate the affairs of the State to which he was accredited. He enjoyed the privileges of extra-territoriality and the immunities that are attached to foreign representatives. In many cases the Residency establishments became a charge upon the State. Indeed, by the beginning of the present century certain personal easements claimed or enjoyed by Political Officers in various States had grown to the dimensions of a scandal which resulted in the Government of India taking cognisance of the matter. Such an "easement," if forced by the Government upon an unwilling State, was an unjustifiable imposition: if volunteered by a State to the officials of an acquiescent or unconscious Government, it was or might easily degenerate into bribery and become tolerated blackmail.

Apart from the definite duties which were assigned to Political Agents, according to the treaties or according to the arbitrary action of Government, there grew up in the course of time the theory of giving "advice" to the Indian rulers. Originally inserted only in agreements with States over which the British Government had acquired a lawful right of control, the provision for compliance with advice served the purpose of the individual Resident whose policy it was to watch the action of the ruler. Under such circumstances conflicts inevitably arose from time to time, and in the evolution of relations the authority of the Resident naturally tended to become dominant. But in the practice which grew up round the theory of giving advice the distinction was soon lost between the States in which the Political Agent had the right to "advise," and those in which he had no right, and between questions on which the British Government might legitimately intervene, like defence, and those in which it had no such right. Instances abound where a real or assumed right of "advice" has been used by Political Officers to secure the cession of valuable rights to the Government of India, even to the financial loss of the State concerned, *e.g.* the Inter-Portal Convention of Travancore, which was signed, after much protest, because the ruler was officially "advised" by the Resident to do so; and many cases to be found in the printed evidence tendered to the Indian States Committee.

The presence of the Political Officers in the States has led to yet another vital change in the status of Indian rulers. During the minority of a ruler, power automatically passes into the hands of the Resident (or other Political Officer appointed for the purpose), irrespective of the circumstances in which the British originally found a footing in, or in relation to, the States. The Government of India assume responsibility, and as a matter of course immediate authority is conferred by them upon their local representative. He becomes either the sole administrator or the President of the Council of Administration, or, failing these two alternatives, other arrangements are made for the States to be run under his "supervision and guidance." He then unites in himself two capacities and three functions. He stands as the representative of the British Government and also as the administrator acting in the interest and on behalf of the ruler, a strange combination of *parusha* and *Prakrti*, in which, unfortunately for the States, the characteristics of the dominant partner assert themselves, often to the exclusion of those of the junior. But as representative of the Government of India he fulfils two quite different functions. He is still diplomatic agent of the Crown to the State. He is also the local officer of the Paramount Power controlling the administration of the State. This function it is the duty of the Paramount Power to perform as a Trustee for the State in a wholly disinterested manner, making no profit out of its trust. But unfortunately the discharge of this duty has in historical fact—as was inevitable—been delegated by the Crown as Paramount Power to the Government of British India, a party which is by the nature of its position very far from disinterested. Hence the policy underlying the directions given by Government to its officers administering a State during minority is biased consciously, or unconsciously, by a consideration of the needs, requirements and advantages of British India, and in particular is influenced by the departmental view of the department of that Government which is concerned in the particular topic under consideration between the State and the Government of India at any given moment. There are fundamental forces working underneath the surface, like the economic forces of supply and demand, and they are bound to exercise an incalculable influence on events, given the conditions described above. The balance of tendencies in this respect of " subordinate co-operation " has been always adverse to the States and they have suffered to a varying and unmeasured extent in consequence. Similar considerations apply in differing degrees to every case of Government administration of a State, whether total or partial, whether absolute or supervisory, whether during a minority after a deposition or in consequence of the mental incapacity of a ruler, or whenever partial control is assumed, whatever be the occasion, either a lawful intervention or an unauthorised encroachment.

We believe the above to be a plain but correct statement of the actual tendencies which have had so much effect in the history of the States; and we are not here discussing their legal aspects.

With the help of the misinterpretation of a phrase—" subordinate co-operation "—the Political Agent has become the repository of almost unique powers. He is a judicial officer entrusted with the enforcement of law against Europeans in all States and against British Indians in some. He is the sole channel of communication with the Government of India, whose deputy he is in all matters. He also enjoys extra-territoriality, freedom from customs, special personal honours, etc. He also represents the Government of India in an executive capacity. The combination of such diverse authority makes the Residents of Indian States specially prone to interpret the obligations of "subordinate co-operation" of States as meaning compliance without question with any wish they may express. As long as the phrase subordinate co-operation is left undefined and the limitations within which "advice" may be given are not understood and prescribed, the Indian States must continue to be placed at the mercy of the Executive Government of India and its officers in the Political Department.

XX.

CERTAIN ASPECTS OF THE RELATIONSHIP BETWEEN THE STATES AND THE PARAMOUNT POWER.

1.—*The use of the word "Feudatory."*

On p. 62 of Sir Charles Tupper's treatise, *Our Indian Protectorate*,[1] occur the words:

"If we distinguish between the Indian Political system and Indian Political law, we may say that the former was almost wholly constructed in the first twenty years of the present (nineteenth) century, while the latter, though based upon occurrences of year after year from the middle of the last (eighteenth) century to the present day, only really took shape during the twenty years next after the Mutiny."

We may accept this historical statement by the author of the secret hand-book, *Political Practice*, which the Government of India give to officers in the Political Department to guide their conduct but never reveal to the Indian Princes or the public, even though we disagree with his theory of "Indian Political Law." In passing, it may, however, be said that the difference in our understanding of the nature of the rights and obligations attaching to the relationship from Tupper's does not rest merely on our disagreement with his contention that the States are Feudatories. Indeed, that view was shown by Lee-Warner[2] to be a fallacy in his *Protected Princes of India*, within a year of the publication of Tupper's book.

Before, however, dismissing the idea of the States being bound to the Empire by the feudal tie, we may point out that the existence of such a tie, which Lord

[1] Tupper, Sir Charles, *Our Indian Protectorate*. London, 1893.
[2] Lee-Warner, W., *Protected Princes of India*. London, 1894.

Ellenborough first broaches in his letters to Queen Victoria, and which Lord Dalhousie asserts on several occasions, was never asserted in correspondence between the Company and the States. While the Company's Government was recognised by all as the Paramount Power in India, the States were officially held to be in alliance with that Power. Even if that Power was on occasions called the Suzerain Power, it was never asserted that the States stood in a feudatory position towards it. The terms of the treaties contained no hint of feudal relations even in the case of the so-called "dependent" States.

2.—*No Official Tendency to treat all States alike in pre-Mutiny Period.*

Another point which is worth noticing in the relations of the States with the Government of India before its assumption by the Crown, is that in their dealings with the States the Political Officers of the Company made no attempt to reduce all the States to one uniform level of subjection (or to the Procrustean policies of the British Provinces). The view was clearly held that the position of one State *vis-à-vis* the Company was different from that of another. What the difference was depended on the terms of the particular treaty which each individual State had made with the Company. From the days of Lord Hastings onwards it had been clear to all that the power of the Company was in actual fact supreme, and that no State or combination of States could hope to compete with it. But the predominant strength of one partner in an alliance was not considered to be a legitimate reason for forcing exactions from the other partner. Public opinion in England as a whole, and not merely the judgment of the Court of Directors, condemned Lord Ellenborough's treatment of Gwalior in 1844. A decade later, enlightened British opinion in India was averse to some of the special methods practised by Lord Dalhousie in his policy of annexation or reduction of allowances paid to ex-rulers. The *Madras Athenæum*, for instance, did not follow the line of the *Friend of India*.

Prior to 1860 there was little uniformity in the policy adopted towards the States. It is impossible to imagine the Political Department of the Company in pre-Mutiny days issuing a circular to its agents detailing a line of action to which all the States were supposed to subscribe. Even from the Company's point of view there would have been no necessity for such a proceeding. The relations of the Company with the States were purely political. Communications had not been much developed, and economic considerations generally did not then possess the importance which they have later assumed.

3.—*Non-Interference in Internal Sovereignty in the pre-Mutiny Period.*

Again, the sovereignty of the States, except in matters in which it had been curtailed by special treaties, was generally recognised, and while the Company in no way neglected its own interests, as it was ready enough to admit, it was also ready enough to admit that the larger Indian States had an independence which they thought made the principles of international law applicable. The fact that by its treaties it had engaged to protect the States against external aggression or to support the authority of their rulers within the bounds of their dominions was never pleaded as an excuse for interference with the domestic affairs of any principality unless the interference were in accordance with some particular engagement mediated between the Prince and his aristocracy. Such intervention as that made in 1831, when the Mysore State was taken under British Administration, was an interposition amply justified by the terms of the Treaty of Rendition made by Lord Wellesley with that State.

During the pre-Mutiny period it was the honest belief

of many that interference in the affairs of the States was unjustifiable, whilst others felt that if the States were left alone, their backward condition would be a standing contrast to the superior administration and improved means of livelihood and happiness prevailing in the British Provinces and help to make the subjects of British India content with their lot.

In the period hitherto described, no detailed attempts had been made by British officers to define the position of the States in their relationship with the Government of India, or to theorise on the obligations of the States to that Government as "the price of union."[1] In return for a very substantial *quid pro quo* in the form of an abandonment of external sovereignty, of territories ceded by the States or of tributes or other money payments or other concessions, the Company had undertaken to protect the States. For this consideration was regarded by both sides as ample. Some States which had engaged to act in subordinate co-operation were under express contract to render military assistance to the Company when called upon to do so, but the meaning of the phrase "subordinate co-operation" had not yet been perverted into the claim that the States must make whatever political or economic concession the Government of India chose to direct. No lengthy list of obligations unexpressed in their treaties and engagements directing the States as to what they ought to do or ought not to do had as yet been evolved by the Political Department, either in the form of Sanads or as so-called "political practices." Political Officers gave advice, but that advice they did not intimate was to be obeyed as the indirect expression of the Company's commands. In certain particular States advantage was taken of successions or minority administrations to further the Company's interests, but such cases only occurred from time to time (whereas at Nagpur, or Gwalior (1843), the disturbances connected with such a succession had first called for the employment of the forces of the Company).

[1] Lee-Warner, Chap. VII.

And generally there appears to have been a desire to avoid any attempt at coercing a State during the minority of its ruler. The age of closing State mints during minority regimes had not yet arrived.

4.—"*Political Practices*" *a post-Mutiny Conception.*

It is perhaps well to lay stress on the fact that before the year 1860 the Government of India never claimed to apply principles of "usage" in its relations with States as a whole. To begin with, thanks to the varying policies applied by successive Governors-General, there was little opportunity for the establishment of general usage, apart from the fact that the dealings of the Company's officers with each State were, as has been said above, not conducted on uniform lines, but in accordance with the treaty position of each State and with the customary methods of diplomatic relations established when first a State had entered into an alliance with the Company.

5.—*No Reliance on Precedent and Prescription.*

"Prescriptive rights" too were not claimed in these days by the Company's Political Officers as a lever for forcing upon the States some system which the Government of India desired to see introduced. Whatever prescription there was, was that urged by the Indian Princes, the ancient customs of whose dominions were often definitely mentioned in treaties or correspondence as worthy of the respect of their ally, John Company. Still less were individual precedents erected into general principles.

6.—*Recognition that Consent is necessary for Measures affecting Internal Sovereignty.*

In various social reforms, such as the prohibition of *sati* and the abolition of infanticide which the States adopted from British India in the first half of the nineteenth century, the desired results were brought about either by perfectly legitimate influence diplomatically exerted through the Residents accredited to the Courts of the Indian Princes or by definite agreements entered into with the States. Those were not the days when a resolution of the League of Nations could have been accepted by the Government of British India, and the States then informed by the Political Department that they must acquiesce in that decision whether it suited their sentiments and pockets or not. It was realised that to introduce a change in internal matters the consent of the State was essential.

In reading through the treaties to be found in Aitchison, the impression left is that they appear more personal than do the treaties of to-day. Not merely in form, but in spirit, they are engagements entered into by the East India Company with individual Princes who are treated as individuals. The subjects of the States are not mentioned unless it be in some stipulation that the Company will not in any manner interfere with the relations, subjects and servants of some ruler over whom the Prince's authority will be supreme. The treaties may not be framed on modern lines, but such as they are, they exist and cannot be got rid of under the plea that they are out of date. The Company recognised not merely the injustice but also the impolicy of interfering between a Prince and his subjects. That this view was a correct one can hardly be denied. It may be affirmed that those States where, thanks to a contingent or subsidiary force being stationed near the capital, there could hardly fail to be some interference (though interference of an indirect and unacknowledged nature), took the longest time to settle down into clearly defined political entities. Hyderabad and Gwalior may be quoted as cases in point.

Whether the States during this period were well or ill administered, the condition of their subjects was no concern of the Company unless a particular Governor-General had designs upon the integrity of the dominions of some Indian Prince, in which case the removal of the oppression of the people by their ruler was made the ostensible ground of interference in order to salve the consciences of the Honourable Court of Directors.[1]

7.—*The Drawbacks of the Protection by the Paramount Power.*

At the time when the Crown took over the administration of India from the Company, the political life of the States was still in a condition of flux. Isolated from one another by a general lack of communications and by Government's strict insistence on the treaty stipulation forbidding any communication between one ruler and another, and possessing as a whole a population which was racially more turbulent and less civilised than that of British India, the States found less opportunity than the British Provinces to adapt themselves to the great economic changes which from the middle of the nineteenth century altered so radically the life of India as a whole.

Though Political Officers in the "forties" and "fifties" of the last century do not seem to have been so prone as their successors to expatiate on the inestimable benefit of the protection which the ægis of the Company extended to the Princes of India, it cannot be gainsaid that such protection was from the first no unmixed blessing to them as autocratic rulers. It was not that this protection in the period under review was utilised as an excuse for undue interference in the domestic concerns of the States, such a grievance may be said to have been almost non-existent in these days. It was rather that it detracted from the merits of autocracy as a system of government. An autocrat justifies his despotical rule if he retains his power by his own personality and ability, but not otherwise. Whether a Government be an autocracy, an oligarchy or a democracy is of little moment, if the administration be strong without

[1] See Parliamentary Paper, Gwalior 1843.

being unduly meddlesome with the liberty of the subject, and if the type of administration suit the stage of political development which the State to be administered has reached. The "blessing" of external protection removes what is, perhaps, the greatest incentive to able administration, the ruler's fear of his own subjects if he does not give them satisfaction. It is a Greek gift which indirectly has done more than anything else to keep the Indian Princes and their States from progressing at the pace of British India.

In conclusion, a short reference may be made to the incorrect theory that the Company and thereby the Crown inherited from the Mughal Empire certain quasi-feudal rights over the States, even though the first assertion of this claim dates from post-Mutiny days.

Before the Mutiny the Company did claim to be the Paramount Power in India, an assertion to be found in the speeches and writings of various Governors-General, but that Paramountcy rested on the fact that by treaties with the States, the Indian Princes had been isolated one from another and had, as a whole, given up the right of foreign relations in return for protection from the Company.

In the beginning, while the Company was still a trading rather than a political corporation, it suited the purpose of its officers on occasion to have the treaties they had made with the rulers of provinces, still nominally under the control of the Great Mughal, acknowledged by the Emperor, and to claim that they acted as his delegates, but in such cases they acted as delegates in the territories under their own control and never in the lands ruled over by the Indian Princes, *e.g.* Madras.

Later, when they were stronger, the Company's officers refused to recognise the claims of the Mughal Emperor, as, for example, when in 1773 Hastings refused to entertain the claim to tribute demanded by the Emperor or to restore to him the territories of Kora and Allahabad.

From the time of Warren Hastings the Company made treaties with the States without any reference to the Emperor, and in no way, when thus acting, claimed to be exercising powers delegated to them by that potentate.

Parliament, too, legislated for the British Provinces without any reference to, or thought of, the Great Mughal, regardless of the fact that they held the Diwani of Bengal from him.

In these days, up to 1804, the Company could hardly claim to be acting as the Emperor's delegate, since the delegate of the Great Mughal was nominally the Peishwa, and in reality his deputy Scindia.

When the Emperor passed under the protection of the Company, the latter made no claim to have assumed the delegated powers of the Great Mughal. Such a claim was quite unnecessary, their *de facto* Paramountcy was ample for them for the purpose of dealing freely with the States.

In the States the impotent Emperor had by 1804 lost all his rights and the Company did not claim them. When they agreed to raise the dignity of the ruler of Oudh to that of Kingship, they did so by their own power and certainly not under powers delegated to them by the Great Mughal.

In fact it is impossible to assert with any show of reason that in pre-Mutiny days the Company made any claim on the States in the name of the Emperor. The theory was evolved as a picturesque thesis, for which no basis had existed in fact, after the Crown had assumed charge of the destinies of India and certain Viceroys and Cabinet Ministers in England had become imbued with the idea that by the use of Oriental imagery the Great Indian Empire would be impressed.[1] As a matter of fact, Great Britain one day woke up to the idea that by accident she had acquired an Empire and was glad enough to accept a romantic explanation of her justification for Eastern rule.

[1] "The tie is not feudal." Lee-Warner's marginal title of his para. 151 (p. 393).

XXI.

CERTAIN CONTEMPORANEOUS DOCUMENTS IN THE TIMES OF LORD MORNINGTON AND LORD HASTINGS.

Extract from Lord Mornington's letter to the Resident in Hyderabad, dated FORT WILLIAM, *6th November*, 1799.

" It is therefore now as necessary that the succession to the Subaship of the Deccan should be settled by the Company's authority as it was in July 1798.

" In every view which I am enabled to take of this question, it continues to appear to me desirable that we should raise Secunder Shah to the Masnad (throne) in preference to any of his brothers. The right of primogeniture is in his favour; his connections are among those persons best affected to our interest; he is the only son of the Nizam who has ever maintained any authorised intercourse with us, or who has ever manifested any desire to cultivate our friendship. Alee Jah was disposed to connect his views with those of Tipu Sultan. Feridon Jah has carried on intrigues in the same quarter; and Jehandar Shah has been suspected of endeavouring to engage the Marathas to take him under their protection.

" In favouring the pretensions of Secunder Jah, we must not overlook what is requisite to the improvement of our connection with the Court of Hyderabad and to the establishment of that connection on a basis of the most solid advantage and of the most permanent security.

" No objection of treaty binds us to take part in any contested succession arising either from the total silence of the Nizam respecting his intended successor or from a disputable declaration of His Highness's intention on the subject. Even in the case of an unequivocal nomination of a successor by His Highness, we should not be bound by the treaty of September, 1798, or by any other objection, to support that successor against any rival whose cause might be espoused by the Marathas. Whatever secret or political motives, therefore, may exist to induce us either to interpose our influence in the settlement of the succession or to prefer the pretensions of Secunder Jah, our faith is not pledged to raise that prince to the Masnad, or unconditionally to support him upon it against any effort of the Marathas, or of any other Power in favour of another candidate.

" Having stated the general principles which should govern our conduct in the conjunction under contemplation, I shall proceed to furnish you with an outline of the particular conditions on which I am willing to support the succession of Secunder Jah against all competitions.

" The conditions are as follows:

(1) " The treaty of September 1798 shall be confirmed by Secunder Jah, for himself and his heirs, in all points not expressly altered by the new treaty.

(2) " The subsidiary force shall be augmented to four regiments of Native Infantry, two regiments of Native Cavalry and three companies of Artillery, including a proportionable increase of gun-lascars.

(3) " The additional force shall be subsidised at the same rate as that now serving in the Nizam's dominions.

(4) " A territory to be selected by the Company producing a net revenue at least adequate to the payment of the subsidy (under the treaty of 1798 as well as under the new engagement) shall be assigned to the sole and absolute management of the Company: the Company to account to the reigning Prince for any surplus of revenue exceeding the amount of the subsidy which may be realised from the said territory under their management.

(5) " The Peshcush (tribute) at present payable by the Company to the Nizam on account of the Northern Circars shall be remitted for ever.

(6) " If the number of troops stipulated to be subsidised should at any time appear to be inadequate to the purpose of securing Secunder Jah on the Masnad against the attempts of any competition, whether supported or not by the Marathas or by any other Power, the Company will augment the subsidised force to such an extent as the Company may judge necessary, and Secunder Jah shall in that case defray the expense of such temporary addition of force.

(7) " All rahdary (transit) duties on goods passing to and from the respective territories of the contracting parties shall be abolished. No articles of merchandise shall pay duty more than once, and a proper tariff shall be established for the regulation of the single duties to be so levied; and a treaty of commerce shall be concluded between the two

States, on just and equitable principles of reciprocal interest and common benefit.

(8) "Secunder Jah shall engage to pay at all times the utmost attention to such advice as the Company's Government shall occasionally judge it necessary to offer to him, with a view to any objects connected with the advancement of his interests, the happiness of his people, and the mutual welfare of both States.

"Such is the outline of the terms upon which I propose to support and maintain the succession of Secunder Jah, whether he should obtain the previous nomination of his father or not, or even if it should be pretended that His Highness had declared in favour of some other of his sons. You will prepare, without delay, an instrument in the Persian language, in conformity to the foregoing outline, in order that Secunder Jah (at the moment of his father's death, or whenever that event shall appear to approach) may be apprised of the terms on which we are ready to support his cause, and may be enabled by immediately executing a formal instrument to accede to my propositions in a regular manner.

"I think it necessary to permit you either totally to suppress or to modify the 8th Article, according to your discretion, apprising you, however, that I consider it to be of great importance to obtain such an ascendancy over the Councils of the Nizam as is described in that Article.

"Secunder Jah must not be allowed to procrastinate his determination. If at the end of a stated and short period of time he should not determine to accept the proffered treaty, you will proceed in concert with Azeem-ul-Umara and Mir Allum, to place one of the younger sons of the Nizam on the Masnad; previously stipulating that the prince succeeding to the Masnad shall fulfil all the conditions of the treaty proposed to Secunder Jah.

"I am aware that the objects proposed might be obtained from Secunder Jah with less difficulty previously to the death of the Nizam, and that it would on that account be desirable that a negotiation should be opened immediately with Secunder Jah. But many objections occur to deter me from such a step. The attempt, if it should transpire (either by accident or design), would probably lead to mischievous consequences. I am therefore of opinion that no such attempt should be hazarded until the Nizam shall be at the point of death.

"It is manifest that our power of settling the succession in the manner described, and of obtaining the advantages which I have enumerated, will depend in an eminent degree, if not absolutely, on the local position of the subsidiary force at the time of His Highness's death. It is, therefore, of the last importance that that force should not only be kept together, but stationed as near as possible to the residence of the Nizam; and I accordingly direct you to adopt every practicable means of accomplishing these most desirable and essential objects without delay.

"I am, etc.,

"MORNINGTON."

SUBSIDIARY FORCES IN INDIAN STATES.

EXTRACT FROM THE LETTER OF SIR THOMAS MUNRO TO LORD HASTINGS IN 1817.

"There are many weighty objections to the employment of a subsidiary force. It has a natural tendency to render the Government of every country in which it exists, weak and oppressive; to extinguish all honourable spirit among the higher classes of society and to degrade and impoverish the whole people. The usual remedy of a bad Government in India is a quiet revolution in the palace, or a violent one by rebellion or foreign conquests. But the presence of a British force cuts off every chance of remedy, by supporting the Prince on the throne against every foreign or domestic enemy. It renders him indolent by teaching him to trust to strangers for his security; and cruel and avaricious, by showing him that he has nothing to fear from the hatred of his subjects. Wherever the subsidiary system is introduced, unless the reigning Prince be a man of great abilities, the country will soon bear the marks of it in decaying villages and decreasing population. This has long been observed in the dominions of the Peishwa and the Nizam, and is now beginning to be seen in Mysore. . . .

"A subsidiary force would be a most useful establishment if it could be directed solely to the support of our ascendancy, without nourishing all the vices of a bad Government; but this seems to be almost impossible. The only way in which this object has ever, in any degree, been attained is by the appointment of a Dewan. This measure is, no doubt, liable to numerous objections; but still it is the only one by which any amends can be made to the people of the country for the miseries brought upon them by the subsidiary force, in giving stability to a vicious Government. The great difficulty is to prevent the Prince from counteracting the Dewan, and the Resident from meddling too much;

but when this is avoided, the Dewan may be made a most useful instrument of Government.

"There is, however, another view under which the subsidiary system may be considered—I mean that of its inevitable tendency to bring every Native State into which it is introduced sooner or later under the exclusive dominion of the British Government. It has already done this completely in the case of the Nawab of the Carnatic. It has made some progress in that of the Peishwa and Nizam; and the whole of the territory of these Princes will unquestionably suffer the same fate as the Carnatic. The observation of Moro Dekshet, in speaking of the late treaty to Major Ford, that 'no native power could, from its habits, conduct itself with such strict fidelity as we seemed to demand,' is perfectly just. This very Peishwa will probably again commit a breach of the alliance. The Nizam will do the same, and the same consequence, a farther reduction of their power for their own safety, must again follow. Even if the Prince himself were disposed to adhere rigidly to the alliance, there will always be some among his principal officers who will urge him to break it. As long as there remains in the country any high-minded independence, which seeks to throw off the control of strangers, such counsellors will be found. I have a better opinion of the natives of India than to think that this spirit will ever be completely extinguished, and I can therefore have no doubt that the subsidiary system must everywhere run its full course, and destroy every Government which it undertakes to protect.

"In this progress of things, the evil of a weak and oppressive Government supported by a subsidiary alliance will at least be removed. But even if all India could be brought under the British dominion, it is very questionable whether such a change, either as regards the natives or ourselves, ought to be desired. One effect of such a conquest would be that the Indian army, having no longer any warlike neighbours to combat, would gradually lose its military habits and discipline, and that the native troops would have leisure to feel their own strength, and for want of other employment to turn it against their European masters. But even if we could be secured against every internal convulsion, and could retain the country quietly in subjection, I doubt much if the condition of the people would be better than under their Native Princes. The strength of the British Government enables it to put down every rebellion, to repel every foreign invasion, and to give to its subjects a degree of protection which those of no Native Power enjoy. Its laws and institutions also afford them a security from domestic oppression, unknown to those States; but these advantages are dearly bought. They are purchased by the sacrifice of independence—of national character, and of whatever renders a people respectable. The natives of the British Provinces may without fear pursue their different occupations, as traders, Merrasidars or husbandmen, and enjoy the fruits of their labour in tranquillity; but none of them can aspire to anything beyond this mere animal state of thriving peace—none of them can look forward to any share in the legislation, or civil or military government of their country. It is from men who either hold or are eligible to hold public office that natives take their characters; where no such men exist there can be no energy in any other class of the community. The effect of this state of things is observable in all the British Provinces, whose inhabitants are certainly the most abject race in India. No elevation of character can be expected among men who, in the military line, cannot attain to any rank above that of Subedar, where they are as much below an ensign as an ensign is below the Commander-in-Chief, and who in the civil line can hope for nothing beyond some petty judicial or revenue office, in which they may, by corrupt means, make up for their slender salary.

"The consequence, therefore, of the conquest of India by the British arms would be in place of raising to debase the whole people. There is perhaps no example of any conquest in which the natives have been so completely excluded from all share of the government of their country as in British India.

"Among all the disorders of the Native States the field is open for every man to raise himself; and hence among them there is a spirit of emulation, of restless enterprise and independence, far preferable to the servility of our Indian subjects. The existence of independent Native States is also useful in drawing off the turbulent and disaffected among our native troops. Many of these men, belonging to the Madras army, formerly sought service in Mysore.

"If the British Government is not favourable to the improvement of Indian character, that of its control through a subsidiary force is still less so. Its power is now so great that it has nothing to fear from any combination, and it is perfectly able to take satisfaction for any insult, without any extension of the subsidiary system being necessary. It will generally be found much more convenient to carry on war where it has not been introduced. This was the case in both the wars with Tippu Sultan. The conquest was complete because our operations were not perplexed by any subsidiary alliance with him. The simple and direct mode of conquest from without is more creditable both to our armies and to our national character than that of dismemberment from within by the aid of a subsidiary force. However just the motives may be from which such a force acts, yet the situation in which it is placed renders its acting at all too much like the movements of the Prætorian bands. It acts, it is true, only by the orders of its own Government, and only for public objects, but still it is always ready in the neighbourhood of the capital to dictate terms to, or to depose the Prince whom it is stationed there to defend.

"In our treaties with them (the Indian Princes) we recognise them as independent sovereigns. Then we send a Resident to their Courts. Instead of acting in the character of ambassador, he assumes the functions of a dictator, interferes in all their private concerns, countenances refractory subjects against them, and makes the most ostentatious exhibition of this exercise of authority. To secure to himself the support of our Government, he urges some interest which, under the colour thrown upon it by him, is strenuously taken up by our Council; and the Government identifies itself with the Resident not only on the single point but on the whole tenor of his conduct. In nothing do we violate the feelings of the Native Princes so much as in the decisions in which we claim the privilege of pronouncing with regard to the succession to the Musnud."

Sir Charles Metcalfe, when Mr. Metcalfe and Resident at Hyderabad, had requested the interference of the British Government in the affairs of the Nizam's dominions on the grounds of misgovernment and, as has been stated earlier in the chapter, had received a very definite refusal. Evidently his further experience of political life had taught him the wisdom of that refusal, for in 1835, as acting Governor-General, in his paper on the affairs of Jaipur he writes:

"Another evil of interference is that it gives too much power to our Agents at foreign Courts, and makes Princes and Ministers very much the slaves of subjects of their will. An interfering Agent is an abominable nuisance wherever he may be, and our Agents are apt to take that turn. They like to be masters instead of mere negotiators. They imagine, often very erroneously, that they can do good by meddling in other people's affairs; and they are impatient in witnessing any disorder which they think may be remedied by our interference, forgetting that one step in this course will unavoidably be followed by others, which will most probably lead to the destruction of the independence of the State concerned.

"It must be admitted to be an evil of the non-interference

policy that temporary and local disorder may occasionally ensue, and must be tolerated if we mean to adhere strictly to that principle. But this is a consequence which we naturally dislike. We are not disposed to wait until things settle themselves in their natural course. *We think ourselves called on to interfere, and some bungling or unnatural arrangement is made by our will, which, because it is our own, we ever after support against the inclination of the people and their notions of right ond justice.*

"The true basis of non-interference is a respect for the rights of others—for the rights of all, people as well as Princes. The treaties by which we are connected with Native States are, with rare exceptions, founded on their independence in internal affairs. In several instances the States are, with respect to external relations, dependent and under our protection but still independent in internal affairs. It is customary with the advocates of interference to twist our obligation of protection against enemies into a right to interfere in the internal affairs of protected States, a right, however, which our treaties generally do not give us, otherwise than as the supporters of the legitimate Sovereign against usurpation or dethronement, in the event of his not having merited the disaffection of his subjects.

"The advocates for interference would probably maintain that it is right to anticipate mischief and prevent it by decided interference, and, as disorder will sometimes follow our adherence to non-interference, there would be much weight in that argument if our interference were always productive of good. But we often create or aggravate mischief and disorder by injudicious settlement of affairs which would not otherwise take place. One of the strongest arguments in my mind against interference is that it is more apt to work evil than good. There is nothing in our political administration that requires so much circumspection and caution, and discreet judgment, as interference in the affairs of other States. A single mistake on the part of an Agent may cause irreparable mischief; and the power left to Agents on such occasions is immense. Almost everything depends on their judgment. The effects of interference are anything but certain. It is not, therefore, a conclusive argument in favour of interference, although it is best, that we may thereby prevent evil, for, on the contrary, we are just as likely to create it; I should indeed say, infinitively more so. And the evil created by interference is generally irremediable. It virtually, if not ostensibly, destroys the State to which it is applied and leaves it only a nominal, if any, existence.

"Our attempts to interfere for the better Government of other States have often been wretched failures as to our purpose, but we have nevertheless had all the bad effects of interference on the States concerned, as well as on the minds of other States. Where interference shall begin, and where end, and to what object it shall be confined, and how that object shall be accomplished without involving further and unnecessary interference, are all nice points to determine. The question of interference altogether is so likely to do evil, and so little certain of doing good, that it ought, I conceive, to be avoided as much as possible. The evils of non-interference may certainly be such sometimes as we would not like to permit to continue, but their effects are generally temporary, and leave the State independent in internal affairs as before. The effects of interference are permanent, and degrade the State for ever, if they do not destroy it."

BENGAL POLITICAL LETTER.

20TH OF DECEMBER, 1822.

"1. Your letters of the 31st August, and 3rd and 5th September, have been laid before the Governor-General in Council, and I am directed to communicate the observations which occurred on their perusal.

"2. In the second paragraph of your first letter you say that 'you suppose our interference in the Nizam's affairs to be not merely right, but also a duty, arising out of our supremacy in India, which imposed on us the obligation of maintaining the tranquillity of all countries connected with us, and consequently of protecting the people from oppressions, as no less necessary than the guaranteeing of their rulers against revolution.' The assumption of our possessing a universal supremacy in India involving such rights as you have described is a mistake. Over States which have, by particular engagements, rendered themselves professedly feudatory, the British Government does, no doubt, exercise supremacy; but it never has been claimed, and certainly never has been acknowledged in the case of Native Powers standing within the denomination of allies. Although a virtual supremacy may undoubtedly be said to exist in the British Government, from the inability of other States to contend with its strength, the making such a superiority a principle singly sufficient for any exertion of our will would be to misapply and to pervert it to tyrannic purposes.

"3. In your third paragraph you observe, 'the only refuge of a people intolerably vexed is in emigration or insurrection; and as we secure the Nizam's Government against rebellion, it seems to be incumbent on us to save his subjects from grievous oppressions.' The argument of supremacy having been set aside, nothing but the tenure of some special engagement could render us liable to the call, or allot to us the title for such interposition. Our treaties, characterising the Nizam as an independent sovereign, authorise no such lassitude. When, for our private views, that Prince was constrained to support a body of our troops, to be stationed near his capital, the then Government disguised the interested oppressiveness of making him pay a portion of our army for holding him in thraldom, by a sturdy declaration that His Highness had spontaneously sought the aid of a subsidiary force to secure his person and territories. The veil thus thrown over our policy required that any stipulations which could mark the prostration of his power should be forborne, so that in appearance he legitimately retained his freedom. The measure, however, really placed him at our mercy. It was hardly to be imagined that our advantage would not be abused, and it was abused; the independence which the very conditions of the compact recognised and pledged us to respect was set at naught. Gradual but unequivocal encroachment on the Nizam's just authority were perceived by the honourable court, and a more becoming system was enjoined. The Governor-General in Council laboured to introduce it—a work of no small difficulty when the country was so disorganised—and having established an understanding with Rajah Chundoo Loll for the correction and future conduct of affairs (this Government, in return, binding itself to support that Minister), the Resident was directed to adopt a course of conciliatory counsel instead of those starts of despotic dictation which had before been in use. That limited degree of interference would still be objectionable but for the common interests between the two governments, that His Highness's territories should be restored to prosperity; yet even that excuse would be insufficient were not our influence to be managed with delicacy, and to be unavowed. Such is the distinct nature of our relations with the Nizam; and a disregard of its terms would be no less repugnant to general principles than to the orders of this Government.

"4. Paragraphs 4 and 5 plead necessity for our interposition because the Nizam does not rule his subjects with equity and prudence. The fact of maladministration is unquestionable and must be deplored. Does that, however, decide the mode in which alteration is to be effected? Where is our right to determine that the amount of the evil is such as to demand our taking the remedy into our hands? His Lordship in Council observes that the necessity stated is altogether constructive. Were such a pretence allowable, a powerful State should never want a colour for subjugating a weak neighbour. The consequence is so obvious that no principle in the law of nations leaves room for acting on such a presumption. It is admitted that if convulsions rage so violently in one State as clearly to threaten the excitation of ferment in a bordering one, the latter may be justified in reducing to order the nation by which its tranquillity was menaced. This, however, is an extreme case, at the same time that it is of a description strictly defined. No analogy exists between indisputable exigency and an asserted convenience, where vague arbitrary charges, if tolerated as a ground of procedure, would furnish ready pretext for the foulest usurpations."

PART II

AN EXAMINATION OF SOME ASPECTS OF THE FISCAL QUESTIONS AT ISSUE BETWEEN THE STATES AND THE GOVERNMENT OF INDIA

In the following pages an attempt is made to examine some aspects of the economic relationships between the Indian States and British India.

The situation of the Indian States is unique in history and no known relationship provides precedents to solve the problems they present. The analogy with a federation of independent States is not complete; the analogy with the subject provinces of an Empire is not complete, and international law is of hardly any assistance at all. The problem is full of difficulties, of which probably the chief is the scantiness and inaccuracy of the statistics from which estimates can be made. Our object has been rather to show the nature of the problem from such data as have been available than to establish definite figures. Where figures have been used we have aimed at moderation. In not a few cases we believe that we have under-estimated the contributions of the States, and where for some reason we accept an estimated figure which we suspect to be over-favourable to them the effect of the error is not great. In any instance where it is thought that we have over-estimated we would ask the reader to substitute his own figure and to see how far, if at all, the change affects our general argument.

We do not claim that our figures are exact. A committee of experts with full access to all available information would be necessary to make them so. Nevertheless, we believe that within reasonable limits the estimates which we have made are accurate.

Economic and fiscal relationships are partly a question of fact and partly of law. It is necessary to ascertain and record what payments are in fact made by one side to the other and what are the services rendered in return, and what are the agreements or claims made by one side with or against the other. But a further inquiry is essential whenever as now a revision of economic relationships is in contemplation. It is necessary to ask what are the rights and obligations on each side—primarily legal or constitutional rights—" créances et responsabilités de plein droit," as a French constitutionalist would say (which is the meaning to be attached throughout this Note to the phrase " legal or constitutional "); and secondarily of a political or moral order (*i.e.* where the obligation is " imperfect ") if there be any ground for supposing that such rights exist.

The views upon which the Princes rely, so far as the legal or constitutional position is concerned, are stated in principle in the Legal Opinion dated 24th July, 1928. The greater part of the relevant facts appear in the collected evidence, gathered from the actual experience of the various States, which has been placed before the Indian States Committee. The examination of the fiscal questions here attempted is intended to put the economic relations between the States and British India in a conspectus of fact and law, bringing together the main facts as they exist; applying the legal principles enunciated in Counsel's opinion; and drawing conclusions as to what financial changes ought to be made in order to make the adjustment of the burdens fair to both sides. But no reference is made to any future constitutional changes which may be introduced in the relations between the States and British India.

Such a reconsideration of the existing position is politically desirable and right for this reason, if for no other, that no such investigation has ever before taken place. It is the first in the whole history of India. Existing financial and economic relations have grown up without any thought being taken of the relationship as a whole and of what it imports in the way of right and obligation. And so far as the Princes know, no such investigation by way of reconsideration and revision of the position has been attempted by either the Government of British India or by the Viceroy as representative in India of the Crown in its capacity of party to the treaties with the Indian Princes; or the India Office and Secretary of State; or the Cabinet in London. Certainly the Princes have never been invited to take part in any such deliberation. We recognise that between 1916 and 1927 endeavours were made to reach agreement between the Political Department and Representatives of the Princes upon certain formulæ in relation to so-called "political practices." But those pourparlers never had the remotest resemblance to a fundamental inquiry of the kind of which we speak, and they never resulted in the actual conclusion of any agreement.

And there are two reasons for instituting such a fundamental inquiry. If the payments from one side to the other are either greater or less than they ought to be, adjustment is needed imperatively in order to preserve good relations as well as to effect justice. But secondly, if any new constitutional machinery is to be set up by which the economic unity of India may be made a reality and the States be asked of their own free will to come into such an arrangement, federal or other, it is absolutely vital to know exactly what the economic foundations are upon which to build. The object of this note is to make some contribution towards the preparation of the site.

XXII.

The Indian States form an almost continuous chain of landlocked territories down the spine of India, surrounded by the narrow strips of sea-coast which were occupied by the English in the course of their acquisition of power. These narrow strips have been somewhat enlarged in the course of time, but British India retains, for the most part, the richer and more accessible sea-coast, and the fertile valleys of the Ganges and Jumna, and of the Indus and its tributaries. The hinterland was left unappropriated, because it was less accessible to forces dependent in no small measure for their security upon sea-power, and less profitable to those who thought largely in terms of exports by sea. The formation of the Central Provinces by the lapse of the Bhosla kingdom in 1852 broke the geographical continuity of the States from Kashmir to Cape Comorin, but the geographical basis of their present existence remains. The Indian States are, in general, the inaccessible and less fertile parts of the Indian Peninsula whose conquest was less justifiable in terms of profits for a trading company, or whose existence was tolerated from reasons of policy.

Despite the building of railways, the States, for the most part, have continued inaccessible, and their general remoteness, combined with their smaller natural fertility, has precluded the growth and advance seen in the last three generations in British India. Whereas the territory of the States is 711,000 square miles, as compared with 1,094,000 square miles of British India, the population of the Indian States is, roughly, 72,000,000, compared with 247,000,000 in British India, that is, the area of the States is 38·8 per cent. of the whole and the population 22·5 per cent.

These two factors, the comparative isolation and the relative sparseness of population, apart from all other considerations, have made the States slower than British India to be affected by the changed economic conditions which have resulted from British occupation. The continuity of their political forms has helped also the survival of their earlier economic organisations, and, viewed from the standpoint of Western industrialism, the States are more backward than British India.

In a vast country possessing few natural waterways, where the temperature is unfavourable to great exertion, where wants are of the simplest, where war made elaborate interdependence risky, it was natural that the unit of economic self-sufficiency should be the smallest, the village. The village grew its crops, spun and wove its cotton, made and mended its simple ploughs and looms, and built by its own labour the mud-walled and thatched cottages which gave such shelter as was needed in a climate where the sky is the natural roof. The village artisans were the servants of the village, paid a recognised yearly tribute of grain per plough and doing in return whatever work was called for.

Such an organisation had very much to recommend it. The workers were dealing and thinking in terms of real goods, they shared alike in the good and the bad fortunes of agriculture. The market was at their own door, or in their own bellies. To misjudge it was impossible. There might be gluts and famines, but starvation in the midst of plenty was at least unknown. But its full virtues can only be recognised if it be remembered that budgets of the Indian worker's consumption have, in exceptional circumstances, shown a proportion even so high as 95 per cent. spent on food. Even to-day 73 per cent. of the Indian population is agricultural, and only some 20 per cent. of its products are exported.[1] The argument for division of labour and specialisation as a ground for a new organisation of Indian society is therefore meaningless. India is already so organised that 73 per cent. of her population are specialists wholly, or almost wholly, occupied in agriculture, and a further 17 per cent. are resident in villages, and dependent for their living upon the village agriculture economy. The urge to the break-up of the old village organisation was therefore in itself small. Manufactured products in any form covered less than 4 per cent. in a typical budget of a poor family, and only some 10–15 per cent. of a middle-class family. The urge was, in fact, at first as much sentimental and political in origin as economic. In 1913 imports of Manchester cottons represented less than Rs. 2 per head of population, and in 1926 the total imports into India represented only Rs. 7–6–0 per head of population.

If, therefore, at first the States were slower to adopt

[1] Wadia Joshi (*The Wealth of India*, p. 105) estimates the value of agricultural produce (crops and yield of live-stock) for British India in 1913–14 at Rs. 1,000 crores. Taking the value for all India (including the States) at Rs. 1,250 crores, and the total exports at Rs. 249 crores, the proportion would be about 20 per cent.

new forms and to make industrialisation their aim, they were in their own generation wise. The gains, even if they could have been calculated, were too small, and the risks too great to justify the break-up of the traditional village organisation, even had available means of transport made it possible. But such railways as were built were mainly constructed from the ports to the fertile areas of British India, skirting or cutting briefly through the States. They were built partly, no doubt, with an eye to military necessities, but even more with an eye to the development of an export and import trade. They were admirably devised to bring Manchester cottons to the areas which produced exportable goods. They were less well designed to develop an internal trade between one part of India and another. This has in some measure been remedied in recent years, but a generation back the break-up of the village implied not the risks of specialisation inside an Indian economic unity, but the additional dangers of an international trade.

To one accustomed to think in terms of European conditions and standards, hesitancy to embark on such a trade would appear foolish. But it must be remembered that the Indian villager is in even worse position to carry risks and dangers than a European farmer. In an average year he secures barely enough to fill the mouths of his household. In a bad year they go short. So long as he is growing crops to feed himself and to pay his rent, he feels as safe as he can be in his circumstances. To grow crops for an unknown and uncertain market brings an additional risk which he was at first without more knowledge unwilling to accept. He is not slow to adopt a proved success, but he cannot afford to experiment.

Such considerations may in some measure explain the economic backwardness of the States. Their rulers were not necessarily conservative, though many of them were; they were not even necessarily apathetic. They simply did not happen to be Europeans, convinced without argument or experiment that whatever was best for Europe was best for India. Their attitude to the situation was that of *lassez-faire*. They neither particularly encouraged industrial developments nor expressly discouraged them.

Gradually the experiment in British India has worked itself out. The old village economy has, to a great extent, come to be superseded by a more elaborate money economy. Rent and land revenue are now almost everywhere paid in money. The competition of machine-made goods has made itself felt in the furthest village, prices of country cloth are affected, and the old village industries depressed. In British India the competition was in the early days that of Europe, and particularly of Lancashire. In the States not only the competition of Europe, but also of the slowly advancing British Indian enterprises, has contributed to undermine the older system. Bombay and the up-country mills have competed with the village weaver for custom as severely as Lancashire, or, in more recent years, Japan.

Whether or not the transition from a village to a world economy could have been eased by a sympathetic use of the customs duties it is not to the purpose to discuss. It is enough that during the vital period India happened to be ruled by a school of thought to which such an idea was inconceivable.

Experience has now shown that industrially produced goods can undersell the laborious products of the village artisan. It has not shown, as has sometimes been claimed, that therefore India should concentrate all her efforts upon agriculture, and import all industrial products from abroad. On the other hand, it has not shown yet, what many politicians have claimed, that India is perfectly adapted for an industrial future. All that is really clear is that the village industry cannot, in its original form, compete on a money basis with machine-made goods. The situation is in many ways analogous to that of England at the beginning of the Industrial Revolution, and India has many stages of European economic history yet to pass through. But whereas in British India much of the initial dislocation is gradually beginning to adjust itself, in many of the States the problem has only of late begun to arise, and the consequent changes are even now in progress.

What are the political and economic consequences of this Industrial Revolution, which, beginning in British India, has now entered the Indian States? The chief political consequence is a growing interdependence. The States vary much in size. Hyderabad has a population of over twelve millions, Mysore of nearly six millions, Kashmir of three. Complete economic self-sufficiency is impossible even for these States; but the majority are much smaller. Nor, as has been already pointed out, is the consumption per head of industrial products large. The individual States must therefore exchange goods much more freely than has been done in the past, both with each other and with British India. Such economic interdependence must lead on to closer political working, since matters which were of little account, so long as internal trade was undeveloped, have now become of considerable moment. Until lately it has been possible for decisions on such matters as banking and currency, railway and postal policy, customs rates and internal duties, to be fixed without consulting the interests of the Indian States, and without inflicting immediately noticeable damage on them. This is now no longer the case. In all matters affecting commercial policy, it is now as essential to consider and to hear the interests of the 72 million inhabitants of the States as of the 247 million of British India.

The economic consequence is the imperative need for the means to finance the industrial reorganisation of the States. The problems of economic reconstruction are in broad outlines the same as in British India. Increased education, better sanitation and medical aid, the improvement of agriculture, the resuscitation and reorganisation of handicrafts—assisted when necessary by modern mechanical improvements—these all involve increased governmental revenue and expenditure.

Moreover, a hundred years in which peace has been interrupted by only one or two brief and localised wars has led to an unprecedented increase in population, and this itself, in a country of hereditary employments and static organisation, imposes unusual demands for material equipment if, even without raising it, the standard of living is to be merely maintained.

The States are not so wealthy as British India. They have no considerable rich middle class, and their banking system is in general less developed. It is absolutely essential to the building up of a sound new industrial system that every anna which is available should be left in the States to assist in their reconstruction, and that the load of taxation, not only for internal purposes, where it may in many cases be devoted to uses which will be helpful to future development, but more especially for external purposes, should be reduced to a minimum.

It is this urgent need for capital which has led the Princes to review the payments made by them to central revenues and to examine the justice of the claims on which those payments are demanded.

As economic interdependence grows, the States must join more and more with British India not only in the upheaval of a rapid change in economic organisation, but also in the benefit of modern developments which in time will bring about readjustment. In those developments, such as railways, which are of necessity common to the two, they must unquestionably pay their fair share of expenses, but, in such cases as those of the railways and the Post Office, by the fact of this payment they become unwittingly involved in the fiscal system of British India, of which these concerns are profit-making enterprises.

In the case also of sea customs, a growing trade will involve a greater expenditure by the States' nationals on imported goods liable to duty and on the protected products of Bombay and Calcutta. Until the comparatively recent past import duties were light and hardly affected the States. The effects of the war and of recent constitutional changes have been to raise import duties. And the Central Government will apparently rely on them more and more as years go on for their income.

These impositions may be just, but without any review of the liabilities of the States for contributions to central revenues, or any examination of the amount of the sea customs duties which fall upon the States, it is impossible to declare whether they are equitable or not, and it is difficult to believe that at all the different levels at which the customs tariff has stood in recent years, with all the different amounts that the railways have contributed to and required from central revenues, a benign Providence has arranged that the States should be paying, in every case, no more and no less than perfect justice would require.

The Princes are asking that their obligations to contribute to central revenues may be examined both in the light of their treaties and of the services rendered to them by Government. They ask also that an expert estimate may be made of actual contributions which are in fact drawn from the States, and that obligations and payments may be brought into accord with each other.

XXIII.

LIABILITY IN REGARD TO DEFENCE.

The services which the Central Government provide for the States may be considered conveniently in three main groups : First, Security ; secondly, Communications ; thirdly, Miscellaneous Services.

Of the three groups, the first, the provision of security, is both the most important and the most expensive. The whole economic development of India in the nineteenth and twentieth centuries has depended upon it. The word Security is here used to cover not only the cost of the armies in India, but also of those services which in other ways contribute to security : the Viceroy, the Political Department and other Departments of Government which are concerned with the foreign relations of India as a whole, or with the external relations and internal security of the States, the Police Services, so far as they give assistance to the States, and the Secretary of State.

First of all let us consider the army. This is by far the largest expense falling upon the central revenue. On the Budget of 1926–7, out of a total expenditure of Rs. 108 crores (excluding Railways), the army alone represents a cost of Rs. 56 crores. Is any part of this properly chargeable to the States ? This question cannot be answered off hand.

The functions of the army maintained by the British in India would appear to fall into four main categories. First, it defends India from external aggression, and in cases where the Empire is threatened in a way that might react upon the welfare of India as a whole (that is to say, in practice in any considerable emergency), it is used to furnish an expeditionary force outside India.

Secondly, it is the means by which the Crown as Paramount Power performs its contractual obligation to the States to preserve their external and internal security. Thirdly, it maintains the internal peace of India as a whole, that is to say, it suppresses rebellions and risings and prevents the innumerable internal wars and organised raiding expeditions to which India was accustomed in the period preceding the establishment of the British power. Finally, in British India it supplies the necessary military power behind the police upon which all Government rests, and maintains order in ordinary cases of civil commotion.

The question of the obligation of the States to contribute is obviously subject, in each of the above four cases, to different considerations. In the first case—defence from external attack—the States undoubtedly have an interest at stake. But it does not follow that an obligation attaches to them to contribute. They are, speaking generally, debarred by the Paramountcy Agreement (whether the term is expressed in a treaty or not) from any relations with outside Powers; they are without voice in the foreign policy by which external wars may be caused or averted; they cannot control the military expenditure of the Governments of Great Britain or British India. On what legal or constitutional ground then can they justly be charged with the costs of war which they have done nothing to bring about, or of an establishment which they are unable to criticise?

If there be such an obligation, plainly it must be found either in the Paramountcy Agreement into which every State alike has entered, or in the special terms of some particular agreement made with the Crown by an individual State. With the latter type of liability we are not in this Section concerned. But we venture to treat as self-evident the answer to the question whether any such general obligation is created by the Paramountcy Agreement. The States were independent of the Crown until by the agreement conferring Paramountcy they became dependent on it. As independent States they could be under no such obligation. If it exists to-day it must be because they have agreed to assume it, *i.e.* it must be a consequence of the only general agreement that there is between them and the Crown, viz. the agreement of Paramountcy.

If it be urged that they have an undefined obligation to help defend the British Empire, the answer is that this is to suggest not a different, but the same source of obligation. Having joined the Empire by agreement, the part which the States play in the Empire is determined by the agreement. It remains wholly voluntary except in so far as by the agreement they have assumed obligations; and that agreement is the very agreement of Paramountcy itself. They have made no other general agreement with the Crown. The British Empire argument is therefore merely the Paramountcy position in another garb.

That the Princes do voluntarily contribute to defence and do it with both hands is *nihil ad rem*. Their loyalty to the King is the pride of the Empire and the glory of the Indian States. But free gifts import no obligation, however often repeated.

What, then, does the agreement of Paramountcy provide?

Its terms are, generally speaking, that the State abandons its wholly independent status, commits to the Crown the conduct of its foreign relations, gives up the sovereign right of making war, and undertakes to restrict its military organisation to such troops and equipment as may be needed for internal purposes. In return the Crown undertakes the conduct of the State's foreign affairs [1] and the whole obligation of defence, guaranteeing the security of the State, both external and internal. The agreement thus consists, like most contracts, of mutual promises, the promise of one party being the consideration for the promise of the other.

[1] *Sc.* Without getting any right to bind the States (without their specific consent) to any obligations affecting the sovereignty which they still retain.

The terms of this contract clearly impose no express obligation upon the States to pay contributions towards the cost of the Crown's military forces; and there is no justification for reading into the contract an implied one. Indeed the fact that with many States the Crown has made special treaties and agreements containing express terms dealing with the amount of subsidy or tribute to be paid or the number of troops to be provided, makes it impossible to maintain that any such general obligation can be implied.

If it be contended on some vague theory that there is a political or moral obligation to contribute, the answer obviously is that the Crown and the States by their legal or constitutional agreement about Paramountcy and by their subsidiary agreements have created such definite obligations as they thought proper and have thereby excluded the notion of any undefined further obligation. For the plain truth must not be forgotten that there can be no obligation to contribute unless it has been undertaken by contract—either in the Paramountcy Agreement or by some particular agreement.

Indeed, the second of the functions of the army mentioned above (to enable the Crown to discharge its obligation to protect the States) shows that the Crown, in consideration of the cession of certain sovereign powers which the States have made under the Paramountcy Agreement, has by the same agreement taken upon itself the obligation to maintain the army; and this undertaking must, in the absence of any express stipulation for contribution by the States, mean at the Crown's own cost.

In respect of the third function of the army, the preservation of the internal peace of India, the Crown can have no more claim upon the States for contribution than out of the first two. What contribution it wanted for maintaining the internal peace of India it presumably asked for and got—or failed to get—when it made the various specific treaties and agreements which fill the pages of Aitchison. There is here again no room to imply any undertaking by the States. Indeed, in this matter of internal peace, primarily the armed forces of the Crown in India are only concerned with the territory of British India. The Crown has no duty to send its army into a State unless the security of that State is imperilled; the army then intervenes, not in discharge of any duty to keep the peace of India, but in order to enable the Crown to carry out its specific duty under the contract of Paramountcy, by which it has undertaken to protect the internal as well as the external security of each State. But in that event for the reasons already given (*prima facie* and apart from special contract) no obligation to pay attaches to the State—although a liability might accrue if the State had rendered the intervention necessary by its own conduct in breach of its contractual obligations to the Crown. But such an exceptional liability depending upon particular facts on a special occasion is irrelevant to the present discussion and need not further be considered in this context.

So, too, the fact that the Crown may have been guilty of a breach of its contractual obligations in failing to intervene when called upon by the ruler of a State having an express contractual right to special assistance in certain events is irrelevant. The point is worth mentioning here, but solely to show that it has no real bearing on the subject of this Section. There are certain treaties with States by which the Crown is pledged in very specific language to intervene—either to protect the persons of their rulers or to suppress rebellion or otherwise to maintain the internal tranquillity of the State. In certain cases complaints have been made that when the ruler has appealed for protection it has either been denied to him or only provided at his own expense.[1]

But these cases of specific engagements and breaches

[1] For instance, the treaty of 1818 with Indore bound the British Government, in return for certain cessions of tribute and territory, " to support a field force to maintain the internal tranquillity of the territories of Malhar Rao Holkar, and to defend them from foreign enemies "; but in 1836, when a pretender to the throne attacked the ruling Maharaja,

of them by either the States or the British Government do not affect the present discussion any more than would a breach of the general Paramountcy duty of the Crown, if established.

No doubt the States have an interest in the internal peace of British India, just as British India has an interest in the internal peace of the States. But there is no reason for one party to subsidise the other for the maintenance of order. Indeed the recent history of the Provinces seems to indicate that the present military cost of preserving internal peace in India is less than it would have been if there had been no States, and the whole country had been under British administration. The change which followed immediately upon the Mutiny from a policy of annexation on every pretext to the policy of preserving the States in existence whenever possible, was no doubt in part due to this very consideration in the minds of the statesmen of that time.[1] If the existence of the States in fact relieved the British Government of part of the cost of maintaining order, by reducing the area of territory over which the maintenance of order is their concern, then, although the Princes cannot rightly claim a contribution from British India to their own revenues on that account, yet they can at least make plain to all that the claim of British India to put upon the States any part of the cost of the troops whose function is to maintain order is wholly inadmissible.

It is, perhaps, also relevant to consider the case of the relations between two States becoming so embittered that but for the restraining hand of the Government they

---

the assistance of the British forces was refused. Scindia, whose treaties include similar engagements, was denied help in reducing rebellious subjects both in 1824 and 1830.

[1] *E.g.* "After the Mutiny and Rebellion of 1857–58, Lord Canning . . . had seen, in his own words, 'a few patches of Native Government prove breakwaters to the storm which would otherwise have swept over us in one great wave,' and he dreaded to think what would be the consequences if the Native Chiefs were not heartily on our side in case India should be threatened by an external enemy."—Major Evans Bell, *Last Counsels of an Unknown Counsellor, John Dickinson.* London, 1883.

would go to war. But in the first place this is not a real danger. The States as a whole know that they are the gainers from the peace of India. For some generations they have been learning the habits of peace, and whatever may be the regrets of races and dynasties with a tradition of conquest behind them, it cannot be argued that any additional British force is necessary to-day in order to restrain their aggressive ambitions beyond that which the Government of India would be compelled to maintain in any case for foreign defence and the general maintenance of order. But, secondly, this particular case, the prevention of inter-State disorder, belongs not to the third but to the second category of military functions in our classification. Were State A to attack State B, the Crown's undertaking to defend the security of B would come into immediate operation, and the Crown would have to employ its armed forces at its own cost in order to perform its pre-existing contract, viz. its agreement of Paramountcy; and no obligation to pay money would attach to B. A would no doubt have broken its contract and would incur a liability to the Crown for the expense to which the Crown was thereby put, but that liability does not touch the general question under discussion.

In the fourth function, that of police duties in British India, the States have obviously no concern. They perform similar duties for themselves, partly with their police forces, partly with their armies; but they claim no contribution from the Central Government for the cost. When, as in cases of dacoity, the interests of both a State and the Central Government are involved, the States have always shown themselves willing to co-operate with Government.

XXIV.

THE CONTRACTUAL ASPECT.

In Section XXIII we have endeavoured to show that from the actual relationship established between the Crown and the States by the agreement of Paramountcy there arises no obligation upon the States to contribute financially to the general expenditure upon the armed forces of the Crown in India.

In the present Section we reconsider the position in the light of the various express treaties and engagements other than the agreement of Paramountcy itself. But we have asked the Indian States Committee to bear in mind what is said by Counsel in their Opinion of the 24th July, 1925, and particularly upon Paramountcy in paragraph 6 of the Opinion. The different States came into their present relations with the Crown, or with its predecessor, the Company, in many different ways at many different times. The treaties which bind the States and the Crown reflect the conditions of the times when they were made. The earliest treaties, such as those with the Nizam concluded in 1766, 1768 and 1790, were those of an equal or inferior Power made with an equal or greater Power. Moreover, they were, as in the case of treaties made in the nineteenth century between European Powers, agreements between parties who regarded their natural state rather as one of enmity than of federal co-operation in a common unity. Gradually the attitude of the Company changed. It ceased to be merely the leading Power among a number of independent Powers, and began to assert its superiority to the States. It required its allies to surrender their right to negotiate with foreign Powers and with States in alliance with itself. Their right to maintain armies was recognised, but at the same time subsidiary forces, maintained at their expense, were put under the control of the Company. In the internal affairs of the States it disavowed all concern, and its external policy was dictated by military considerations and the fear of French intrigue. But as the French danger disappeared and the ascendancy of British power in India was secured, the tone of the treaties altered, and gradually the States, even when their independence was admitted, came to be considered and treated as units in an Indian Empire over the whole of which some measure of ultimate authority and responsibility rested with the British Crown. But the recognition that the change of relationship thus unconsciously, or at least unobtrusively, effected was radical in character, followed in only comparatively recent times; and indeed the change appears not to have been the subject of legal analysis until the year 1928.[1]

The makers of the old treaties were concerned to secure the interests of the parts of India subject to their rule at the least possible cost to themselves. To regard the States as a responsibility of the Crown possessing any community or equality of interest with British India itself was a new idea, only gradually emerging. The earlier treaties were aimed rather at securing an immediate *modus vivendi* between two more or less equal Powers, Powers which could, and very likely would, rescind and recast their agreement in a few years' time, than as establishing a permanent set of constitutional relationships in that curious conglomeration that has come to be the Indian Empire. Nevertheless, chance has preserved them as binding agreements. But the *fact* that the earlier treaties were made with reservations in the minds of the makers does not render them less valid. Lee-Warner writes (Chapter 8):

> "In the next period of intercourse the Company had nothing to fear from a French invasion; and since it was engaged in the work of political settlement and general disarmament, its desire was to reduce the forces of the States rather than to undertake the task of organising a general scheme of defence. The violence of Sindhia's idle troops at Maharajpur in 1843, the inability of Ranjit Singh's successors to prevent the Sikh Khalsa from invading British India, and finally the collapse of the system of contingents, led to the conclusion that the problem of military co-operation had better be left alone until India had quieted down. Under these circumstances, the Paramount Power has hitherto been content with its indefinitive claim upon the resources of the States in case of emergency, rather than assess the precise share which each of them must contribute, whether in arms or money, for the defence of the Empire."

---

[1] The main results of the examination are contained in the legal opinion obtained by the Princes in July 1928.

In other words, Lee-Warner declares that the policy of Government was to disarm the States by a system of treaties guaranteeing them defence free of cost, and then to make the States, at a later date, provide for their own defence in a way that was convenient and safe for Government, despite the existence of the treaties. But "hitherto" the Government have been satisfied with finding a way round the treaties. In fact, disregarding the existence of the treaties, the Government have thrown a gradually increasing load of payment for defence on to the States, until to-day, despite the often reiterated promises of successive Sovereigns that their treaty rights shall be respected, the Princes feel, in consequence of the taxation to which their people are subjected, that States are dealt with in matters of defence almost as if no treaties existed at all.

The States contribute, as we shall presently show, a considerable sum to central revenues by various indirect means, and it is loosely assumed by some apologists for the Government of British India that the States' total contribution merely covers their obligations for defence. We have seen in XXIII that the agreement of Paramountcy does not entitle the Crown to demand payment for the defence of the States which it thereby undertook. But do the terms of the actual treaties authorise such a view? No attempt has ever been made either to repudiate or to revise the treaties. Kings and Viceroys affirm their sacred character. They stand as the bulwark of the States' freedom, and the Government of India, as the agent of the Crown, are necessarily bound by them. We proceed, therefore, to an examination of their provisions.

A large number of States hold treaties in which the Crown has promisec them protection against external aggression in the clearest terms. Other States have, strictly speaking, no treaties, but their relationship with the Crown is determined by Sanads and other consensual engagements. The essence of that relationship is the guarantee of defence by the Paramount Power. The

Government have assured them in various official pronouncements [1] that their territories should be preserved from invasion, and it is assumed that the duty of defending them rests upon Government. The States with which treaties were made are, with one or two exceptions, explicitly guaranteed protection. For instance, the treaty of 1818 with Udaipur (Article 2) [2] contains these words: "The British Government engages to protect the principality and territory of Udaipur," and again by Article 1 of the Treaty of 1888 with Dewas,[3] "The British Government . . . will grant its protection," and by Article 3, "The British Government will further protect the Rajahs of Dewas against the attacks of enemies, and will aid them in the settlement of any of their rebellious subjects, and will mediate in a just and amicable manner in any dispute that may arise between them and other States and petty Chiefs." In the treaty concluded in 1853 with the Nizam,[4] reaffirming all the treaties with his State, it is specifically mentioned that by the agreement then reached the Nizam was relieved of any further obligation in respect of defence. Similarly, in the case of Indore, in reward for services rendered during the Mutiny the Maharaja was permitted to capitalise his contributions towards the Malwa contingent and the Malwa Bhil Corps; accordingly, the State deposited Rs. 23,81,520 with the Government of India, the interest thereon at 5 per cent. being assigned as the payment for the future, "thereby relieving His Highness from all demands on account of the said contingent and Bhil Corps, as well as from all pecuniary demands present and future from service with troops." [5] These are typical instances of the guarantees contained in the treaties with the States.[6]

[1] See, *e.g.*, Aitchison, *Treaties*, Vol. V. p. 112, Pannah: "Whereas your possessions are in the Province of Bundehlcund, it is improbable that any foreign force shall attack them, but should this unexpected event happen, your possessions will be protected by the British Government."

[2] *Id.*, *ib.*, Vol. II.

[3] *Id.*, *ib.*, Vol. IV.

[4] *Id.*, *ib.*, Vol. IX.

[5] *Id.*, *ib.*, p. 1889.

[6] See Appendix B.

Certain of the States engaged in return to supply troops in time of war,[1] at the requisition of the British Government; but upon their financial resources or upon their armies in time of peace the Government have no claim. Lee-Warner has sought to argue from the existence of this clause in certain treaties, that the Government have in time of war a claim on *all* the efforts and *all* the resources of such States without limit, and he would extend this claim to *all* States on the ground that the natural duty of a Sovereign to put forth the full efforts of his State to defend his subjects "cannot be weakened by the fact that he has entered into combination with other States for the common defence." Now clearly the existence of the treaties no more weakens this duty of the Princes to their subjects than the existence of a police force abolishes the occasional need for a law-abiding citizen to defend himself with his own fists. But the chief duty of the defence of the said citizen remains the function of the police force and not of himself. The fact that, should the Government fail to fulfil their obligations, the State would be obliged to provide for itself does not abate one jot or tittle of the obligations of Government. For if, as Lee-Warner asserts, in time of war the onus of their defence is automatically transferred to the States, then Government's obligation to defend the States becomes simply an obligation to defend them when no defence is required, which is manifestly absurd.

Moreover, such treaties as do call for the State's assistance in time of war expressly limit that assistance to available and existing military resources, and declare that the Prince is obliged in the event of war to furnish assistance to the British forces "according to his means." [2] Thus it cannot seriously be argued that the duty to assist Government in time of war implies not only putting forces at their disposal, but also subjecting themselves

[1] See Appendix A, Part 5.

[2] *E.g.* Treaty with Bikaner, 1818, Article 8. Aitchison, Vol. II. Oudaipur, 1818, Article 8. Aitchison, Vol. II. See Appendix B, Part 5.

equally with British India to taxation imposed for the purpose of providing the defence which had been guaranteed to them by Government.

XXV.

DEFENCE AND ARMED FORCES. I.

In taking their stand upon their treaty rights the States are not merely attempting to hold the Crown to the letter of a bad bargain. Apart from various actual payments in land or money, every State, as has already been affirmed, has made one concession of the greatest importance. It has committed the whole of its external relationships to the Paramount Power. In the treaties concluded with the Rajputana States it is expressly mentioned that the guarantee of defence is given in return for this concession, in the other treaties it is implied. But it is not merely a matter of treaty bargains, but of elementary justice. By this means the British power was able to establish itself in India without constant war and turmoil, and now that it has gained the full advantage of general peace and security, it will not repudiate the guarantee which made pacification possible.

But beside this general concession which every State has made in return for the guarantee of defence, the greater number have also made definite payments. Some pay annual tributes in money, some ceded territories whose revenues were estimated to be adequate to support a given number of troops, some pay a subsidy for the same object. It is not known accurately what is the present yield of the territories ceded, but it is known that the revenue has very greatly increased, has increased indeed faster than the cost of maintaining troops. It was found, for instance, that in 1902, Berar, which had been assigned to Government in 1853, in order to discharge a payment of Rs. 32 lakhs, was yielding a revenue of Rs. 119 lakhs (an increase of 270 per

CONTRIBUTIONS.

No.	Name.	Infantry.	Cavalry.	Artillery.	Lascars.	Remarks.
1	Udaipur .	660	—	—	—	Refer to Aitchison's Treaties, Vol. III. Udaipur's contribution is Rs. 16,000 for the Merwara Battalion and Rs. 50,000 for the Mewar Bhil Corps. This total sum of Rs. 66,000 is realised from Udaipur's share of Mewar-Merwara. At Rs. 1,00,000 per battalion of 1,000 men this works out to 660 men. The pay of one sepoy was Rs. 6 per mensem, or 77s. per year. For 1,000 men the cost would be 72,000 rupees. Making allowance for the higher salary of officers, the estimated cost of one battalion is Rs. one lakh per annum. *See* Art. 2 of the treaty of 1812 with Rewa.
2	Jodhpur .	—	1,500	—	—	By the 8th Article of the treaty of 1818 Jodhpur State was bound to furnish a contingent of 1,500 horse. In 1835 this obligation was commuted to an annual payment of Rs. 1,15,000 towards the Jodhpur Legion which was then raised.
3	Kotah . .	2,000	—	—	—	In 1838, on the creation of a new State, Jhalawar, Kotah was also compelled to contribute Rs. 2 lakhs a year for the maintenance of the Deoli Regiment. Rs. 2 lakhs being taken as equivalent to 2,000 men as in the case of Udaipur.
4	Gwalior .	5,000	—	24 guns.	—	Refer to Aitchison's Treaties, Vol. IV. Treaty of Sarje Anjangam 1803 and of Burhanpore 1804. Territories ceded by Scindia, and the East India Company agreed to maintain these troops, out of the revenue of the territories ceded.

CONTRIBUTIONS—*continued*.

No.	Name.	Infantry.	Cavalry.	Artillery.	Lascars.	Remarks.
						By the treaty of 1817, Scindia was required to supply 5,000 horses for the Pindari war, and to pay for it by the assignment of tributes from the Rajput States (aggregating 3½ lakhs) and of certain payments (aggregating 7 lakhs annually) made to him and his family by the British Government. This force was maintained on a reduced scale of 2,000 horses up to 1844, when it was merged in the increased contingent force which was imposed upon Scindia, and for which additional assignments of large districts belonging to the State were required.
—	—	7,000	1,000	4 batts. 24 guns.	—	Increased contingent to be maintained by Scindia by the treaty of 1844. What this treaty meant to the British Government may be gathered from the despatch of the Governor-General to the Secret Committee dated the 21st January, 1844: "The sum appropriated to the future maintenance of the contingent will be sufficient, I hope, to provide seven battalions of infantry, two regiments of cavalry and four batteries of artillery, commanded by our officers, for the preservation of order within the Gwalior State." [1]
5	Indore . .	—	3,000	—	—	By Art. 11 of the treaty of 1818, Holkar agreed to retain in his service, ready to co-operate with the

[1] By the treaty of 1860 Government engaged to maintain a force costing "not less than Rs. 16 lakhs." It is therefore possible that the contingent was reduced at that date, and that the figures which we have given are too high by perhaps 1,000 men.

CONTRIBUTIONS—*continued.*

No.	Name.	In-fantry.	Cavalry.	Artillery.	Lascars.	Remarks.
						British troops, a body of not less than 3,000 horse. In lieu of his obligation under Art. 11, Holkar paid Rs. 1,11,214 as an annual subvention, and in reward for services rendered during the Mutiny the Maharajah was permitted to capitalise his contribution, and accordingly the State deposited Rs. 23,81,520 with the Government of India, the interest thereon at 5 per cent. being assigned as the payment for the future, "thereby relieving His Highness from all demands on account of the said contingent and Bhil Corps, as well as from all pecuniary demands, present or future, and from service with troops."
6	Dewas . .	200	75	—	—	In 1827 the contingent to be provided by the Dewas States under the treaty of 1818 was fixed at 75 horse and 200 foot. This obligation was afterwards commuted to an annual contribution of Rs. 28,474-9-2.
7	Bhopal . .	400	600	—	—	Art. 6 of the treaty of 1818 reads: "The State of Bhopal shall furnish a contingent of 600 horse and 400 infantry for the service of the British Government." Bhopal paid a contribution for the maintenance of this contingent, and since 1849 its amount has been fixed at Rs. 1,61,000.
9	Dhar . .	—	—	—	—	These States, besides Gwalior and Indore, contribute for the maintenance of the Malwa Bhil Corps.
10	Jhabua . .	—	—	—	—	
11	Alirajpur .	—	—	—	—	
12	Barwani .	—	—	—	—	

CONTRIBUTIONS—*continued.*

No.	Name.	Infantry.	Cavalry.	Artillery.	Lascars.	Remarks.
13	Cutch . .	1,800	—	—	—	By Art. 6 of the treaty of 1819, Cutch agreed to pay for a subsidiary force, and in 1832 the demand on account of the subsidiary force was limited to two lakhs of Sikka rupees, to be reduced in proportion to reductions made in the subsidiary force provided that the sum to be paid should not be less than 88,000 Sikka rupees. At present the State pays a contribution of Rs. 1,86,949 to the British Government. Assuming, as in the case of Udaipur, the cost of one battalion of infantry 1,000 strong to be Rs. 1,00,000 this figure works out at 1,800 men.
14	Akalkot . .	—	100	—	—	In 1868 the contingent of 100 horsemen, which the Chief was bound to maintain under the treaty of 1820, was disbanded, and a money payment of Rs. 1,45,921 a year was established.
15	Jath . . .	—	50	—	—	The Jagirdar pays to the British Government Rs. 6,500 a year in lieu of a service of 50 horsemen besides a tribute of Rs. 4,847.
16	Phaltan . .	—	75	—	—	The Chief pays Rs. 9,600 a year to the British Government in lieu of a service of 75 horses.
	SOUTHERN MARATHA JAGIRDARS.					
17	Sangli . .	—	450	—	—	Service of 450 horse was commuted by ceding land yielding Rs. 1,35,000 a year at the rate of Rs. 300 per horse. *See* Aitchison, Vol. VII. p. 225, and Engagement Nos. XCVI.
18	Miraj-Senior Branch.	—	50	—	—	Aitchison, Vol. VII. p. 282.

CONTRIBUTIONS—*continued.*

No.	Name.	Infantry	Cavalry.	Artillery.	Lascars.	Remarks.
19	Miraj-Junior	—	24	—	—	Aitchison, Vol. VII. Letter on p. 283.
20	Jamkhandi .	—	78	—	—	Letter on p. 282. Aitchison, Vol. VII.
21	Karundwar Senior and Junior.	—	36	—	—	No. XCIX, p. 281. Aitchison, Vol. VII.
22	Mudhol .	—	10	—	—	Letter, p. 283. Aitchison, Vol. VII.
23	Baroda . .	3,000	—	1 Coy. 4 guns.	2 Coys.	Treaty of 1805.
		1,000	1,000	—	—	Treaty of 1817.
24	Nabha . .	133	100	—	—	A portion of the territory of Nabha was confiscated owing to its refusal to help the British army during the first Sikh war, and the share of this (valued at Rs. 28,766), which the British took, was regarded as payment for a contingent; Nabha State being exempted from furnishing one.
25	Hyderabad .	6,000	500	24 guns.	—	Treaty of 1798.
		2,000	500	8 guns.	—	Treaty of 1800. See pp. 68 and 69. Aitchison, Vol. IX.
		2,000	—	—	—	Raised in 1813.
		5,000	2,000	4 field batts., 24 guns.	—	Treaty of 1853.
26	Mysore . .	3,000	500	—	—	[1]Treaty of 1799. Mysore to pay 7 lakhs of pagodas annually for a military force. In 1807 the Maharajah was required to maintain 4,000 horse in addition to the subsidy.
		—	4,000	—	—	

[1] From the treaty of 1800 with Hyderabad, Articles 3 and 5, it is clear that the cost of 8,000 infantry and 1,000 horse with their complement of guns, European artillerymen, lascars and pioneers, was 18 lakhs of pagodas. In like proportion 7 lakhs of pagodas may be assumed to have sufficed for a force $\frac{7}{18}$th of above, or 3,000 infantry and 500 horse with their complement of guns and European artillerymen, lascars and pioneers.

CONTRIBUTIONS—*continued.*

No.	Name.	Infantry.	Cavalry.	Artillery.	Lascars.	Remarks.
27	Travancore .	3,000	—	1 Coy. 4 guns.	2 Coys.	Treaty of 1795.
		2,000	—	—	—	Added in 1804.
28	Cochin . .	1,000	—	—	—	Treaty of 1809.
	Total .	46,693	19,148	92 guns.	4 Coys.	

cent.), while the total cost of the army in India had increased during that period by less than 140 per cent.[1] It is not possible to find comparable figures for other districts or other years, and we cannot exactly estimate the present share contributed by the States towards the cost of defence as represented by their cessions of territory, their tributes and subsidies. But in any case the cessions, subsidies and tributes were designed to bring in a sufficient income, allowing in every case a handsome margin, to maintain certain stated forces. If the fixed tributes and subsidies have proved a bad bargain for Government, the territories have turned out an exceedingly profitable one. These stated forces are given in the table above. In most cases, as may be seen from the remarks column, the forces to be maintained were mentioned in the treaty. Where they are not, we have converted the fixed money sum into troops at the then prevailing cost of providing troops.

It will be seen that in total the cessions of territory and the subsidies maintain 46,693 infantry, 19,148 cavalry, and a certain number of batteries of artillery. To these must be added the troops which it was possible to maintain at the cost of the tributes, for those tributes were demanded and received by the British representatives of that time as payments made for security and immunity, and later

[1] In 1850 the total cost of the Company's army was £12 million, and in 1902 net expenditure on the army in India was £19 million, and in 1850 Rs. 12 crores, and in 1902 Rs. 28·5 crores.

actually for defence.[1] These tributes amount to about Rs. 20 lakhs;[2] not including Rs. 2 lakhs originally payable to Scindia, which were assigned to Government by the Gwalior Darbar in payment of the contingent forces, and have therefore already been counted. When Gwalior in 1844 ceded territory yielding Rs. 18 lakhs, the Governor-General informed the authorities in England that this would be sufficient to maintain seven battalions of infantry, two regiments of cavalry with the necessary complement of artillery, and the required European officers.[3] We have chosen this figure in preference to other figures contained in the above table, although by this calculation the Company clearly left itself a considerable margin of profit when fixing the subsidy, in order to make our estimate err (since it cannot be exact) on the side of moderation. If we add 7,000 infantry, and 1,000 cavalry to the totals already given in the table we find that the States have by their past cessions of land and money, and by their present tributes and subsidies, provided 53,693 infantry and 20,148 cavalry, with a certain amount of artillery, or say 74,500 troops in all.

The Government over a long period of years made bargains extremely favourable to themselves. How favourable can be seen from the fact that at the time of the Mutiny more than 40 per cent. of the Company's armies were maintained at the cost of the States, without taking into account the payments which had been received from such States as Oudh and Nagpur, which had been annexed during the preceding decade. Even when the Company made treaties guaranteeing defence without exacting a definite payment, the saving effected by removing a possible enemy, and reducing the need for troops, was in itself a sufficient advantage.

[1] Aitchison, Vol. III. p. 1. The tributes were demanded "in order to secure the British Government such pecuniary aid as might be adapted to the means of the several States, in order to indemnify the British Government for the charges incidental to the obligation of protecting them." See also Treaty with Cochin, 1791, Article 8, Aitchison, Vol. X., 1809, Article 1.

[2] See Appendix A, Part III.

[3] Despatch of Governor-General to Secret Committee, January 21st, 1844.

XXVI.

DEFENCE AND ARMED FORCES. II.

Although by reason of the agreement of Paramountcy and of the treaties the Crown is precluded from imposing upon the States any general obligation to contribute to the cost of the army, it is of some interest to discover to what such an obligation would amount if no such agreements existed, and the States, irrespective of their history, were treated as members of a federation with British India.

Firstly, it may be noted that the four functions of the army mentioned on p. 145 in Section XXIII do not interest the States in an equal degree. The first—the defence of the Empire and of India as a whole against external attack—may be said to interest each subject of a State equally with each subject of British Indi On the other hand, the fourth—the policing of British India—cannot be said to interest the States any more than the policing of the States interests British India. Nobody could say that any duty attached to either territory to contribute to the expenses of the other. The matter is purely domestic in each case.

The second of our categories—the contractual obligation of the Crown to maintain an army in order to protect the States—is irrelevant to the present number because we have assumed the hypothesis of no contractual relationship.

The name we have given to the third function—the general preservation of peace in India—is ambiguous because it relates to India as a whole, and the conclusion might conceivably be different according as it were the peace of British India or the peace of the States that was in question. The preservation of peace in British India is analogous to our fourth function—the duty of supporting the British Indian police in the maintenance of law and order; it is a difference of degree, not of kind; and if there is no duty on the States to pay for the one, there can hardly be such a duty to pay for the other. So far as the States are concerned, it is in either case the domestic affair of British India.

Preservation of peace within the States is primarily the duty of the Governments of the several States. The Central Government have no concern therein except as a corollary of the contractual relationship between the Paramount Power as such and the States, or of some special agreement. The position is the same as in the second category; the duty of the Crown when it attaches is contractual, and the duty of the States to pay cannot exist unless the contract imposes it. But these contractual aspects are, *ex hypothesi*, irrelevant. It follows, therefore, that on neither side of the preservation of peace in India (neither in British India nor in the States) is there scope for discerning any duty upon the States to make any money contribution to the central revenue.

The result, therefore, of our examination (apart from contract) of the four functions of the armed forces of the Crown in India is that there is only one of them, defence against external attack, in respect of which (if the contractual relationship be ignored) the duty would rest upon the States to carry a share of the financial burden. Let us then examine this question and see what is fair.

We must, of course, assume that the armed forces kept by the Crown in India are reasonable—in total, in type and in distribution—for the performance of their four functions.

The Government of India so far as we know have never published any statement of the number or fraction of troops needed for purposes of internal security. But in *The Army in India and its Evolution*, officially published by the Government of India in 1924, the topic is dealt with very definitely on p. 42 as follows:

"Internal security troops are a necessary feature of every military organisation. That they are specially necessary in India is a matter of common knowledge, emphasised in recent times by the Moplah rebellion of 1921, and the numerous occasions on which in the years 1920–22 troops were called out in support of the civil administration. In times of external peace the field army is available to assist in internal security duties. But in time of war the field army must be free to carry out its legitimate rôle, undisturbed by internal calls. It should not be forgotten that there are in India some 4,000 miles of strategic railway to be guarded, the working of which must be ensured on mobilisation.

" It is necessary to add that, while the total of the forces maintained for different rôles taken together is regarded as, in present circumstances, an irreducible minimum, the actual allotment of troops to each category of duty must inevitably vary from time to time."

We have to put the best quantitative interpretation we can upon the requirements laid down in the above quotation. If we take into account merely those troops which, when the fighting forces and their fixed bases and subsidiaries of all kinds are eliminated, would remain available for police duties anywhere in India, it is difficult to put the proportion of the whole at less than one-third, having regard to the size and population of India. But to be on the safe side let us put it at one-fourth.

The total strength of military forces at the disposal of the Government in British India is roughly 230,000. One-fourth of this would be 57,500 men, leaving 172,500 as the measure of the burden of foreign defence, in comparison with the other duties of the army.

To calculate the cost of these troops is exceedingly difficult. Lord Rawlinson notes in his diary in July 1921, that 28 British infantry battalions and 21 Indian battalions were then maintained for internal security, and that he proposed to reduce the proportion of British troops allotted to this purpose. We may, therefore, suppose that the number of Indian and of British battalions devoted to internal security is now equal or very nearly equal. A British unit is at least twice as expensive to maintain as an Indian unit, and there are a higher proportion of British battalions among the internal security troops than among the external defence troops. Their average cost is therefore unlikely to be less than the average for the army as a whole in spite of the fact that the external defence troops must be provided with artillery and must be maintained in a state of readiness for war, and in default of any other method of estimating the cost of the troops used for purposes other than foreign defence we will allot to them a share in the cost of the army proportionate to their numbers, that is to say, about Rs. 14 crores. The total cost of the army is Rs. 56 crores; we will, therefore, assume that the cost of the troops providing defence in which the States are interested is Rs. 42 crores. The population of the States is 72,000,000 out of 319,000,000 for all India. Dividing this cost of Rs. 42 crores equally in these proportions, we conclude that the States would, if there were no other considerations to be urged, be responsible for about Rs. 9 crores. This must be regarded as a maximum figure.

Unfortunately for our purpose the army accounts can make no distinction between the costs of the four functions which we have mentioned, since the same troops presumably must be capable at need of performing the different functions at different times or even at the same time. The attempt to isolate the cost of external defence, therefore, involves a good deal of guesswork.

This figure involves the assumption that apart from this payment the States are making no direct contribution in kind to the external defence of India.

Let us consider the matter of the direct contributions of the States to defence. The armies maintained by the States amount to some 50,000 men.[1] Of these some part are necessary to secure good order within each State and correspond to that quarter of the British forces with which we have argued that the States have no concern.

[1] The Indian State Forces have a total authorised strength of about 45,000, with an effective strength of about 35,000. But the latter figure does not represent the whole of the forces maintained by the States and available in time of need, since several States (*e.g.* Baroda and Kotah, whose armies amount to 6,000 men) have not included their armies in the Indian States Forces organisation, and others (*e.g.* Rewa, Hyderabad) have included only certain troops. In addition, many States have inferior troops not included, which would be available for home defence duties, and to set free first-class troops for service outside the State. Jodhpur, Rewa, Gwalior, Bharatpur and Bikaner have between them a total strength of 14,783 men, as compared with an authorised strength of 11,181 men in the States Forces scheme.

Moreover, their troops vary greatly in efficiency and in equipment. Some amount to little more than a superior police force, but others, if not so well officered, are as well equipped as the Indian army troops. How these troops would be employed in an emergency can in the nature of things be known only to the Higher Command. But some estimate of the number which could and would be employed outside the borders of their States can be formed from the organisations of the Imperial Service troops before they were superseded by the present organisation. They amounted in all at that time to some 21,000, and the conditions of their service can be seen from a letter of the Resident of Gwalior to the late Maharaja accepting on behalf of Government an additional regiment of cavalry. "I am further requested," he writes, "to explain that on a general mobilisation of the Indian army all Imperial Service troops will be moved to the front, and that consequently none of these regiments should in the event specified be counted upon for the maintenance of order within the borders of Your Highness's State, adequate provision for which, it is assumed, is already separately in existence and will continue to be kept in the necessary condition of efficiency."[1] If it be assumed that at the present time 25,000 out of the 50,000 are efficient enough and well enough equipped to be used on general service, and that they can, in fact, be spared from home duties (which in general the inferior troops will be adequate to perform), then the total force available for the defence of India is increased from 172,000.[2] Of this on a population basis the States would be responsible for 44,500, that is, for nearly 20,000 more troops than they do in fact contribute. The cost of these troops, if despite other considerations it were chargeable to the States, would create a liability for some Rs. 4 crores.

[1] Semi-official letter, No. 5397, July 29th, 1904, Gwalior Residency.

[2] In the Great War 26,000 troops from Indian States armies served abroad, besides a considerable number who released British troops by serving on the frontier or in other parts of India. See *India's Contribution to the Great War*, pp. 198–9.

XXVII.

THE QUESTION OF DEBT.

The cost of the army is not the only item in the Indian Budget connected with the defence. A considerable charge on the revenues of the Central Government is formed by the interest payable on the debts of the State, and a part of this is attributable to defence. In 1926–27 the total payments for interest amounted to Rs. 37,31,00,000. Of this, over Rs. 24,00,00,000 was for amounts chargeable to railways, Rs. 12,00,000 for amounts chargeable to irrigation and Rs. 6,02,00,000 for other productive works. There remained Rs. 6,87,00,000, which is the interest payable on the ordinary debt of the Central Government; to this must be added Rs. 4,97,00,000 provided for the reduction of debt, making a total charge for debt services of Rs. 11,84,00,000. It is necessary to consider how this debt arose.

In the financial year 1914–15, interest on this ordinary debt amounted to no more than Rs. 67,00,000. The table on page 171 gives its subsequent history.

It is hardly necessary, in view of the figures there given, to point out that the bulk of this debt represents the share of the costs of the war assigned to and undertaken by India. The greater part of these charges are purely war charges shouldered by the country. The remainder largely represents the consequences of failure to balance the Budget in the years immediately following the war, partly no doubt owing to actual expenditure resulting from the war, but even more as the result of inability to raise revenue to levels corresponding to the new and higher level of prices.

As regards the war debts, the States' position has never been clearly established. But the liability of the Princes for financial contributions to the costs of any war, however vast, cannot be different from their general liability for foreign defence. The Princes made their contributions unstintingly in men, horses and equipment, and in the provision, at their own cost, of their own armies wherever they were stationed in or outside India. In addition, the Princes placed all their surplus funds at the disposal of Government and subscribed freely and without expectation of return to all the manifold demands upon their generosity. But even if these claims could not be made, there remain their rights under the agreement of Paramountcy and their treaties. If defence is guaranteed to

INTEREST ON GOVERNMENT ORDINARY DEBT.

(Excluding Railway and Irrigation Debt, etc.)

	Lakhs Rs.	
1914–15	67	
1915–16	77	
1916–17	68	
1917–18	9,75	
1918–19	10,50	
1919–20	11,54	
1920–21	14,22	
1921–22	13,39	
1922–23	13,09	Including Sinking Fund.
1923–24	14,32	Including Sinking Fund.
1924–25	15,06	Including Sinking Fund.
1925–26	14,05	Including Sinking Fund.
1926–27	11,84	Including Sinking Fund.
1927–28 (Revised Estimate)	10,31	Including Sinking Fund.
1928–29 (Budget Estimate)	8,68	Including Sinking Fund.

them by the Crown, they cannot be asked to pay the cost of that defence simply because British India accumulates debt instead of meeting its obligations immediately.

The debts incurred in the subsequent years (1919–28) fall into a different category. In so far as the deficits of those years were due to currency causes, the States cannot be held responsible, since they enjoy no influence in deciding the currency policy of the financial authorities of British India. Moreover, they had felt the burden already, since each State has a budget of its own which also must be made to balance. Each State had to contend with just the same difficulties as the Central Government, although they had no hand in the currency policy, which caused them. If part of the failure to balance the Government Budget were due to a failure of the States to provide sufficient revenue to pay for those services of Government for which they are properly liable, then the States would reasonably have been held responsible for that part of the debt which was due to their failure to contribute, but we shall show in a later section that the States do, in fact, contribute considerably more than can properly be demanded of them, and although we have only quoted figures for one particular year, there is no reason to suppose that their contributions varied to a significant extent during the period in question. If then they were not responsible for the origin of the deficit they cannot well be held accountable for its consequences.

The other services which the Government perform for the States in the interests of peace, though equally valuable, are by no means so expensive as military defence.

The assistance given them by the police forces and police officers of British India, though of great utility, costs but little, and it is only provided when a British district is as much concerned as the States in the suppression of crime. When the States' police have co-operated with the police of British India, the Darbars have always borne the full cost of their share in the work. British officers are sent to the States to advise them in training their armies, but of this service also the cost is small.

There remains the Political Department. It is doubtful whether the States can be said to be under the obligation to contribute to the expenses of this department.

In so far as officers of the Political Department are agents of the Crown watching over the due performance of treaties and engagements to which the Crown is a party, their services are diplomatic in character, and the cost of their activities would seem to be chargeable to the Crown and not to the States to which they are accredited—unless there is some express agreement containing such a provision. The country to which an Ambassador is accredited does not pay the expenses of the diplomatic mission which it receives.

Many of the particular activities pursued, or work done, or negotiations carried out by the officers of the Political Department are undertaken at the instance and in the interest of the various departments of the administrations, Central and Provincial, of British India, and in no sense in the interest or on behalf of the States.

It is only certain functions of the Political Department which can be said to be exercised directly in the interests of the States. The Viceroy, with the Political Department of which he is the head and holds the portfolio in Council, has the duty of protecting the States and safeguarding their interests in any conflict of interest between the States and British India, and generally of seeing to the performance of the Crown's obligations to the States. It lies with him to discharge the Paramount Power's contractual duty to settle disputes between States and generally to see that the States, *inter se*, get their fair rights and discharge their fair obligations. This latter duty is purely contractual in character, and no financial charge can be imposed upon the States for its performance.

The Paramount Power in actual practice takes upon itself to perform functions in relation to individual States which involve varying degrees of control over their internal government, from mere advice upon the spontaneous request of a State, through the stage of unsolicited advice which the State is expected to follow, right up to the stage of complete control of the whole administration of a State. In so far as such services, whether welcome or unwelcome, are rendered, pursuant to the terms of a treaty or other contract, no obligation to pay can attach to the State unless the contract imposes it; and in any event it must be a particular obligation of one State and not a general obligation attaching to all. It therefore cannot come into any general reckoning such as is the subject of this Examination.

It follows, therefore, from the above analysis, that there is no obligation upon the States under these heads.

XXVIII.

COMMUNICATIONS.

There remain now to be considered certain other services, apart from defence, which the Government provide for the States. The first group of these can be brought together under the head of Communications, which includes the provision of railways, roads, ports and postal services. In so far as these exist for military purposes or have strategic uses they are subject to the considerations which apply to defence, but their commercial uses have yet to be considered.

The railways are self-supporting, indeed for some years past they have made a large annual contribution to the central revenues. The States are under no obligation to Government for their provision; on the contrary, they provided a considerable amount of the capital necessary for the construction of lines in their own territories, on no very favourable terms, and provided the necessary land without cost, even forfeiting their sovereignty over it. The Holkar State Railway, for example, was built out of a loan of a crore of rupees, at 4½ per cent. from the Indore Darbar, and in this case the terms granted to the Prince were unusually favourable, as half the profits on this line are paid to him, although no allowance is made in calculating them for the additional traffic which it brings to the main line. The Gwalior Darbar amongst other loans (for railway construction) provided Rs. 75 lakhs for the section of main line from Gwalior to Agra, less than half of which lies in Gwalior territory, and supplied not only the necessary land, but also materials for the construction of the line, free of charge.

Each of these railways is useful to the State concerned. The Nizam was less fortunate. He was persuaded to build a length of line (Purna to Hingoli) which was to form a link in a strategic through line from north to south, but when fifty miles had been built it was found necessary to change the alignment and even the gauge of the north and south line, and the Nizam was left with a piece of railway leading nowhere, which yields 2 or 3 per cent. on the money which was invested in it.

Even when the lines financed by the various Darbars were successful they were not always those most suitable to the State in question, and they often contribute more to the general welfare of British India than to the particular State which provided the capital. For instance, it has been argued that industrial development in Mysore is handicapped by the fact that the railways in her territory do not follow the natural channels of trade.

In each case the terms of loans and cessions made by the States are different, but in almost every case the State has made over lands and jurisdiction and has agreed to charge no transit duties on goods passing through its territories. The States have by no means received the railways as a gift from Government. It is true that for many years the railways were run at a loss and the deficit made good out of general taxation, but it is probable that if the same kind of calculation of the liabilities and contributions of the States as we are now making had been made at a time before the railways became self-supporting, the contributions of the States would have been found at least to equal all their obligations, including a fair share of the deficit upon the working of the State railway lines and of the payments made by the Government in respect of guaranteed interest to the commercial lines. It is not, however, necessary to discuss in detail the liability of the States in the past any more than it is possible to claim consideration for past contributions. The question before us is whether there is any liability at present on account of railways.

It has been argued that the existence of a railway confers benefits greater than can be measured by the yield of railway rates and the profits of railway companies, that a railway develops a territory, broadens markets, widens economic life and increases economic values, without taking a tithe of the increase as its toll, and that therefore the States are in reality liable for a contribution to the Central Government which provides them with transport. This argument is based on a confusion. It would be just as true to say that the railway from Dholpur to Agra, built with Gwalior money, yields a gain unmeasured by the profits of the G.I.P., for which the central revenue should pay a tribute to Gwalior. But it is often assumed that the railways belong to British India and ought to sell their services at a monopoly price to the States, who are regarded as purchasers. The same argument is often applied to defence, the postal services and other undertakings run in common. The confusion arises from the uncertainty that has hitherto cloaked the precise relations of the States to the Indian Empire. At one moment the British Government will sell services and goods to the States at monopoly prices, as if they were foreign countries, at another they will justify the imposition of taxes upon them and throw on to them the military responsibilities and economic policies as if they were ordinary districts, without any rights under treaties and agreements. They cannot claim the generous co-operation of the States in building railways for the sake of developing and uniting the whole country and at the same time regard the States' share in that development as a benefit which they had no right to expect and for which they must unquestionably pay whatever price may be asked.

The ports of British India also are a paying concern. The Trust loans are in certain cases guaranteed securities, but as the ports are prosperous this costs the Government nothing. The ports are not subsidised and the States therefore have no liability under this head.

The roads are provided in British India by the Provinces, in the States by themselves. If the population of the States use the roads in British India, the people of British India in their turn use the roads in the States. Considerable distances of highways, such as the Agra-Bombay road, lie through States, and they are kept in better condition than local traffic demands, largely for the benefit of British-Indian motorists. Certain States, moreover, have been saddled with roads or bridges, originally built for strategic purposes, which bring the State no benefit comparable with their cost of upkeep and which have been superseded by railways since they were first made. The States provide their full share of roads and bridges and they are under no liability on this account.

XXIX.

POSTS AND TELEGRAPHS.

The services of the Imperial Post Office are enjoyed by the Indian States in common with the rest of the country. In fifteen States the Darbars also provide Post Offices. Five of these States (Gwalior, Chamla, Jind, Natha and Patiala) have Conventions with the Imperial Post Office and work in co-operation with it. In the rest, Hyderabad, Cochin, Travancore, Jaipur, Chaikari, Junagad, Kishangad, Mewar, Shahpura, Orchha, the greater part of correspondence within the State is carried by the local post offices, while branches of the Imperial Post Office exist at most important places and carry the greater part of correspondence across the State frontiers. In Gwalior, the chief of the Convention States, Imperial Post Offices exist only on territory which is British for purpose of jurisdiction, such as railway stations and the Residency area, and Gwalior postage stamps are valid for correspondence to any part of India, but not overseas.

Although the Imperial Post Office is at present run upon more or less commercial lines it has to receive a grant every year from the central revenue. The figures for the last three years are as follows:

	Net Receipts.	Expenditure.	Balance.
Accounts, 1926–7 . .	70·65 lakhs.	75·82 lakhs.	— 5·17 lakhs.
Revised estimate, 1927–8 .	51·76 „	81·67 „	—29·91 „
Budget estimate, 1928–9 .	57·37 „	81·66 „	—24·29 „

In so far as the States are not permitted to manage their own postal system, there can obviously be no grounds for saddling them with any portion of this deficit. On the other hand, States that desire to be served by the Imperial system can be held responsible for profits and losses calculated upon the operation of the system within their borders.

The Post Office Department made, or was budgeted to make, a considerable profit in each of these years. The Telegraph Department made a loss, while its rival the Telephone Department is expected to show a profit for the first time in 1928–29. The profits on the Post Office have usually been sufficient to cover the loss on the other two branches, and the greater part of the deficit represents new capital development, that is to say, the opening of new Post Offices in areas which are expected to benefit from them, but which are not expected to provide enough business to cover the whole cost of the new offices.

The extent to which the States desiring to be served by the Imperial system are liable for the expenses of the Post Office, therefore, is the extent to which they benefit from the Telegraph Service, and from the capital expansion of the Post Office, for these only are subsidised from general taxation. In so far as the Post Office is self-supporting these States have no liability, since their subjects pay for the services which they receive from it in just the same way as they pay for the services of any commercial institution.

The benefit to the States from the Telegraph is clearly not in proportion to population, since it is largely used for administrative and military purposes, and still more by dealers and the business community in general, and there are very few commercial centres of any importance within the States. Its use by private individuals probably amounts to very little, and although this means that the States do not contribute much to Telegraph receipts, it also means that they are being provided with a service (mainly for strategical reasons) for which they have little real need.

Next as to capital expansion. In most cases when a Durbar applies for the opening of a new office, it is expected to guarantee that office against loss, although it will receive no share in the profits which the new branch may ultimately make, and no share in whatever profits other branches within the State may be making. It therefore remains very difficult to discover to what extent the States are really indebted to a subsidised Post Office.

In return for the benefits which they receive from it, the States which desire to be served by the Imperial system may be held to have surrendered certain rights and opportunities. Chief of these must be reckoned the fact that, with the exception of the fifteen States with their own Post Offices already referred to, the Imperial Post Office enjoys a complete monopoly of the postal services which, as the example of Gwalior and Travancore shows, can be efficiently run and made a considerable source of revenue. An indigenous postal system is known to have existed in Mysore, Cochin and Travancore before the advent of the British. In other States post offices, more or less efficient, grew up under the example of the British before the Imperial Post Office offered to serve the States. Jodhpur, which has only recently given up its own post office, also had a telegraph office, now closed, from which the revenue amounted to Rs. 19,000, and Bikaner owns a railway telegraph line which has suffered from the introduction into the State of the Imperial Telegraph system. It is probably the case that these services were less regular and reliable than the Imperial Post Office, but they were also probably cheaper, as the Travancore post office is to this day, for the Imperial Post Office is obliged to have regular servants at a uniform rate of pay, in all parts of the country, while a State can adjust wages to the cost of living within its own borders, and can make use of part-time workers who are already in the State service in some other capacity.

Some minor services are also provided by the States. For instance, they are obliged to guarantee security to the Post Office servants within their territory and are responsible for the value of goods which are stolen, but they are never credited with any of the money which is paid on registered parcels as an insurance against the risk of robbery. Some States, such as Jodhpur, provide buildings for Post Office branches at very low rents, and the State treasuries make loans to local post offices and manage the business of remittance for them from one part of the State to another. In return for these services certain States receive a fixed number of stamps for official correspondence, but in many instances they find that an allotment, whether adequate or not when it was made, has not been increased when the volume of business has grown, so that the allowances are often quite inadequate at the present time.

The States which guarantee branches of the post offices have reason to complain that they have no control over the expenditure or the methods of accounting which determine whether the branches in question are being run at a loss or not. Neither have they any control over the general policy of the Post Office. They have no influence in determining postal rates, and they cannot fairly be held responsible for a share of the losses upon new branches opened at the initiative of the Imperial Post Office, since when they themselves ask for a branch to be opened in a particular district they are required to provide a guarantee.

For all these reasons it is exceedingly difficult to estimate the obligation of the States, if obligation there is, to make any financial contribution to the Central Government on account of the postal services. Even to calculate it upon a population basis is not easy. First it is necessary to allow for about 5 millions of population in the Convention States which are almost entirely served by the State post offices. The population of the 10 States which have independent post offices amounts to 22 millions, but it would be better to allow only half of this number, as the people of these States are also served by the Imperial Post Office, and it is impossible to estimate more exactly the extent to which they make use of the State post offices. We must therefore subtract 16 millions from the population of India and assign to the States the responsibility of 56/303 of the deficit upon the Post Office. On this basis the liability of the States in 1926–27 (the last year for which accounts are available) would have been Rs. 80,000, and in 1928, when the expenses of the Post Office were increased by a more generous scale of pay to its subordinates, the States' share would be Rs. 4,40,000. But before the States are debited with this amount it is necessary to remember that the deficit on the Post Office is incurred because new branches are opened which cannot immediately pay, so that none of the States served by guaranteed branches share in this liability, while presumably only profitable branches of the Imperial Post Office are opened in the States which run postal services for themselves. For this reason we do not include these four lakhs in our estimate of the States' liabilities. But it is still necessary to add that in order to arrive at a satisfactory adjustment, conventions should be concluded with such States as are free and willing to enter into them.

XXX.

PUBLIC WORKS.

Finally, there are certain commercial services which might now be examined. In the past, irrigation schemes have been undertaken by Government in which States have had an interest. The schemes, however, have been designed to be self-supporting, and they carry their own debt charges. When the additional land revenue due to their existence is taken into account, all the schemes which have been established for any time show a considerable profit.

The States, moreover, shared in the construction of many of these schemes, and, as in the case of railways, ceded the territory which was needed for their construction. The entire management of the various schemes is in the hands of Government, and the States, in most instances, have abandoned their rights to undertake schemes of their own which might interfere with British Indian works; while in certain cases the Government schemes actually divert water with which nature had endowed the States. For instance, the surface water of a large area of the territory of Kishengarh State has been drained away to supply the Sambhar salt lake, and the district deprived of water has been reduced to a wilderness. During a minority administration the Darbar was prevented from constructing bundhs, or wells, on the ground that by such means their own water would have been kept within their own territory and prevented from flowing to swell the Sambhar Lake. The Darbar has received no compensation for the water which it has lost, but when, on the other hand, water rising in British India is distributed to a State the Government is accustomed to charge seigniorage for its use.

Treaties were drawn up with the various States concerned as each scheme was undertaken. The first of these was made in 1873 between the British Government and the States of Patiala, Jind and Nabha. Under its terms, each of the four parties was to bear a share both of capital and running expenses in proportion to the benefit received, and this practice has been followed in most of the later treaties. Many States without natural waters of their own have been benefited by British irrigation works, but to others they have been denied. For instance, the State of Alipura, in Bundelkhand, ceded land for part of the length of the Dhasan canal, but the State receives no water from it. The Bharatpur Darbar entered into an agreement with the Government of the United Provinces in which it was promised water from the Agra canal, which flows along the border of the State. The Darbar accordingly constructed channels to receive the promised water, but after they were built the Provincial Government refused to supply it, the capital sunk in the channels was wasted, and the cultivators of Bharatpur disappointed of their hopes.

XXXI.

CUSTOMS AND TARIFFS.

It is necessary to examine how much, in fact, the States contribute to the central revenue. Certain of them pay tributes and subsidies which have already been mentioned. It remains to discuss the indirect and uncovenanted contributions which are paid by the subjects of the Darbars. Of these we will endeavour to make an estimate.

The chief among them is the customs revenue levied on goods which are consumed in the States.

It might be argued that all Governments have a right to levy duties at their own ports on all goods imported, whatever their destination, without inquiring where that ultimate consumer lives on whom the weight of the tax must fall, but a moment's consideration of the case of Switzerland,[1] or Austria will show that this is a right which it would be impossible to claim. The Government of India, moreover, demands no such right in respect of independent States, such as Nepal and Afghanistan. Again, it might be urged that these duties are in effect transit duties, a form of taxation long familiar in India, but this plea would come ill from a Government whose aim has always been to abolish transit duties wherever they are found, and which is justly proud of the stimulus to Indian prosperity which has followed their abolition.

If it be recognised that international relationships present no analogy relevant to this question, the *prima facie* case against these payments becomes even stronger. It is clearly unjust to tax the whole of a nation or of a confederacy and to exclude a particular part of it from participation in the revenue which that tax yields. If a motor tax was imposed on all owners throughout England and no share of the Road Fund spent in Yorkshire, the

[1] For arrangements made by land-locked countries in Europe, South America and the British Dominions, see Stanley Jevons, *Evidence before the Fiscal Commission*, Vol. I. p. 281.

inhabitants of Yorkshire would certainly be justified in complaining. We are forced to return, therefore, to the plain question of what, in fact, consumers in the States contribute to the yield of customs, and what they receive in return.

The contribution which the inhabitants of the States make to customs revenue has only lately become important. In the days of a 5 per cent. tariff the injustice may have been theoretically as great, but the economic loss was small. It could not exceed at most 22 per cent., or about Rs. 5 crores. Since the war two very important changes have come about. In the first place, the peoples of the States are becoming more and more dependent on imported goods. The old economy of the self-supporting village is fast breaking up, and as communications of every kind develop, the inhabitants of even the most remote parts of India are increasingly affected by the results of her foreign trade. Secondly, the Government of India appear definitely to have abandoned the ideal of free trade. This came about by two stages. First, under pressure of war finance the tariff was raised in 1917, and an even greater pressure from unbalanced budgets raised it still further after the war. Then came the Reforms and a rising tide of nationalism which found an expression in the policy of protection advocated by the Fiscal Commission in 1922. Even when the Budget was balanced, the claims of Salt and of Provincial Contributions were preferred to those of Customs, and in present conditions there seems little chance of the tariff being considerably reduced.

The States feel both the sentimental attractions and the solid benefits of protection far less than the people of British India, for they are much less developed either in political views or in industrial organisation. Of cotton yarn produced in India in 1921 less than 6 per cent. came from the States,[1] of piece goods 7·7 per cent., and of the total value of goods woven in cotton mills less than 4 per cent. Of woollen goods the States produced 11 per

[1] Industrial Census, 1921.

cent., of coal 5 per cent., of other minerals about 6 per cent., of iron and steel goods none at all.[1] The population of the States is 22·5 per cent. of the whole. It can easily be seen, therefore, that it is yet hardly time for the States to begin asking for protection, since they are still so preponderantly importers and consumers rather than producers of manufactured goods. But even if the protective policy was just as useful or more useful to the States than it is to British India, that would be no reason for depriving the States of their share in the revenue which is incidentally raised.

As we have seen, the customs revenue grew up from causes quite unconnected with the States. It was not imposed consciously in order to exact a predetermined contribution from them, and the haphazard manner in which this burden has fallen upon the States makes it all the more distressing.

The States, with the single exception of Hyderabad, are not guaranteed by their treaties against this kind of exaction, for when the treaties were made there was no reason to expect that such duties would be charged. As long as India was looked upon mainly as a market for British goods, import duties were out of the question, and at the same time there was no reason to expect that the States would share to anything like the extent which they now do in the import trade of India. One or two States, however, owing to their geographical circumstances, have been given special concessions. Apart from the agreement of 1917 with the Kathiawar States, the dispute in respect of which is not yet settled, the chief of these concessions is the arrangement by which the Kashmir Darbar receives a drawback of customs duties on goods consigned to Kashmir, in return for an engagement not to charge transit duties on goods entering India through its territory. With these exceptions every inhabitant of a State must contribute to the central revenue whenever he buys a dutiable article which has entered India from abroad.

[1] Since that date an Iron and Steel Works has been opened in Mysore.

To how much does this contribution amount? The receipts from import duties in 1926–27 amounted to some 40 crores, so that a division *per capita* would show that the States contributed Rs. 9 crores. This figure does not include export duties, in which the States have little interest.

It is hard to estimate how much allowance should be made for the relative poverty of the States, and impossible to collect exact figures of the amount of overseas goods which cross their frontiers. The figures from the Industrial Census which were quoted above suggest that the States must take less than their full 22 per cent. of raw materials. They probably take less than 22 per cent. of machinery, though their earlier industrial backwardness and their present efforts to catch up are an influence in the contrary direction. Of consumable goods it is more difficult to judge. The general poverty of their populations would suggest a rather smaller proportion. On the other hand, the mills and factories of British India compete with foreign exports most successfully in their own neighbourhood, where transport costs make the greatest difference. The industrial backwardness of the States may then result in their importing more than other districts of foreign manufactures. Thus in 1925–26 the import of cotton piece goods was 1,563,713 yards, the Indian mill production was 1,954,461 yards, making a total of 3,518,174 yards. Now if we assume that instead of consuming 22 per cent. of the mill-produced cotton goods the States because of their greater poverty consume only 18 per cent., but draw 60 per cent. of it from abroad,[1] their consumption of imported cotton will then be 280,063 yards, or 24·3 per cent. of the total of imported cotton piece-goods. These figures are

[1] The only State for which actual information on this point is available is Kashmir. While excise duty was charged on Indian manufactured cotton, Kashmir received a rebate of that duty, as well as of the customs duties, and records were therefore kept of all cotton crossing the Kashmir frontiers. In 1925 Kashmir imported Rs. 28 lakhs worth of foreign piece goods and Rs. 6 lakhs worth of Indian piece goods: that is to say, the foreign goods were as much as 80 per cent. of the whole.

intended to be illustrative only, and it is not claimed that they represent the actual facts. It is here only our purpose to show that when an article is manufactured both in British India and abroad for import into India, even if the States consumption per head is demonstrably lower than that in British India, it may nevertheless happen that the States' proportion of the consumption of imported goods is as high or higher than the proportion that their population bears to the whole. And even where it is not, but when the States, or some given State has no manufacture of that particular commodity and no intention of undertaking it, that State may not unreasonably plead that its interest lies solely in the price of the article, and it makes little or no difference to it whether the article is to be imported from abroad or from British India, that its loss through the customs, on cotton goods for instance, is spread not only over the goods which pay sea customs, but also over the piece goods manufactured in the protected mills of British India. This is no argument for a refund to the States of the customs rate on their whole importation of cotton goods, whether from British India or abroad. It does nevertheless show that in an economically interdependent area, whether or not in the strictest sense of the word Federation exists, there must be a great deal of give and take between different districts. No simple tax system can be uniformly fair (though that is no sufficient reason for not endeavouring to make it as fair as possible), and the best that can be hoped is that the unfairnesses may to some extent cancel out. The States can reasonably claim that if one tax in its results, other than upon revenue, is adverse to their interests, those interests deserve favourable consideration in other matters.

In order to make a quantitative estimate of the contributions of the States, it is necessary to attempt to estimate the proportion of the total customs revenue which is derived immediately or ultimately from their population. The means to obtain accurate figures or even an intelligent estimate are lacking. The Government do not tabulate their sea customs according to destination, and if they did, the vast quantity of things which break bulk at the ports, and are re-consigned in smaller packages to the States, or are bought by individuals in the States from traders in British India, would escape tabulation. Nor do the States in general record their imports by countries of origin. The State import duties do not distinguish between English, Japanese and Bombay cotton goods or between sugar originating abroad and in British India or another State. Few States indeed keep accurate statistics at all. Such as are available are extremely difficult to reconcile either with probability or with known facts. Further, the heads under which they record imports are wholly different from those used by the Imperial customs authorities, and differ also between State and State. Some have records of quantities only and not values. Some record values only, not quantities. The measures used are in many cases not easily changeable into the measures used by the Imperial customs. Imports of cotton may be reckoned in maunds, or yards, or values, and sometimes the only returns available show the yield of a specific duty on a miscellaneous group of goods.

Moreover, even where there is reason to believe that the statistics have been honestly and carefully kept, they may not for many reasons accurately represent the imports into that State of goods on which British Indian customs duty has been paid. Where frontiers are mainly long and intricate land boundaries, to prevent evasion entirely would, even if it were possible, be financially ruinous. For all classes there are ways and means of avoiding the tax. Where the Imperial Post Office is operating, the States have sometimes considerable difficulty in securing knowledge of imported goods. One Darbar remarks that "it may perhaps be a genuine coincidence, but it is not free from a certain amount of legitimate suspicion, that during the last twenty years no duty has ever been paid by any employee of the Post Office on any parcel sent to him through the post." The richer residents in the States spend money in British India, using their purchases in the district where they are bought and importing them later into the States without paying duty. Again, a considerable proportion of the goods imported from Europe into the States are bought on account of their Governments. While these goods pay duty at the ports, they do not in most cases pay the duties imposed by the States, and do not, therefore, appear in their statistics.

For these reasons such statistics as are available tend to under-estimate the consumption of imported goods. Further, several States who, either voluntarily or under treaty obligations, impose no customs duties have no record of the quantities and values imported.

We have examined in great detail the statistics provided by the States. Since, as we have already stated, they are not homogeneous, and since statistics of one commodity may be available only from certain States and not from others, it has proved quite impossible to compile them into a table. Instead, we have employed the knowledge thus gained as the basis of an estimate for the whole area. The method we have adopted in making this estimate is to take the various heads of customs revenue and group them into four classes according to our ideas of the probable consumption of each article in the States, compared with its consumption in British India. The result is mainly guesswork, but there is unfortunately no alternative, and our utmost hope is that the errors of our guesses may in some measure cancel out and that the total guess may be nearer the truth than if we guessed simply from one total to the other.

We have placed the different articles or groups of articles in four categories. The first we assume to be consumed as much by people in the States as by people in British India, and therefore we assign 22·5 per cent. of the revenue to the States. In the second group we assume that 18 per cent. of the revenue is derived from the States, that is, that the consumption per head in the States is 78 per cent. of the consumption per head in British India. In the third group we have assumed that

15 per cent. of the revenue is derived from the States, and in the fourth 10 per cent. of revenue. In no case have we assumed a larger average consumption in the States than in British India.

YIELD OF CUSTOMS.

(*See Review of Trade of India*, 1926–27, *pp.* 200–1.)

Figures of 1926–27.

Lakhs of Rupees.

I.		II.		III.		IV.	
Articles 22·5%.	Yield of Customs.	Articles 18%.	Yield of Customs.	Articles 15%.	Yield of Customs.	Articles 10%.	Yield of Customs.
Sugar	701	Articles wholly or mainly manufactured (other than cotton or silk).	814	Liquor	261	Machinery	38
Mineral Oil	129	Cars and Cycles	105	Tobacco	191	Railway Materials.	24
Cotton Yarn	36	Rubber Tyres and Tubes.	39	Iron Steel (10% duty).	43	Railway Tracks	8
Cotton Piece Goods.	621	Paper and Stationery.	24	Iron and Steel (Protective special duty).	268	Miscellaneous (10% duty).	1
Matches	89	Portland Cement.	9	Articles of Food and Drink.	175		
Others (non-protective special duties).	15	Coal Tubs	1	Raw Materials	65		
				Miscellaneous (15% duty).	61		
				Miscellaneous (30% duty).	104		
				Silk	78		
Total Revenue	1,591		992		1,246		71
Assumed % taken by States.	% 22·5		% 18		% 15		% 10
Consumption in States as % of consumption in British India.	100[1]		78[2]		62[3]		38
Tax paid by population of States.	358		179		187		7
Total Sea Customs paid by States.	731		—		—		—

1 $\dfrac{22{\cdot}5 \times 100}{(22{\cdot}5 \times 100) + 77{\cdot}5 \times 100} = 22{\cdot}5\%.$

2 $\dfrac{22{\cdot}5 \times 78}{(22{\cdot}5 \times 78) + (77{\cdot}5 \times 100)} = 18\%.$

3 $\dfrac{22{\cdot}5 \times 62}{(22{\cdot}5 \times 62) + 77{\cdot}5 \times 100)} = 15\%.$

4 $\dfrac{22{\cdot}5 \times 38}{(22{\cdot}5 \times 38) + (77{\cdot}5 \times 100)} = 10\%.$

The States Contribution to Customs Revenue.

	Lakhs of Rupees.
Total Sea Customs paid by State . .	731
Total Customs Revenue (Import, Export and other duties)	4,738
Percentage of total paid by the States. .	15·4%
Total cost of collection and other charges .	81
15·5% of cost	12·5
Net Customs duties paid by the States .	718
Deduct 77·5% of refunds paid to certain States [1]	12
Net contribution of States to Customs Revenue	706

States Share of Customs Revenue in Proportion to Population.

	Lakhs of Rupees.
Total Import duties	3,996
Gross share of States in proportion to population	899
Cost of collection	15
Net share of States	884

We conclude, as can be seen from the above calculation, that the States contribute to the customs revenue 706 lakhs, or Rs. 1¾ crores less than 22·5 per cent. of the whole. The injury to the States from sea customs is not limited to the payment which they make. Besides

[1] Certain States already receive a refund of a part of their contribution towards customs revenue. Under the Interportal Agreement, Cochin receives Rs. 1,00,000, and Travancore receives Rs. 40,000, annually. Kashmir receives a rebate on goods imported in bond which in 1926 amounted to about Rs. 14,00,000. 22·5 per cent. of these sums have already been deducted from the States contribution to customs, as they are included among the charges on customs revenue. We must, therefore, deduct 77·5 per cent. of Rs. 15,40,000 in order to obtain the net contribution of the States as a whole.

the actual burden of the tax there are many incidental hardships. The chief of these is that they have no say in the tariff policy of the country. In so far as the States are consumers rather than producers of industrial goods, they must have the natural bias of the consumer towards free trade, but they may have particular industries which, if protection is being given at all, wish to claim their share of protection. For instance, the silk industry of Mysore (the principal silk-growing district of India) suffers from the competition of Japan and China and might well ask for protection. The same State also might, with the help of export duties, be able to develop industries which would use the rare minerals, such as chrome and magnesium, that are found within its borders.

The Indian tariff, moreover, does not only cover consumable goods. Machinery and raw materials are taxed, though at a comparatively low rate, and the States which have come late into the field, when they wish to lay down industrial plant, find themselves in competition with factories in British India which were established before the duties on machinery were imposed, and whose capital charges are therefore on a lower scale.

The States are ready to co-operate in any policy which will benefit Indian industry, provided their own wishes and interests as consumers and producers are given due weight when policy is being decided.

XXXII.

EXCISE DUTIES.

The excise revenue of the Central Government at the present time is small. The excise on cotton was removed in 1925 in deference to Indian opinion, and the only duties which it will be necessary to include in our calculations are those on motor-spirit and on kerosene. The State of Kashmir is exempted from these duties, and the rebate which it receives has already been deducted from the figures for customs. Some three millions of population must, therefore, be deducted from both sides before estimating the relative share of the States and British India in excise revenue. In the case of motor-spirit we will assume the same rate of consumption by the States as we have assumed to be their share in the importation of cars, that is to say, 78 per cent. of the average consumption per head in British India, and for kerosene we will assume the same rate of consumption as we did when considering the custom duty upon mineral oil, that is to say, a full proportionate share, that is, eliminating the population of Kashmir, 21·5 per cent. of the whole.

Our estimate of the States contribution to the central excise is therefore shown in the following table:

	Excise on Motor Spirit.	Share of States [1] 17·6%.	Excise on Kerosene.	Share of States [2] 21·5%.
Accounts, 1926–27 .	96·4	17·0	104·7	22·5
Revised estimate .	124·6	21·9	101·2	21·8
Budget estimate .	124·8	21·9	110·6	23·8

[1] If the rate of consumption per head of 21·5 per cent. of the population is 78 per cent. of the rate of the remainder, the first group consume

$$\frac{21·5 \times 78}{(21·5 \times 78) + (78·5 \times 100)}$$ or 17·6 per cent. of the whole.

[2] Population of States excluding Kashmir . 68·7 69 = 21·5 per
„ India „ „ . 316·7 cent. of 316.

This shows a total contribution (in the last year for which accounts are available) of Rs. 39.6 lakhs, from which must be deducted Rs. 60,000 for expenses [1] of collection, leaving a net contribution of exactly Rs. 39 lakhs.

Opium revenue, which is mainly in the form of excise, is an item of some importance in the central Budget. The contributions which the inhabitants of the States make under this head vary very considerably from one

[1] Calculated in the same way as for customs.

part of the country to another, both because opium is used much more in some parts of India than in others, and because some States are still able to grow opium for their own use. We have, therefore, found it impossible to include an estimate of this contribution in our calculations, but when an authoritative examination is made of the payments received by central revenue from the peoples of the States, their contribution to opium revenue will have to be included.

The policy of the Government in regard to opium and the losses which have fallen upon the opium-growing States in their co-operation with that policy have been many times discussed. It is not proposed to open the question here. The burden upon the States from that policy must be regarded as a loss rather than as a contribution, and cannot be reckoned in our estimate of the share of the States in the central revenue.

The Provinces charge excise upon liquor and goods, such as hemp drugs, of which a partial monopoly has been secured to them by the various treaties and agreements which prevent the States which produce these goods from exporting them. So far as they are partly consumed by the inhabitants of States, this must be regarded as an export tax, the burden of which the taxing authority is in a position to throw partly upon a foreign consumer. In so far as these duties are similar to customs duties, the reasoning of the last chapter is applicable. If they are in the nature of an export duty, they can only be legitimate if the States are to be regarded as foreign countries. But such an attitude would be politically wrong; and in practice the only sensible arrangement is for a common policy to be negotiated between the Provincial Governments and the States with which they are in geographical contact, subject to such qualifications as may be necessary through States being in contact with more than one Province. Plainly, co-operation between the States as a whole, and the Central Government and the Provinces, is politically desirable. But these considerations do not affect the estimation of the actual burden upon the States, which is our present task.

The duty on *charas* is unlike the rest in that it is in fact a transit duty. *Charas* is not produced in India, but is all imported from Central Asia and distributed from Hoshiarpur in the Punjab, where the tax is levied. It is as unjustifiable in principle that the burden of this tax should fall upon the people of the States as that the burden of customs duties should fall upon them, but as it is a question between the Provincial Government and the Durbars, we do not propose to include it in our present estimate of the States' contributions to central revenue.

Although we have not included any part of the Provincial Excise Duties in our estimate, it is necessary to examine certain disabilities which the States suffer in connection with them. The first disadvantage to the States which we must note is that certain minor States agreed to give up their excise revenue in return for a compensation equal to the amount of revenue which was sacrificed at the time. The revenue which is now raised is very much larger than that which was originally sacrificed, partly because of the general rise of prices, but mainly because of the very high rates of duty which are now charged.

The more common arrangement is that by which the States levy their own excise duties, but by which they are compelled to follow the policy of the adjoining Provinces. If a Province wishes to raise its rates of duties the neighbouring States are compelled to follow suit, in order to avoid competition and the temptation to smuggling. If, on the other hand, a State wishes to raise its duties, the Province is unaffected. It is right that there should be co-operation between the States and the Provinces in this matter, but the interests of the States concerned should be allowed at least some weight in the determination of the policy in which they are obliged to share.

A third type of arrangement is that by which a State

and a Province each with its own excise system agree to have a shopless zone for a certain number of miles on each side of their mutual boundary. Such an area is likely to represent a far higher proportion of the whole area of the State than it does of the Province, especially as the territory of many States consists of scattered islands, the whole of which is covered by the two-mile ring, and the revenue that is foregone by this means is a correspondingly greater loss.

A minor disadvantage of the States is that liquor may be sold at railway station refreshment rooms within the territory of a State. This liquor will have paid Provincial excise or Government customs duty, but as the railway premises are treated as a part of British India it will not be charged with the States' duties. It often has the advantage of preferential railway rates from the ports, and for both these reasons it can compete unfairly with other liquor sold in the State and offers a great temptation to a very easy form of smuggling.

Although the excise duties of British India yield a considerable revenue, their motive is partly social, and they are designed as much to check the consumption of liquor and drugs as to raise funds for the Provincial Governments. The duties, therefore, are imposed at a very high rate. But while the States are obliged to follow the moral views of the Provinces in their excise policy, the Mohammedan State of Bhopal, which was entirely prohibitionist, received no co-operation from the Provincial excise offices upon its borders, and was not even able to forbid the sale of liquor on the railway stations within its territory.

These are minor disadvantages to the States in addition to the contributions that many of them are compelled to make to Provincial revenues.

XXXIII.

THE SALT MONOPOLY.

The Government of India derive some Rs. 6 crores of revenue from the taxation of salt. Some of this is raised by means of customs duties on salt entering the country; some by an excise duty on salt manufactured locally, part of which is mined, part taken from lakes and part from the sea; and some by the sale of salt produced in Government works. In effect the Government fix the price of salt and every purchaser of salt is contributing to revenue.

The taxation of salt dates from the early days of British rule in India, and since a large part of the salt consumed in India comes from Rajputana, it was necessary for the taxing authority to draw a customs line across India, which was maintained at great expense both of trouble and of money. In 1870 Lord Mayo initiated a fresh policy by negotiating a treaty with the States of Jodhpur and Jaipur by which the Sambhar Lake was leased to Government, and by later agreements all other important sources for the supply of salt came under Government control, and the customs line was abolished.

But the methods by which the Government of India acquired the monopoly of salt are not our immediate concern. It is the States regarded as consumers rather than as producers of salt that we must consider. Their peoples, with every pound of salt that they buy, make a contribution to the central revenue, and it is the amount of that contribution which we are concerned to discover.

There is no reason to suppose that the States consume less than their proportionate share of salt, since it is a commodity which the poorest must buy, and it is least needed in the wealthiest and most populous places, the large towns where there are almost no cattle.

Rough estimates can be made of the amount of salt consumed in certain States. The figures of the annual consumption of seven States, taken at random, which cover a population of some eight millions, show an average of 12·2 lbs. per head. The returns published in the Statistical Abstract for British India show that the average consumption for all India is 12·3 lbs. per head. These calculations are not accurate enough for a difference of 0·1 lb. to have any significance, and we may safely assume that the average consumption in the States is roughly the same as in the rest of India.

The States, therefore, can fairly claim that they contribute a share of the salt revenue proportionate to their population. During the last five years the salt revenue has varied between five and six crores of rupees, of which 22 per cent. is something over Rs. 1 crore. From this it is necessary to deduct the compensation which is paid to certain salt-producing States to the amount of some 40 lakhs.

NET SALT REVENUE AFTER PAYING CHARGES AND CAPITAL OUTLAY.

		22·5% of net Revenue.	*Less* Compensation.
	Lakhs Rs.	Lakhs Rs.	Lakhs Rs.
1924–25	6,49	1,46	1,10
1925–26	5,41	1,21	81
1926–27	5,83	1,31	93
1927–28 (Revised estimate) .	5,89	1,33	94
1928–29 (Budget) . .	6,14	1,38	99

One or two of the salt-producing States are allowed a certain quantity of salt free of duty, and to this extent the above calculation is inaccurate.[1] But this privilege is only one of the concessions by which they were induced to give up the revenue which they had formerly made from salt and to turn their productive resources over to

[1] Certain States are allowed to produce salt for their own consumption; but the amount thus produced is negligible. Kashmir is only allowed a rebate on salt imported from overseas, and in practice she imports almost no salt in this way.

the control of the British authorities, so that if they had not been compensated in this way it would have been necessary to compensate them in some other way. If the States which merely consume salt can justly be credited with the amount of the tax that their subjects pay, the States which formerly owned salt works, and which are already exempted from the tax, can claim to be credited with something more. We therefore do not exclude the population (which amounts to three millions) of the States which enjoy this concession from the general calculation, and we conclude that the States' populations bear the burden of some 90 lakhs of rupees taxation which they contribute to the salt revenue.

Besides the direct burden of the tax there are various disadvantages to the States from this payment. The whole control of salt revenue is taken out of their hands and they are unable to influence the policy of the Government in regard to the price which they choose to charge for salt. An illustration of this is afforded by the fact that pressure was brought to bear upon the States in whose territory salt is produced, and which are allowed a certain quantity for their own consumption, to raise the price of salt to their own peoples at the time when an increase in the rates of the salt tax happened to suit the needs of the British Indian budget. A dispute over this point with Jodhpur lingered on until it was brought to an end by an improvement in the British Indian financial position which made it possible for the tax to be lowered again, but the States which have no source of supply within their own borders were unable to protest against the rise in the price of salt.

The States in which salt is found suffer, besides the payment which all must make, various special disadvantages.

The treaties under which States agreed to refrain from the production of salt or by which they put their resources under the control of Government provide for certain forms of compensation. The terms granted to the different States vary considerably. Some received compensation for the transit duties which they had been accustomed to charge and which they were obliged to abandon, some received compensation for the price of the salt consumed by their subjects, some received compensation only for transit duties, some received no compensation at all. Some were allowed to produce salt on condition it was not exported, some were induced to treat other excisable goods in the same way. Some were obliged to give up production altogether. In every case the convenience of the Government excise system was considered above everything, and in most compensation was inadequate and was fixed in an arbitrary way. Sir John Strachey, the Finance Minister of the time, advanced the argument that the States were also compensated by "the removal from April 1st, 1878, of the duties formerly levied on all sugar exported across the customs line from our own territories, which fell mainly upon the people of the Native States of Rajputana." But he did not explain how the removal of export duties on a commodity of which the Rajputana States had their own sources of supply could be a benefit to them, nor did he mention that the benefit of the abolition of the duty must in any case have been far greater to the British Indian exporters. That such contentions were made at the time suggests that a doubt lurked in the Government mind as to the justice of the arrangement, but no change has been made in it up to the present day.

It is not only the States which suffer from the fact that Government drove so hard a bargain with them.

In some States sources of supply are available, the use of which is prohibited, and certain Darbars are even required to destroy natural salt which occurs in the ground without the necessity of human effort. Several States which formerly produced salt from brine wells find that since the salt workings have been stopped the land grows saline and unfit for cultivation. Sir Michael O'Dwyer, when he was Settlement Commissioner (1897–1900), wrote of a part of Bharatpur State:

"This was a great seat of salt manufacture and was one of the most busy and prosperous parts of the State, but it has now a forlorn and depressed appearance, with large areas of land lying waste or deserted owing to bad soil, bad water, want of hands and the inroads of wild cattle. . . . Since the abolition of the salt trade population has become sparse and the jungle has speedily encroached upon cultivation. . . . The village sites have a forlorn and desolate appearance aggravated by the belts of dismal farrash trees which alone thrive in the ungenerous soil."

Colonel Brockman, who was in Bharatpur in 1905, writes:

"The continual abstraction of water from Katcha wells, dug for the purpose of drawing lime water from the salt-bearing strata, annually removed from the soil tons of lime which now, owing to the suspension of salt manufacture in the State, remains in the soil, and contaminates the water with enormous quantities, chiefly of chloride of sodium, which accounts for its brackish nature."

Not only do the salt-producing States suffer these indirect losses, and not only are their exchequers deprived of a source of revenue, but a part of their natural wealth remains undeveloped and their peoples are often compelled to pay an unduly high price for salt which has been transported from a distance, or even imported from abroad, while a nearer and sometimes better supply remains unused. This is not only a disadvantage to the States concerned, but a loss of real wealth to the country as a whole.

XXXIV.

RAILWAYS.

We have hitherto been considering the contributions made by the States to central revenues as the result of taxation. There is a further group of contributions which is represented by their share in the profits of the profit-making enterprises of Government. The Government already possess in many districts, and is gradually acquiring in others, a monopoly of the railway services. The sales of monopoly products have long been recognised both in India and in other countries as a fruitful source of income for Governments. In India the salt duties are largely of that nature; in France, matches and tobacco have long been Government monopolies. While, strictly speaking, a monopoly price is different in nature from a tax, in practice the two converge. A tax imposed upon liquor by a Government is as dependent on the demand for liquor, and has the same effects in diminishing that demand, as an excessive monopoly price imposed by a producer. Between direct taxation and the extortions of a monopolist there is considerable difference, between indirect taxation and monopoly revenue very little.

The history of Indian railways has been a chequered one. For many years they failed to produce a sufficient surplus above their running expenses to pay in full the interest on the capital sunk in their originally rather extravagant construction. In the last few years they have come into their own as a sound profit-making concern of Government. The separation of the Railway Budget from the General Budget has made it much easier than it was to distinguish the profits and losses attributable to the railways, and the present system of accounting specifically separates the part of profits which is retained in the Railway Reserve Fund, to balance good and bad years and build up a general reserve for the railway finances, from that part which is transferred as a contribution from railway to general revenues. The table on next page shows the financial results of working in the two last available years.

The figure with which we are at the moment concerned is that of the contribution from railways to general revenues. This contribution comes from charging railway travellers, and people who consign goods by railway, more than the services have cost to provide. That is to say, it is in the nature of a tax paid by the consumers of railway services, either by travelling or consuming goods which have been carried. The incidence of the tax is therefore on travellers and consumers in the States as much as in British India. To make an accurate estimate of the incidence it would be necessary to know

FINANCIAL RESULTS OF RAILWAYS.

	(Figures in thousands.) 1925–26. Rs.	1926–27. Rs.
(1) (*a*) Gross earnings	9,97,000	9,90,398
(*b*) Surplus profits from subsidised companies	3,507	3,972
(*c*) Interest and Depreciation and Reserve Funds	5,377	6,392
(*d*) Other miscellaneous railway receipts	66	475
	10,05,950	10,01,237
(2) (*a*) Working expenses excluding depreciation	5,37,508	5,35,114
(*b*) Depreciation	1,06,688	1,08,858
(*c*) Surplus profits paid to companies	17,742	16,556
(*d*) Land and subsidy to companies	438	521
(*e*) Interest	2,48,112	2,58,670
(*f*) Miscellaneous railway expenditure	2,628	6,552
	9,13,116	9,26,271
(3) Net gain	92,834	74,966
(4) (*a*) Contribution from railway to general revenues	54,904	60,113
(*b*) Surplus railway revenue transferred to Railway Reserve Fund	37,930	14,853
	92,834	74,966

exactly to what extent the inhabitants of the States do, in fact, consume the services of the railway companies which contribute to the Government balance, that is, those railways which are owned by the State or in which it has an interest as a guarantor. This includes directly and indirectly (for a guaranteed minimum profit goes to the main line operating company in the case of those of the State-owned railways worked by a main line) some 34,000 miles out of the 39,000 miles of railway in the country. It is true that the Darbars own and work some 3,000 miles of line of their own, apart from lines leased to main lines, and to some extent these lines must provide for local travellers the services which in British India are provided for such people by the State-owned lines. On the other hand, these bring profitable traffic to them which would not otherwise have been available. Furthermore, the average length of haul for export and import goods from an India State to a seaport is probably greater than from British Indian districts, since the latter lie for the most part nearer the coast.

If we take the share of the States in the traffic to be in proportion to population, their share of the contribution to revenue would be (in 1926–27) 22·5 per cent. of Rs. 6,01,13,000, or about Rs. 135 lakhs. It is possible that this would be an over-estimate, and for the purpose of our calculations we will take the figure of Rs. 120 lakhs which would result from an average use of the railways by the peoples of the States, 85 per cent. of the average in British India.

In the case of railways, as of excise, of customs, and of salt duty, the money payment is not the only burden of which the States complain. They feel that the policy of the Railway Board is often inimical to their interests, and that the decisions of the railway officials carry more weight with Government than protests from a State which feels itself unfairly treated.

The Rewa Darbar, for instance, find that their collieries which they have lately electrified at considerable cost, are unable to develop because the railway companies serving the Central Provinces have recently lowered the rates on coal coming from that district without allowing a similar concession to the coalfields in Rewa. There may be some good reason for this action, but if so it should at least be made clear to the Darbar. Again, the Gwalior State suffers from the fact that the lines which are owned by the Darbar, but managed by the companies, do not receive their fair share of traffic. For instance, there are two possible routes between Howrah and Ahmedabad. Of these the shorter route, via Ujjain, lies partly over line owned by the Darbar. The company concerned fixes the minimum rates for goods traffic allowed by the Railway Board, upon the longer route, and the maximum rates upon the shorter route, thus diverting traffic from the Darbar's lines. It would be possible to multiply instances of injustice suffered by the States at the hands of railway authorities, but here it is our purpose merely to point out that the States are treated by them as taxpayers, and yet denied the taxpayer's right to make his views respected.

XXXV.

CURRENCY AND MINTS.

Another service from the provision of which the Government make a profit is the supply of currency. The minting of rupees and small coins and the printing of notes each yield a surplus measured by the difference between their respective nominal value and their costs of production. This surplus is used to build up a reserve, part of which is invested in income-yielding securities, and so contributes to revenue. This income has amounted in the last four years to sums varying from 3 to 6 crores of rupees per year.

The right of coinage is one of the dearest privileges of sovereignty, and it was with great reluctance that the various Princes gave up their mints. Some, such as Hyderabad, Udaipur and Jaipur, to this day coin their own rupees, and many coin their own pice. Originally a great number of States had their own separate currencies, and the business of exchanging one against another or against the Company's money was no doubt exceedingly annoying to the public and a great hindrance to trade. As long, however, as the value of the rupee was determined by the value of its silver content the existence of these various currencies was nothing worse than a nuisance.

In 1873–93 there was a severe fall in the value of silver and at the same time a rise in the value of gold. The result of this was that the price level in India was agitated and the exchange value of the rupee fell. The lowest point which it touched was a gold value of just over one shilling. The value of the rupee at the beginning of this period had been two shillings sterling.

To save it from further depreciation the Government decided to close the Indian mints to silver. The currency, now limited in amount, gradually rose in value, and was stabilised at the rate 1*s.* 4*d.* sterling. It was obviously impossible to maintain the value of the rupee unless there was a single minting authority for the whole country, and at this time the majority of States were persuaded to close their mints. The Government bought up the currencies of some Darbars at their silver value, and the British rupee became legal tender within their territories.

The value of the rupee now remained above the value of its silver content and the Government made a profit of about 6 annas on each rupee minted. From this profit the Gold Standard Reserve was built up, which was used to support exchange. This reserve amounted in 1913 to £22 million, of which £16·9 million was invested in various ways. In the same year 14 crores of rupees were held in securities in the Currency Note Reserve, which was entirely separate from the Gold Standard Reserve.

Both these reserves, after shrinking in the crisis at the beginning of the war, rose steadily with the increase in circulation during its course. The statutory limitation to the fiduciary issue of notes was raised, the security in the Currency Note Reserve amounted in 1919 to 99·5 crores of rupees, and the Gold Standard Reserve in that year stood at £36 million sterling.

In the following year a misguided attempt to maintain exchange at the level to which inflation in Europe had raised it, involved the Government in a loss of some Rs. 40 crores of rupees, and depleted its sterling resources to the extent of £55 million. The Reserves have since been reconstituted and now stand as follows:

MARCH 1928.

Gold Standard Reserve in Europe.		Currency Notes Account.	
1. Cash at short notice	3,100	Gold, silver coin and bullion . . .	13,560
1. British Treasury Bills . . .	12,194,281 [1]	Securities in India .	3,789 [1]
3. Other Government Securities . .	25,648,285 [1]	Securities in England .	377 [1]
4. Gold . . .	2,152,334		
	£39,998,000		

[1] Earning assets.

The States suffered considerably from the fluctuations in the price level and in exchange which followed the war. These, however, are the kind of misfortunes that any country is liable to suffer under any Government. The control of currency is a difficult task at which no Governments of modern times have been conspicuously successful. It is galling to the population of the States to suffer from a policy against which they have not so much as the right to protest, but it would be unwise to claim that if the control of currency were in their own hands, they would manage it any better. It is only natural, however, that those States who gave up their own currencies to the benefit of the whole country should look with envy at the profits which were made by States who still had their own rupees in circulation and their own mints at work during the war, and were able to take advantage of the rise in the price of silver. The accidents of history have made the original sacrifice appear much greater now even than it did at the time when it was made.

Although such losses cannot be reckoned as part of the contribution of the States, the Darbars can nevertheless justly claim to be credited with a share on the present profits of the currency.

To assess their share in the coinage it is necessary to allow for those States which provide part of their own currency, but it is also necessary to allow for the fact that the use of silver is likely to be greater amongst the relatively poor and backward peoples of the States, and that the velocity of circulation of money is likely to be smaller among them than among the peoples of British India. In spite, therefore, of the smaller real wealth of the States, we may conclude that they make use of silver and token money to the same extent as the rest of India, or, allowing for Darbar currencies, slightly more than the rest of India. The revenue from this source arises in two ways: first, the yearly net profit from the Mint, and secondly, the interest receipts from securities held in the Gold Standard Reserve, which was originally built up out of the profits of coinage. As long as the Reserve is maintained at the sum of £40 million sterling the annual interest receipts are absorbed into revenue.

Next we must consider the Note Issue. The interest receipts from that part of the Paper Currency Reserve which is held in the form of securities varies from year to year between 1½ and 3 crores of rupees. In this the States cannot claim to be credited with a full share, for, as we have already said, their peoples prefer silver to paper. The habit of using cheques, though it is beginning to develop in the industrial centres of British India, is not sufficiently advanced to have displaced the note circulation to a significant extent, and it is probable that notes are still used in British India to almost double the extent to which they are used in the States.

We therefore allow the States 22·5 per cent. of the profits from coinage and 12·6 per cent.[1] of the profits on Paper Currency.

[1] If the rate of consumption of 22·5 of population is half that of the rest, they consume 12·6 per cent. of the whole.

	Net Revenue of Paper Currency Department.	Share of States.
	Lakhs Rs.	Lakhs Rs.
1924–25	295·7	37·2
1925–26	372·8	46·7
1926–27	346·1	43·6
1927–28 (Revised estimate) .	171·9	21·6
1928–29 (Budget estimate) .	173·5	21·9

	NET REVENUE FROM COINAGE IN LAKHS RS.			Shares of States. 22·5% Lakhs Rs.
	I. Mint.	II. Gold Standard Reserve (Interest receipts).	III. Total.	
1924–25. . . .	27·9	134·7	162·6	36·6
1925–26. . . .	17·6	197·8	215·4	48·4
1926–27. . . .	7·1	194·8	187·7	42·2
1927–28 (Revised estimate)	9·6	240·0	249·6	56·1
1928–29 (Budget estimate)	57·0	216·6	222·3	50·0

It will be seen from the above tables that, according to our estimate in the year 1926–27, the States contributed Rs. 86 lakhs towards the profits from currency. These profits vary considerably from year to year. According to the Budget for 1928–29 the States share would be only Rs. 71·9 lakhs, while in 1925–26 it was Rs. 95 lakhs, but it will be necessary to include the figures for 1926–27 in our estimate of the total contribution of the States, as we have chosen that year to provide us with illustrations in the preceding Sections.

XXXVI.

INCOME TAX.

There is a further contribution which the peoples of the States make to central revenue which is on a different footing from those we have so far discussed. This contribution results from the fact that the British Indian income tax, like that of Great Britain, works upon the double principle of taxing income which is derived from a source within its boundaries and also income enjoyed by any person resident within its boundaries. This method of taxation has lately come to be regarded as unjustifiable, for if two countries both use it, any person who lives in the one and draws income from the other will suffer double taxation. This double taxation will impose an unfair burden on individuals who are caught by it unawares, and will also discourage the movement of capital between the two countries concerned.

Let us examine the situation first of a subject of British India holding capital invested in a State.

If there is no income tax in the State his investments will not be touched by the State's fiscal system, and there wil be no double taxation.

If there is an income tax, imposed before the investment was made, the effect will not be a burden on the individual investor, but enterprises in the State will have to offer a higher rate of interest than would otherwise be the case. This may retard development and lower the taxable capacity of the State's subjects.

If the income tax was imposed after the investment was made there will be a burden upon the investor, which will take the form of a fall in the capital value of his investments, and the State will be benefited at his expense. It is open to the States to avoid this kind of injustice and this kind of discouragement to investment in their enterprises by exempting all foreign capital under their income tax schemes, but they not unnaturally feel that the concessions should not be upon one side alone.

Let us next examine the case of a subject of a State the whole or part of whose income arises in British India.

This income will suffer double taxation equally if there is or is not an income tax in the State, as it is likely to be spent in the State and therefore to be subject to indirect taxation.

As before, if the British income tax was in force before the investment was made or the business opened, the effect of the tax will have been to discourage such investment, but it cannot be considered as a burden on the subjects of the States or as a loss to its exchequer.

If the investment was made before the tax was imposed or before any expectation of it had arisen, there will be a burden upon the States subject, and a diminution of his power to pay State taxes. As this type of investment in British India by subjects of States must be fairly common, the exchequers of the States are suffering a real loss and their citizens a considerable burden from this cause. The impediment to the free movement of capital is, however, even more important than the burden of the tax.

It is possible to avoid both by an arrangement relieving such investments of part of the British Indian income tax. The present arrangement between Great Britain and British India, as well as other members of the Empire, is as follows. If an individual is subject to taxation by both Governments, the amount of tax which he has paid to the Dominion or Indian Government is deducted from the amount which is due from him to the British Government. This relief is only granted up to half the rate of the British tax, but the Indian tax does not exceed that amount. The same principle should be applied between the States and British India. At present the subject of a State is only entitled to relief from British Indian taxation to the extent of half the tax paid to the State.[1]

[1] Patiala State has an arrangement slightly different from that here described.

If the justice of granting relief is acknowledged, there can be no reason for granting it in such a niggardly style. Those States which charge income tax do so at a lower rate than British India (except that in some States the exemption limit is lower), and therefore they would stand, if the concession were granted to them, in the same relation to British India in which the latter stands to Great Britain.

Since the principle has been admitted to be just, and since the system has worked satisfactorily, there seems no ground for withholding its full benefits from the States, and every reason to encourage, by granting it, the introduction of an income tax by any State which finds itself in a position to substitute that form of taxation for indirect taxes, which must always be an impediment to trade.

The disadvantage of this system of relieving double taxation is that it can only be made to apply between Governments both of which impose income tax, and, as we have said, income derived from investments in British India and spent in a State is subject to double taxation even when there is no income tax in that State. This, however, is an evil which it is impossible to remedy. Without detailed information from the Revenue Department it is impossible to estimate to how much the refund would amount if this system were introduced. It is, therefore, impossible to include an estimate of this particular figure in our calculation of the contribution of the States to central revenue.

XXXVII.

SUMMARY OF CONCLUSIONS.

In the foregoing Sections we have attempted to estimate the various ways in which the States do, in fact, contribute to the revenues of British India, and the amount of these contributions. In the table below the different heads of payment are collected:

CONTRIBUTION OF STATES.

	Rs. Lakhs
Sea Customs	706
Salt	93
Railways	120
Currency and Mints	86
Income Tax	—
Excise	39
Total	1,044

It will be seen from the above table that the contributions of the States amount to over Rs. 10 crores. As we have already stated, these figures are only tentative. But their accuracy or inaccuracy does not affect our argument. The fact that the subjects of Indian States do contribute to British Indian revenues under these heads is indisputable; and therefore the Princes expect that the Indian States Committee will address themselves to the task of enunciating the necessary principles of adjustment. Before these principles are finally adopted, the Chamber of Princes must be given an opportunity of discussing them. Their detailed application must, however, be entrusted to an expert committee, upon which the Indian States should be adequately represented.

Whatever figures may emerge from the expert committee of the future, it is important to remember that the imposition of this taxation lays upon the States a real burden far greater than can be measured by the actual sum which their peoples sacrifice. In the first place, it must react upon their whole fiscal system. The yield of any tax falls in an increasing ratio, the higher the taxation already imposed on the subjects who pay it. It follows that the yield of the Darbar's own taxes is diminished by this imposition, and the burden upon their peoples is all the greater because none of the proceeds are spent within the States.

In addition to this, the imposition of sea customs for the benefit of central resources throws the whole taxation system of the State into confusion. For goods which arrive at their frontiers, if imported from overseas, will have paid one customs duty, in many cases a considerable one; and, as the British Indian tariff raises the price not only of goods actually imported, but of all goods of the same class, so all such goods which pay a local duty at the frontiers of the States have, in effect, to bear a double tax. Moreover, an *ad valorem* tax at a State's frontier will be calculated on the price of goods already enhanced by the British Indian duty. Thus a State rate of duty of one anna in the rupee, charged on goods which have already paid 25 per cent. duty at the port, will really be a rate of 0—1—3 in the rupee on the original price of the goods.

This is a misfortune for consumers in the States as well as for the States' Governments, since the fact that the price of the goods has been enhanced by sea customs will check the demand for them within the State, besides depriving the Darbar of revenue it would otherwise have been able to collect.

How are they to raise revenue?

The alternative exists of taxing incomes directly. This, while the obvious and most satisfactory course in a Western country is ill adapted to the Indian States. Agricultural income is already taxed by the land revenue. A taxable middle class hardly exists. The chief incomes large enough to pay income tax are those of the officials. These incomes are fixed at the figure which is required to attract men of the necessary ability into the service of the State, and the amount of taxation would naturally be taken into account by any man considering such service. To impose taxation on them would only result in having to raise their salaries. Until, therefore, a strong middle class has grown up in the States there is little scope for an income tax.

Our main purpose in this survey has been to show that in our opinion the peoples of Indian States are at present subjected to a considerable burden of taxation for which they receive no return and for which there can be no justification. The difficulties which we have met in examining this state of affairs have, however, made it clear that an authoritative estimate of the actual amount of the burden can only be made by somebody with powers and with knowledge far greater than our own. We have, moreover, shown that the excessive taxation to which they are subject is only one among a number of economic disabilities from which the States suffer.

We have necessarily avoided embarking upon the still more complicated field of the particular rights and obligations of individual States. That topic lies wholly outside our present task save in so far as we have in Section IV estimated and added up the military contributions of the individual States. And nothing said herein must be read as in any way prejudicing the particular position of any State.

As regards procedure, we have urged that, after the Indian States Committee have reported, and the principles recommended by them have been considered and settled in consultation with the Princes, the expert body we recommend should be set up in order that it may, upon the basis of the principles so agreed, pronounce with authority upon the figures which we have discussed above.

And concurrently we contemplate that arrangements should be made for discussion and negotiation between the Crown and the Princes in order to decide what permanent political machinery should be constituted for regulating the relations of the States to the Crown and to the Government of British India, with a view permanently to protecting the rights of the States, promoting wise and harmonious co-operation between the States and British India, and ensuring the commercial development of the States themselves and India as a whole. We make no attempt here to discuss the above proposals in detail.

APPENDIX I.

GUARANTEES OF PROTECTION.

1. *States which have Treaties.*

ALWAR: Treaty of 1803. Article 2. The friends and enemies of the Honourable Company shall be considered the friends and enemies of Maha Rao Rajah, and the friends and enemies of Maha Rao Rajah shall be the friends and enemies of the Honourable Company.

Article 5. As from the friendship established by the second Article of the present Treaty, the Honourable Company become guarantee to Maha Rao Rajah for the security of his country against external enemies.

BAHAWALPUR: Treaty of 1838. Article 2. The British Government engages to protect the Principality and territory of Bhawulpore.

BANSWARA: Treaty of 1818. Article 2. The British Government engages to protect the principality and territory of Banswarra.

BARODA: Treaty of 1805. Article 2. The friends and enemies of either party shall be the friends and enemies of both, and if any Power shall commit any act of unprovoked hostility or aggression against either of the contracting parties, or against their respective dependents and allies, and after due representations shall refuse to enter into amicable explanations or shall deny the just satisfaction which the contracting parties shall have required, the contracting parties will proceed to prosecute such further measures as the case shall appear to demand. Converted by treaty of 1817 (Article 1) into a definite undertaking to "protect the Gaekwar's Dominions" (which were thereafter considered to include all States paying tribute to Baroda).

BHARATPUR: Treaty of 1805. Article 2. The friends and enemies of one of the parties shall be considered the friends and enemies of both.

Article 7. As by the second Article of the present Treaty the Honourable Company becomes guarantee to Maharajah Runjeet Singh for the security of the country against external enemies . . .

BHOPAL: Treaty of 1818. Article 2. The British Government engages to guarantee and protect the principality and territory of Bhopal against all enemies.

BIKANER: Treaty of 1818. Article 2. The British Government engages to protect the principality and territory of Bikaneer.

BUNDI: Treaty of 1818. Article 2. The British Government takes under its protection the dominions of the Rajah of Boondee.

COCHIN: Treaty of 1809. Article 1. The friends and enemies of either of the contracting parties shall be considered as the friends and enemies of both, the Honourable the East India Company Bahador engaging to defend and protect the territories of the Rajah of Cochin against all enemies whomsoever.

CUTCH: Treaty of 1819. Article 5. The Honourable Company engages to guarantee the power of His Highness the Rao Dessul, his heirs and successors, and the integrity of his dominions from foreign or domestic enemies.

DATIA: Treaty of 1818. Article 4. The British Government hereby agrees to protect the original territory of the Rajah of Dutteeah, as well as the district now granted to the Rajah, from the aggressions of all foreign Powers.

DEWAS (Senior, Junior): Treaty of 1818. Article 3. The British Government will protect the Rajahs of Dewas in their present possessions. . . . The British Government will further protect the Rajahs of Dewas against the attacks of enemies, and will aid them in the settlement of any of their rebellious subjects, and will mediate in a just and amicable manner any dispute that may arise between them and other States and petty Chiefs.

DHAR: Treaty of 1819. Article 3. The British Government agrees to protect the State of Dhar and its dependencies.

DHOLPUR: Treaty of 1806. As by the third Article of the present treaty the districts of Dholpore, Baree and Rajekeerah have, in conformity to the request of the Maharajah Ranah, been granted to him in sovereignty, and will remain exempt from all orders of the Adawlut or other demands of the Honourable Company, Maharajah Ranah hereby agrees to take upon himself the responsibility for adjusting all disputes which may arise, either external or internal, and no responsibility for assistance or protection remains with the Honourable Company.

GWALIOR: Treaty of 1804. Article 2. The British Government will never permit any Power or State whatever to commit with impunity any act of unprovoked hostility or aggression against the rights and territories of the Maharajah Dowlut Ras Sindia, but will, at all times, in compliance with the requisition of the Maharajah, maintain and defend the same, when such requisition is made, in the like manner as the rights and territories of the Honourable Company are now maintained and defended.

Treaty 1844. Article 6. Whereas the British Government is bound by treaty to protect the person of His Highness the Maharajah, his heirs and successors, and to protect his dominions from foreign invasion, and to quell serious disturbances therein ...

HYDERABAD: Treaty of 1800. Article 2. The British Government will never permit any Power or State whatever to commit with impunity any act of unprovoked hostility or aggression against the rights and territories of His Highness the Nizam, but will at all times maintain and defend the same, in the same manner as the rights and territories of the Honourable Company are now maintained and defended.

Treaty of 1853. Article 5. It is also hereby agreed that, excepting the said subsidiary and contingent forces, His Highness shall not under any circumstances be called upon to furnish any other troops whatsoever.

INDORE: Treaty of 1818. Article 1. The British Government will at all times extend the same protection to the territories of Maharajah Mulhar Rao Holkar as to its own.

JAIPUR: Treaty of 1818. Article 2. The British Government engages to protect the territory of Jeypore, and to expel the enemies of that principality.

JAISALMER: Treaty of 1818. Article 3. In the event of any serious invasion directed towards the overthrow of the principality of Jessulmere, or other danger of great magnitude occurring in that principality, the British Government will exert its power for the protection of the principality, provided that the cause of the quarrel be not ascribable to the Rajah of Jessulmere.

JAMMU and KASHMIR: Treaty of 1846. Article 9. The British Government will give aid to Maharajah Gulab Sing in protecting his territories from external enemies.

JHALAWAR: Treaty of 1838. Article 5. The British Government engages to take Rajah Rana Mudun Sing's principality under its protection.

JODHPUR: Treaty of 1818. Article 2. The British Government engages to protect the principality and territory of Jodhpore.

KALAT: Treaty of 1876. Article 3. The British Government on its part engages to respect the independence of Khelat and to aid the Khan, in case of need, in the maintenance of a just authority and the protection of his territories from external attack, by such means as the British Government may at the moment deem expedient.

KARAULI: Treaty of 1817. The British Government

takes under its protection the dominions of the Rajah of Kerowlee.

KHAIPUR: Treaty of 1838. Article 2. The British Government engages to protect the principality and territory of Kheirpore.

KISHENGARH: Treaty of 1818. The British Government engages to protect the principality and territory of Kishengarh.

KOLHAPUR: Treaty of 1812. Article 8. In consideration of the cession of the harbour of Malwan, and on condition of the effectual suppression of piracy, the Honourable Company engages to guarantee such territories as shall remain in the Rajah of Kolhapore's possession against the aggression of all foreign Powers and States.

KOTAH: Treaty of 1817. Article 3. The British Government engages to take under its protection the principality and territory of Kotah.

MYSORE: Instrument of Transfer, 1881. Article 5. The British Government having undertaken to defend and protect the said territories against all external enemies. . . .

ORCHHA: Treaty of 1812. Article 2. The territory which from ancient times has descended to Rajah Mahendra Biskermajeet Bahader by inheritance, and is now in his possession, is hereby guaranteed to the said Rajah and to his heirs and successors. . . . The British Government, moreover, engages to protect and defend the dominions at present in Rajah Mahendra Biskermajeet Bahader's possession from the aggression of any foreign Power.

PARTABGARH: Treaty of 1818. Article 1. The Rajah promises to give up all connection with other States, and to the utmost of his power prove his obedience to the British Government, who in return agree to . . . protect him from the claims and trespasses of all other States.

RAMPUR: Engagement of 1794. Article 2. The said Company engage to guarantee the possession of the said mehals to the said Nabob Ahmed Athy Khan Behander.

REWA: Treaty of 1812. Article 1. The British Government engages to protect the territories at present possessed by the Rajah of Rewah from the aggressions of any foreign Power in the same manner as the dominions of the Honourable Company are protected and defended.

SAMTHAR: Treaty of 1817. Article 2. The British Government, with a view to confirm the attachment and fidelity of the Government of Sumpthur, hereby guarantees to Rajah Runjeet Singh, his heirs and successors, the territory actually possessed by him at the period of the establishment of the British Government in Bundelkhund, and now in his occupation, and the British Government hereby agrees to protect and defend the same from the aggressions of any foreign Power.

SAWANTWARI: Treaty of 1819. Article 2. The British Government engages to protect the principality and territory of Sawant Waree.

SIKKIM: Has no guarantee of protection.

SIROHI: Treaty of 1823. Article 1. The British Government consents to take under its protection, and to receive amongst the number of its dependent and tributary States, the chiefship and territory of Serohi.

TRAVANCORE: Treaty of 1805. Article 1. The friends and enemies of either of the contracting parties shall be considered as the friends and enemies of both; the Honourable Company especially engaging to defend and protect the territories of the Rajah of Travancore against all enemies whatsoever.

TONK: Treaty of 1817. Article 1. The British Government guarantees to Nawab Umurkhan, and his heirs in perpetuity, the possession of the places which he holds in the territories of Maharajah Holkar, under grants from the said Maharajah, and the British Government takes those possessions under its protection.

UDAUPIR: Treaty of 1818. Article 2. The British Government engages to protect the principality and territory of Oudeypore.

2. *States which have no Treaties but which have been Guaranteed Protection in some other Express Form.*

MANIPUR, Sanad 1891: "Be assured that so long as your house is loyal to the Crown and faithful to the conditions of this Sanad, you and your successors will enjoy the favour and protection of the British Government."

TRIBUTARY STATES OF ORISSA: The relationship of these States with the British Government is laid down in the treaty engagements of 1803. By these engagements the States undertook to pay tribute to that Government, and as its tributaries they must be held entitled to its protection.

STATES WITHOUT FORMAL TREATIES IN BOMBAY AND THE WESTERN INDIAN AGENCY: The tributaries of the Peshwa and Gaekwar were originally guaranteed protection by the terms of the alliances between those rulers and the Company. By Article 2 of the treaty of Bassein it was laid down that if any Power or State whatever shall commit any act of unprovoked hostility or aggression against either of the contracting parties or against their respective dependents or others . . . then the contracting parties will proceed to concert and prosecute such further measures as the case shall appear to demand. . . . The British Government will never permit any Power or States whatever to commit with impunity any act of unprovoked hostility or aggression against the rights and territories of His Highness Rao Pundit Purdham Behander, but will at all times maintain and defend the same in the same manner as the rights and territories of the Honourable Company are now maintained and defended.

A number of States, formerly tributary to the Peshwa, became tributary to the Company, and their tributes, many of which consisted of a share in transit or other duties, since commuted to fixed sums, became payable to the Company. The Company thenceforward became responsible, in place of the Peshwa, for the defence of these territories. The rest of the States who paid tribute to the Peshwa came into direct relationship with the Company upon his resignation in 1818, and the Company assumed his obligations towards them.

The States of Kathiawar and Mahi Kantha as well as Rewa Kantha and Palanpur and Rhadanpur are protected under the Walker Settlement of 1807–8 (Kathiawar), the Mahi Kantha Settlement of 1811–12, the Rewa Kantha Settlement of 1821–14, the Palanpur Agreement of 1813, and the Rhadanpur Agreement of 1820. Only in the case of Bariya in Rewa Kantha was the tribute imposed explicitly in return for protection.

The following States were formerly subject either to Gaekwar or to Peshwa:

Sachin.	Panth Piploda.
Cambay.	States of Kathiawar.
Bansda.	Palanpur.
Dharampur.	Radhanpur.
Jaujar.	Kankrej.
Janjira.	States of Mahi Kantha.
Savanur.	States of Rewa Kantha.
Sandur.	

Sanad States in Bundelkhand: These States also were ceded by the Peshwa to the British Government, and though no clause in the Sanads which they received from it guarantees protection to them, it is affirmed in the answers to several of the Papers of Requests submitted by one or other of the chiefs in Bundelkhand.

SOUTHERN MARATHA STATES known as "Jagirdars," Sangli, Miraj Senior, Miraj Junior, Jamphandi, Kurnudwad Senior, Kurnudwad Junior, Ramdurg, Mudhol: Treaty of 1817. Article 13, p. 64. Terms granted by the Honourable East India Company 1819, Article 2: "As long as you shall remain faithful and true to Government, your lands shall be continued to you without interruption."

PUNJAB HILL STATES: These States were conferred by Sanad on their various Chiefs after the Gurkha wars. The Chiefs either pay tribute or were bound to perform feudal services which have since been commuted for money. In answer to a Paper of Requests presented by the Rajah of Bilaspur, he was assured that his territory "shall in every respect be considered to be under the protection of the British Government," and presumably the rest of the Punjab Hill States are to be considered in the same way.

CIS SUTLEJ STATES: Patiala, Jind, Nabha, Kalsia, Maler Kotla, Faridkot, Mandwa, were taken under British protection by a Proclamation in 1809. Patiala received a further guarantee in a Sanad in 1847: "The Rajah of Putteala having requested that he may receive a renewed assurance of protection and guarantee of his rights in his former possessions, the Governor-General is pleased to confer this assurance in the form of a Sanad or Grant."

Jind received a Sanad in the same terms. Nabha was assured of protection in answer to a Paper of Requests and in a Sanad in 1860.

The Chiefs of the so-called "Feudatory" STATES IN THE CENTRAL PROVINCES hold their lands under Sanads containing the following clause: "The British Government will continue, as long as you remain loyal to the Crown and abide by the conditions of the Sanad and of your other engagements with the British Government, to maintain you in the position and privileges which you have hitherto enjoyed or which are now conferred on you." These States pay tributes.

TEHRI, Sanad of 1820: The British Government will guarantee the Rajah and his posterity in the secure possession of the country now conferred upon him and will defend him against his enemies.

APPENDIX II.

PAYMENTS FOR DEFENCE.

I.—Territories Ceded.

UDAIPUR: Udaipur's share of Mewar Merwara was transferred to British management soon after the subjugation of that part of the country. In 1881, with the view of removing difficulties connected with the adjustments of accounts, the British Government proposed to accept in future the revenue of Mewar Merwara in full discharge of the Udaipur State's contribution towards the cost of the administration of the district, the expenses of the Mewar Bhil Corps (Rs. 50,000) and of the Merwara battalions (Rs. 16,000).

It was further stipulated that should the receipts from the district at any time exceed Rs. 66,000, the surplus money should be paid in full to the Udaipur Treasury.—Treaty of 1818. Aitchison, Vol. III.

GWALIOR: By the treaty of 1803 Scindia made large concessions of territories, yielding a revenue of nearly a crore and a half. Out of the land ceded the East India Company offered to maintain a subsidiary force, consisting of six battalions of infantry with their complement of ordnance and artillery.—Treaty of 1804.

By the treaty of 1817 Scindia was required to provide 5,000 horse (known as the Gwalior Contingent, and afterwards as the Auxiliary Horse) out of his own troops to co-operate with the British troops in suppressing the Pindaris. By Article 5 of this treaty Scindia renounced for a period of three years certain payments amounting to Rs. 7 lakhs annually made to him and his family by the British Government under a previous treaty of 1805, and relinquished for two years to the British Government, the tribute amounting to Rs. 3½ lakhs, which he received from the Rajputana States.

In 1844 a new treaty was signed by Article 2, of which the contingent force was to be considerably increased, and in addition to all the revenues and other receipts, already set apart for the purposes, the revenues of other large districts belonging to the State were assigned to the Government for the maintenance of the force, the total cost of which was now estimated at 18 lakhs annually. The sum appropriated was sufficient to provide 7 battalions of infantry, 2 regiments of cavalry, and four batteries of artillery. (Despatch of the Governor-General to the Secret Committee, dated 21st January, 1844.)

As a reward for his services in the Mutiny, Scindia was given in 1860 territory yielding Rs. 3 lakhs. For convenience the territory was found out of the districts he had assigned in 1844 for the expenses of the contingent.

By the treaty of the same year the Maharajah ceded to the British Government in full sovereignty the remainder of the assigned districts; the Government engaged to maintain a subsidiary force at the reduced miniumum cost of Rs. 16 lakhs.—Aitchison, Vol. III.

INDORE: By Article 7 of the treaty of 1818, Holkar was guaranteed protection in return for large cessions of territory.—Aitchison, Vol. IV.

KOLHAPUR. By Article 8 of the treaty of 1812, Kolhapur ceded certain forts and the harbour of Malwan in return for protection guaranteed.—Aitchison, Vol. VII.

SANGLI: Ceded territories yielding a revenue of Rs. 1,35,000 in lieu of subsidy.—Aitchison, Vol. VII. p. 225.

SAWANTWARI.—Ceded the whole line of east coast from the Karli River to the boundaries of the Portuguese possessions in return for protection (treaty of 1819). —Aitchison, Vol. VII.

BARODA: By the treaty of 1802, Baroda agreed to receive a State subsidiary force from the British Government and to cede the Chauthi and Surat and the Pargana of Chorasi on condition of being supported against his rival, Malhar Rao.

In 1805 the subsidiary force was increased and territories yielding Rs. 11,70,000 were ceded for its support.

In 1808, the Gaekwar ceded additional territories yielding Rs. 1,76,168, as the ceded districts were found not to yield a revenue equal to the amount of the cost of the subsidiary force.

By the treaty of 1817 the subsidiary force was again increased, and the Gaekwar ceded to the British Government all the rights which he had acquired by the farm of the Peshwa's territories in Gujerat yielding Rs. 12,61,969. In 1830 lands yielding 15 lakhs were sequestered from the Gaekwar's territories to provide funds for the additional troops which he had agreed to maintain by the treaty of 1817. In 18[illegible]2, however, the districts were restored on the Gaekwar agreeing to deposit Rs. 1,00,00,000 with the British Government. In 1839 the District of Petlad yielding a revenue of Rs. 7,32,000 was sequestered, and a part of the revenue of Petlad was appropriated to the maintenance of a body of cavalry organised by the British Government and called the Gujerat Irregular Horse. In 1841, an agreement made with the Gaekwar revised the treaty of 1817 and provided for a payment of Rs. 3,00,000 for the Gujerat Irregular Horse and for the maintenance of 3,000 horse by the Gaekwar. On the conclusion of this agreement the district of Petlad and the one crore deposited with the British Government in 1832 were returned to the Gaekwar in 1858 as reward for services in the Mutiny. The payment of Rs. 3 lakhs a year for the Gujerat Irregular Horse was remitted.

In 1881 an Agreement was executed by which the British Government allowed the contingent to be disbanded in consideration of an annual payment of Rs. 3,75,000.—Aitchison, Vol. VIII.

NABHA: A portion of the territory of the Nabha State was confiscated owing to its refusal to help the British army during the first Sikh war. This portion was divided between Patiala and Faridkot and the British. The revenue from the British portion was appropriated to the maintenance of 133 infantry and 100 horse, and the Chief was exempted from providing the troops which he had formerly furnished.—Aitchison, Vol. VIII.

HYDERABAD: By the treaty of 1766, in return for the Circars of Ellore, Cricacole, Rajamahendri, Mustfanagar and Murtzanagar or Guntur, the British Government agreed to furnish the Nizam with a subsidiary force when required and to pay 9 lakhs a year when the assistance of the troops was not required. By the treaty of 1800 the subsidiary force was increased, and to secure the regular payment of the troops the Nizam ceded the greater part of the territory which he had acquired under the treaty of Serangapatam (1792) and under the Mysore treaty of 1797, yielding altogether 20,91,428 pagodas, or about 62,74,000 rupees.

By Article 12 of the treaty of 1800 the Nizam was also bound to maintain six thousand infantry and nine thousand horse to co-operate with the subsidiary force. As the Nizam's troops were inefficient, it became necessary to maintain in their place two battalions, armed, clothed and equipped like the Company's troops.

Later it became necessary to make advances from the British Treasury for the payment of this contingent force, and in 1851 territorial cessions were demanded to liquidate the debt, which then amounted to more than Rs. 78,00,000. A payment of Rs. 40,00,000 was at once made, but the balance remained unpaid, and in 1853 the debt had again risen to Rs. 45,00,000. In 1853 a fresh treaty was concluded and the British Government agreed to maintain in addition to the subsidiary force an auxiliary force, called the Hyderabad Contingent, of not less than 5,000 infantry, 2,000 cavalry and 4 field batteries of artillery, and in order to provide for the payment of this force the Nizam assigned in trust districts in Berar, Dharaseo and Raichur Doab estimated to yield a gross revenue of Rs. 50 lakhs a year. It was also agreed that accounts should be annually rendered to the Nizam, and that any surplus that might accrue should be paid to him. By this treaty the services of the subsidiary force and the contingent were to be at the disposal of the British Government in time of war and the Nizam was released from any further obligation in this respect. The contingent ceased to be a part of the Nizam's army and became an auxiliary force kept by the British Government for the Nizam's use.

In 1860 the debt of Rs. 50 lakhs due by the Nizam was cancelled and the district of Dharaseo and Raichur Doab were restored to him. The Nizam had, however, to cede certain districts on the left bank of the Godavari and to agree to free the traffic on that river from all duties. He further agreed that the remaining assigned districts in Berar should be held in trust by the British Government for the purpose specified in the treaty of 1853, and that no demand for accounts of the receipts or expenditure of the districts should be made. In 1902 Berar was re-leased in perpetuity in consideration of the payment to the Nizam of a fixed and perpetual rental of Rs. 25,00,000 per annum. The British Government were also empowered to redistribute, organise and control the force composing the Hyderabad Contingent. The Hyderabad Contingent has now ceased to exist, the artillery having been disbanded and the cavalry and infantry absorbed in the regular army.

II.—Lump Sum Payments.

INDORE: In lieu of his obligation under Article 11 of the treaty of 1818 by which Holkar agreed to retain a body of not less than 3,000 horse in his service ready to co-operate with the British troops, an annual subvention of Rs. 1,11,214 was paid by him. Besides this, the Maharajah also paid Rs. 7,862 annually towards the Malwa Contingent and Bhil Corps. These payments were capitalised by the State depositing Rs. 23,81,520 with the Government of India, the interest thereon at 5 per cent. being assigned as the payment for the future, "thereby relieving His Highness from all demands on account of the said contingent and Bhil Corps, as well as from all pecuniary demands, present or future, and from service with troops."

DHAR. In 1880 Dhar surrendered to the British Government, Government promissory notes amounting to Rs. 3,00,000, thus capitalising the annual payment of a sum of Rs. 12,000, which was a part of its contribution towards the Malwa Bhil Corps.

III.—Subsidies.

JODHPUR: In accordance with the eighth Article of the treaty of 1818, the State was bound to furnish a contingent of 1,500 horse. This obligation was commuted to an assured payment of Rs. 1,15,000 towards the cost of a contingent called the Erinpura Regiment.

KOTAH: The State pays Rs. 2,00,000 a year towards the cost of the Deoli Irregular Force. This sum was fixed by the treaty of 1838.—Aitchison, Vol. III.

DEWAS: By the treaty of 1818 the two States of Dewas were required to provide a contingent of 50 horse and 50 foot to be at the disposal of the British Government, in return for the guarantee of protection. In 1827 the contingent was raised to 75 horse and 200 foot. This obligation was afterwards commuted to an annual contribution of Rs. 28,474-9-2.

BHOPAL: By the treaty of 1818 Bhopal was guaranteed protection and undertook to provide a contingent of 600 horse and 400 infantry. The contribution paid for its maintenance was raised in 1840. After the Mutiny the contingent was replaced by the Bhopal Battalion. Since 1849 the State has paid an annual contribution of Rs. 1,61,290.

JAORA: Pays Rs. 1,59,027-4-4 in place of the quota of troops formerly maintained as part of the Malwa Contingent.

DHAR: Pays an annual contribution of Rs. 7,656 towards the maintenance of the Malwa Bhil Corps.

JHABUA: Pays Rs. 1,271 towards the cost of the Malwa Bhil Corps.

ALIRAJPUR: Pays Rs. 1,271 towards the cost of the Malwa Bhil Corps.

BARWANI: Pays Rs. 3,389 towards the cost of the Malwa Bhil Corps.

CUTCH: By the treaty of 1819, the Maharoa of Cutch agreed to provide a contingent force in return for the guarantee of protection. The State at present pays a contribution of Rs. 1,86,949, which is liable to be reduced to a minimum of Rs. 88,000 if the contingent is reduced.

AKALKOT: Pays Rs. 14,592 in lieu of the service of horsemen.

JATH: Pays Rs. 6,400 in lieu of the service of horsemen.

PHALTAN: Pays Rs. 9,600 in lieu of the service of horsemen.

MIRAJ (Senior): Pays Rs. 12,557 in lieu of the service of horsemen.

MIRAJ (Junior): Pays Rs. 6,412–8 in lieu of the service of horsemen.

JAMKHANDI: Pays Rs. 20,840–10 in lieu of the service of horsemen.

MUDHOL: Pays Rs. 2,671–14 in lieu of the service of horsemen.

KURUNDWAD: Pays Rs. 1,696–8 in lieu of the service of horsemen.

BARODA: In 1881 an agreement was executed by which the British Government agreed to allow the contingent of 3,000 horse maintained by the Gaekwar to be disbanded in consideration of an annual money payment of Rs. 3,75,000.

MYSORE: Used to pay Peshkash and subsidy of Rs. 35,00,000, which has since 1926 been reduced to Rs. 25,00,000.

TRAVANCORE: By the treaty of 1795 the Rajah engaged to pay an annual subsidy adequate to maintain 3 battalions of sepoys. In 1805 one more Regiment was added; eventually the subsidy payable by the Travancore State was fixed definitely at Rs. 80,00,000.

COCHIN: Pays Rs. 2,00,000.

IV.—Tributes.

Name of State.	Tribute (Government Rs.).	Remarks.
	Rs. a. p.	
Udaipur . .	2,00,000 0 0	The tribute under Article 6 of the tieaty, dated the 13th January, 1918, was fixed for the first five years at one-fourth of the revenues of Udaipur, and thereafter at three-eighths in perpetuity. In 1826 it was fixed at 3 lakhs, Udaipur rupees. In consequence of financial embarrassments of the State, the tribute was reduced in June 1846 to Government Rs. 2 lakhs.
Dungarpur . .	17,500 0 0	Tribute payable under Article 9 of treaty, dated 11th December, 1818, Salim Shahi Rs. 35,000.
Banswara . .	17,500 0 0	The tribute payable under Article 9 of th treaty, dated the 25th December, 1818, was Salim Shahi Rs. 35,000 = Government Rs. 17,500-0-0.
Jaipur . . .	4,00,000 0 0	Tribute payable under Article 2 of Agreement, dated 4th September, 1871, taken as part of, and supplementary to, the treaty, dated 2nd April, 1818. The payment of a like amount to the Darbar, under the Salt Treaty, is set off against this tribute.
Lawa (Thakurate)	225 0 0	The tribute has been paid since the 1st April, 1883. Reduced by Government from Rs. 3,000.
Jhalawar . .	30,000 0 0	The tribute payable under Article 11 of the treaty, dated the 8th April, 1838, was Rs. 80,000-0-0. A part of the territories which were made over by Kotah in 1838, for the formation of the Jhalawar States, was restored to Kotah in 1899, and the tribute was reduced to Rs. 30,000 by a Sanad dated the 30th January, 1899.
Kotah . . .	2,34,720 0 0	The tribute payable under Article 7 of the treaty, dated 25th December, 1817, was Rs. 2,89,720. A remission of Rs. 25,000 was sanctioned by Sanad, dated 25th September, 1819; and on the formation of the State of Jhalawar, a further reduction of Rs. 80,000 was granted under Article 4 of the treaty, dated 10th April, 1838. The tribute was enhanced in 1898 by Rs. 50,000 when certain territories were restored to Kotah from Jhalawar.
Bundi . . .	40,000 0 0	Tribute payable under Article 5 of the treaty dated 10th February, 1818, as *chauth* of Bundi and other places.
Shahpura (Chiefship) . .	10,000 0 0	The tribute is paid on account of Pargana of Phulia under the Sanad dated 27th June, 1848.

TRIBUTES—*continued.*

Name of State.	Tribute (Government Rs.). Rs.	a.	p.	Remarks.
Sirohi . . .	6,881	4	0	The tribute originally payable under Article 8 of the treaty, dated 11th September, 1823, was Bhilari Rs. 15,000 or Government Rs. 13,762–8–0. The Chief, having rendered meritorious service during the mutinies, a remission of half his tribute was sanctioned by the Government of India on the 18th December, 1857.—Aitchison, Vol. III.
Bundhelkhand .	27,194	5	6	The following five States in the Bundhelkhand Agency pay tribute for certain villages or districts in their territories, namely, Charkhari, Panna, Ajaigarh, Bihat, and Paldeo.—Aitchison, Vol. V.
Junagarh . .	28,394	0	0	—
Nawanagar . .	50,312	0	0	—
Bhavnagar . .	1,28,060	0	0	—
Porbandar . .	21,202	0	0	—
Dhrangadhara .	40,671	0	0	—
Rajkot . . .	18,991	0	0	—
Wadhwan . .	26,009	8	0	—
States of Mahi Kantha Agency.	921	11	2	—
States of Rewa Kantha Agency.	24,382	0	0	—
Cambay . .	—			Tribute remitted in return for admission of salt excise.—Aitchison, Vol. VI.
Bansda . . .	7,351	8	0	In 1858 the Rajah of Bansda agreed to pay Rs. 1,500, in addition to this tribute, in consideration of the British Government foregoing its share in transit duties. In 1873 the Rajah was granted Rs. 8,698 per annum as compensation for abolishing transit duties. The net payment made by the State to the British Government is, therefore, now Rs. 153–8–0.
Dharampur . .	9,000	0	0	By an agreement signed in 1870, this sum was made payable in place of the British share in transit duties which were then abolished.
Bhor . . .	4,684	0	0	—
Jath . . .	4,847	0	0	—
Hindur . . . (Nalagarh)	5,000	0	0	Sanad 1860.
Bashahr . .	3,945	0	0	Sanad of 1816 required a tribute of Rs. 15,000 which was reduced in 1847 in compensation for the abolition of transit duties.
Baghat . . .	2,000	0	0	Sanad of 1862 required a tribute of this amount, but the actual payment is now Rs. 132–6–0, as part was remitted on account of lands ceded at Solon and Kasauli.
Jubbal . . .	2,520	0	0	—
Kapurthala . .	1,31,000	0	0	In commutation of military service.
Mandi . . .	1,00,000	0	0	—

TRIBUTES—*continued.*

Name of State.	Tribute (Government Rs.). Rs.	a.	p.	Remarks.
Chamba	10,000	0	0	Part of the tribute was remitted on account of lands made over to Government. The actual payment is now Rs. 3,800.
Suket	11,000	0	0	Sanad 1846.—Aitchison, Vol. VIII.
Travancore	13,319	8	0	Paid as equivalent of the Peshkash and Nazrana formerly due to the Nawab of the Carnatic.—Aitchison, Vol. X.
Benares	2,19,000	0	0	—
Manipur	15,000	0	0	Sanad 1891.—Aitchison, Vol. XI.
Cooch-Behar	67,700	15	0	Sum fixed in 1780.

The following 17 States in Orissa received Sanads in 1894, redefining their status and mentioning the tribute which they are liable to pay :

Name of State.	Rs.	a.	p.	Remarks.
Athgarh	2,800	0	0	—
Athmallik	480	0	0	—
Baramba	1,397	15	5	—
Bod	800	0	0	—
Daspalla	661	7	11	—
Dhenkanal	5,099	0	9	—
Hindol	551	3	11	—
Keunjhar	1,701	1	3	—
Khandpara	4,211	8	8	—
Morbhanj	1,067	11	9	—
Narsinghpur	1,455	8	3	—
Nayagarh	5,525	4	1	—
Nilgiri	3,900	7	8	—
Pal Lahara	266	10	8	—
Ranpur	1,400	13	2	—
Talcher	1,039	10	5	—
Tigaria	9,158	0	0	—
Bonai and Gangapur.	1,750	0	0	Sanad of 1899.
Bamra	1,500	0	0	Sanad 1905.
Kalahandi or Karound.	12,000	0	0	Sanad 1905.
Patna	8,500	0	0	Sanad 1905.
Rairakhol	800	0	0	Sanad 1905.
Sonpur	9,000	0	0	Sanad 1905.—Aitchison, Vol. I.

Feudatory States in the Central Provinces.

Name of State.	Rs.	a.	p.	Remarks.
Bastar	17,200	0	0	—
Chang Bhakar	387	0	0	—
Jashpur	1,250	0	0	—
Kanker	—			Tribute remitted in consequence of resumption by Government of sugar duties.
Kawardha	32,000	0	0	—
Khairagarh	70,000	0	0	—
Kondka	15,000	0	0	—

TRIBUTES—*continued.*

Name of State.	Tribute (Government Rs.). Rs.	a.	p.	Remarks.
Korea . . .	500	0	0	—
Nandgaon . .	70,000	0	0	—
Raigarh . .	4,000	0	0	—
Sakti . . .	1,300	0	0	—
Sarangarh . .	1,350	0	0	—
Sarguja . . .	2,500	0	0	—
Udaipur . .	800	0	0	—
Baghat . . .	2,000	0	0	Sanad of 1862 required a tribute of this amount, but the actual payment is now Rs. 132–6–0, as part was remitted on account of lands ceded at Solon and Kasuli.

The following States were granted Sanads which required the provision of forced labour. This was afterwards commuted for money payments.

Name of State.	Rs.	a.	p.	Remarks.
Bhajji . . .	1,440	0	0	—
Kothar . . .	1,000	0	0	—
Kumharsain . .	2,000	0	0	—
Dhami . . .	360	0	0	—
Balsar . . .	1,080	0	0	—
Mailog . . .	1,440	0	0	—
Beja . . .	180	0	0	—
Taroch . . .	280	0	0	—
Kunhiar . .	180	0	0	—
Mangal . . .	72	0	0	—

The following States paid tribute to Scindia which were assigned to the British Government as part of the payment for the Gwalior Contingent under the treaties of 1844 and 1860.

Name of State.	Rs.	a.	p.	Remarks.
Khilchipur . .	11,134	3	6	—
Ratlam . . .	65,520	0	0	—
Sailana . . .	32,760	0	0	—
Jodhpur . .	1,08,000	0	0	Reduced by Rs. 10,000 on account of cession of land at Amarkot.—Aitchison, Vol. IV.

APPENDIX III.

SUPPLY OF TROOPS IN TIME OF WAR.

UDAIPUR: By Article 8 of the treaty of 1818 the troops of the States shall be furnished according to its means at the requisition of the British Government.

DUNGARPUR: By Article 10 of the treaty of 1818 the Maharawal, his heirs and successors engaged to afford what military force they might possess to the British Government upon their requisition.

BANSWARA: Engaged to furnish troops according to its means to the British Government on requisition.

JAIPUR: The Maharajah agreed to furnish troops on the requisition of the British Government. (Treaty of 1818.)

KISHENGARH: Engaged to furnish troops on the requisition of the British Government, according to its means.

KARAULI: Engaged to furnish troops on the requisition of the British Government, according to its means. (Treaty of 1817.)

ALWAR: Alwar troops to co-operate with those of the British Government. (Treaty of 1803.)

BIKANER: The Maharajah of Bikaner will furnish troops on the requisition of the British Government, according to his means. (Article 8 of the treaty of 1818.)

KOTAH: "Furnish troops according to his means when required." (Treaty of 1817.)

JHALAWAR: The Maharajah Rana agreed to supply troops according to his means.

BHOPAL: Article 6, treaty of 1818. "The State of Bhopal shall furnish a contingent of six hundred (600) horse and four hundred (400) infantry for the service of the British Government. Whenever required and when necessary, the whole of the Bhopal forces shall join the British army excepting such a portion as may be requisite for the internal administration of the country."

DATIA: By the treaty of 1818, Article 6, "the Rajah hereby binds himself to employ his troops at his own expenses whenever required to do so in co-operation with those of the British Government on all occasions in which the interest of the two States may be mutually concerned."

SAMTHAR: Provision similar to that of Datia.

CUTCH: By Article 14 of the treaty of 1819 the Rao, his heirs and successors, engaged to afford what military force they might possess to the aid of the Honourable Company's Government upon requisition.

PATIALA: By the Sanad granted in 1847, the Maharajah, among other things, engaged himself to attend in person with his forces should the Cis Sutlej territories be invaded by the enemies, while the British Government gave up all claims to tribute or revenue or commutation in lieu of troops or otherwise.

JIND and NABHA: Same as above.

The following States are bound to render service, presumably when called upon in time of war:

Sirmur.	Kothar.
Kahlur.	Taroch.
Jubbal.	Kunhiar.

JAMMU and KASHMIR: By the treaty of 1846 the Maharajah engaged for himself and heirs to join the whole of his military forces with the British troops when employed within the hills or in territories adjoining his possessions.

SUPPLY OF GRAIN AND OTHER MATERIAL.

PATIALA: By the Sanad of 1860 the Maharajah is bound to co-operate with British forces on an enemy appearing and to provide carriage and supplies of grains, etc. free to the British troops.

JIND and NABHA; Same as above.

INDEX